Deciding What We Watch

Taste, Decency, and Media Ethics in the UK and the USA

Colin Shaw

Clarendon Press · Oxford
1999

Oxford University Press, Great Clarendon Street, Oxford OX2 6DP

Oxford New York

Athens Auckland Bangkok Bogotá Buenos Aires Calcutta
Cape Town Chennai Dar es Salaam Delhi Florence Hong Kong Istanbul
Karachi Kuala Lumpur Madrid Melbourne Mexico City Mumbai
Nairobi Paris São Paulo Singapore Taipei Tokyo Toronto Warsaw
and associated companies in
Berlin Ibadan

Oxford is a registered trade mark of Oxford University Press

Published in the United States
by Oxford University Press Inc., New York

First published 1999

British Library Cataloguing in Publication Data
Data available

Library of Congress Cataloging in Publication Data
Shaw, Colin, 1928–
Deciding what we watch: taste, decency, and media ethics in the
UK and the USA / Colin Shaw.
Includes bibliographical references and index.
1. Mass media—Moral and ethical aspects. 2. Mass media—
Great Britain. 3. Mass media—United States. I. Title.
P94.S53 1990 175—dc21 98–37842
ISBN 0–19–815937–4
ISBN 0–19–815936–6 (pbk.)

1 3 5 7 9 10 8 6 4 2

Typeset by Best-set Typesetter Ltd., Hong Kong
Printed in Great Britain
on acid-free paper by
Biddles Ltd.,
Guildford and King's Lynn

Deciding What We Watch

Preface

I would not wish this book to sail under false colours. As much as a look into the future, it is a personal enquiry into the past, but more rigorous than a simple essay in nostalgia. It has as much to do with personal experiences as with abstract principles. I spent a large part of the forty-three years in which I worked in British broadcasting attempting to deal with many of the issues of taste and decency described in the following pages. Although there were codes and guidelines, some of which I helped to write, much of what had to be done then, as now, was done pragmatically. I and my colleagues applied what we hoped was common sense to situations which, in the nature of both radio and television, rarely had a precise parallel.

Time passed and the rate of change in the broadcasting industry accelerated. It had always had a special dynamic, moving in sixty years from radio to television, black-and-white to colour, AM to FM, monaural to stereophonic, and, in Britain, from monopoly to competition. But from the 1980s the dynamic was charged with fresh energies, economic and technological. Cable and satellite services became large-scale realities, ending the scarcity of frequencies which had been used in arguments to justify the existence of content-regulators like myself and my colleagues. The majority of us believed that we had been acting in the public interest, attempting to ensure that a sense of public morality was maintained in the use of the scarce public resource which frequencies represented.

With the evaporation of the scarcity argument, the existence of content-regulators became more problematical. In the United States, a commercial broadcasting system constitutionally averse, in more senses than one, to intervention by a regulator had maintained an almost permanent challenge to the Federal Communications Commission over matters of content. The deregulation fever which struck America under the Reagan administration left commerce firmly in the saddle and the FCC further constrained in the expression of any concerns with content. At the same time, however, American courts, as well as Congress, have indicated a willingness to continue to treat broadcasting differently from print, citing its pervasiveness, for example, as a reason for affording a measure of protection for the child-audience.

Britain caught the fever a little later, but, as I hope to show, the British have continued to demonstrate an interest in the regulation of programmes as an assurance of quality in the broadest sense. Yet they too face the prospect, with the coming of digital broadcasting, of so many new channels that the detailed regulation of content, programme by programme, would not be practical even if it were considered desirable. In such circumstances, quality must be secured by other means: through the will of programme-makers themselves and the demands of the audience within structures of regulation which recognize both the promise and the dangers of the new realities.

A darker ground-bass, however, had sounded throughout the early years of regulation. Critics asked in whose name the regulators were acting. The state put them in place: did the state then give them their orders, directly or implicitly, on how they were to do their job? Were they acting as agents of social control, imposing a conformity in the interests of the state? In the United States, there are constitutional blocks on anything of that kind happening, but, in an area so full of subjective judgements as content regulation, value judgements have to be made every day. Whose values prevailed, therefore? One official at the FCC in Washington was apparently known as 'the national nanny' for supplying answers to questions which could not, if broadcasting were to continue, be left without them. He may have relied, as other regulators have done, on common sense, but what constitutes common sense is itself a matter for contention.

So I wanted to find out in the name of what the questions had been asked in the past and how, if at all, they are to be answered in the future. I thought it would be valuable to explore the American broadcasting system, of which I knew only enough to know how much more I had to learn. It is a system which is enormously popular, generated by an industry which is enormously successful. Britain, by contrast, has a system at least as popular and also, in its commercial sector, very profitable, but achieving its success within a much tighter framework of regulation than exists in the United States. I thought that a contrast between the two systems, emerging from two different societies, one the reluctant progenitor of the other, might be valuable, perhaps enabling the future to be seen a little more clearly in the light of the past.

I was fortunate enough to be given a generous grant by the John & Mary Markle Foundation in New York. It enabled me to spend nearly six months in the United States during the winter of 1996/7. In the first three months I benefited from the generous hospitality of the Center for Policy Studies at Duke University, North Carolina. My particular hosts were Dr Ellen

Mickiewicz, Director of the De Witt Wallace Center for Communications and Journalism, and Professor Joel Fleishman, of the Department of Ethics. I am very grateful to them both and to other members of the University who enriched my stay by sharing their knowledge and experience. My final weeks were spent at the Benjamin N. Cardozo Law School, part of Yeshiva University in New York, for which my thanks are due to Professor Monroe E. Price. From these bases, I was able to travel north as far as Minneapolis, west to Los Angeles, and up and down the East Coast between New York and Charlottesville. I carried out a number of interviews to continue the series I had already begun in Britain and would resume again on my return home in the spring of 1997. Some of the interviews are quoted in the succeeding chapters, a measure of their immediate relevance, but not of the worth of all the thoughts and insights that I gathered from words unquoted and people unnamed. I made constant companions of Asa Briggs and Erik Barnouw whose histories, respectively, of British and American broadcasting are indispensable to anyone embarked on a task of this kind and to whom I owe special thanks. Finally, I must express my gratitude for advice and guidance from two long-standing friends, Professor Jay Blumler and Stephen Hearst, who patiently saw me through successive drafts.

There are two further matters with which I would like to end this Preface. The first of them has to do with style. When the parliamentary draftsmen were drafting terms of reference in 1989 for the Broadcasting Standards Council which the British Government was proposing to set up, they used the formula 'sex and violence'. It seemed to those of us who were to run the new body that this was to reinforce a dangerous stereotype. Equating sex and violence as if they were always a single phenomenon obscured the gravity of the latter, a judgement in which the majority of people concurred, while giving an undue emphasis to the former about which public attitudes in Britain were continuing to undergo radical changes. For the same reason, it would be sensible to reverse taste and decency so that the more important of them, in my view, received priority. I have not done so, concluding that to reverse them on the relatively few occasions when they appear together would be an unnecessary underlining, irritating by its unfamiliarity, of a distinction which, I hope, quickly makes itself apparent.

The final matter is more personal. I was described in 1990 by the left-leaning *Guardian* as 'suspiciously liberal'. I am as proud of that description as any since I believe the *Guardian* and I would agree on its meaning. I abhor the way in which the word 'liberal' has been abused in the past twenty years, its humanity and generosity hijacked for an economic system which has seemed to me to be lacking in either quality. I am aware that, as a liberal, I should be suspicious of regulation, but its absence offers a bleak alternative for the values which, again as a liberal, I believe broadcasting should uphold. I hope that my deep affection for Charles Hill, a former Chairman of the BBC, entitles me, now that I cannot seek his permission, to quote some words which he used in his last public address before retiring more than twenty-five years ago. He spoke of television, but the words apply no less to radio:

A liberal, tolerant society of the kind we have had in this country represents an immense gamble with the goodwill of its citizens . . . It is a collective gamble and, if it is to be successful, it depends on an enlightened, rather than an ignorant, population. Television has, I believe, a major part to play in the process of enlightenment, setting the facts before the people and providing contexts in which the facts can be properly judged. It is not, I suggest, the business of television to influence people in the judgements they make. Nor, however, is it the business of television to work in a moral vacuum anywhere where there are moral values to be found.[1]

The words were originally mine. I would not want to amend them today. I hope they do not impugn my liberal credentials.

1 May 1998   C.S.

---

[1] Reprinted in the *Listener*, 7 Dec. 1972.

Contents

Definitions

Some clarification may be useful at the start of this book. 'Broadcaster' is applied here to organizations responsible for transmission, with the words 'programme-maker' used for producers, directors, and production teams. Regulation, with two exceptions in Britain, is the responsibility of organizations independent of the broadcasters: the Federal Communications Commission in the United States, the Independent Television Commission and the Radio Authority in Britain, none of them having anything to do with individual programmes prior to transmission. The exceptions are the British Broadcasting Corporation and the Welsh Fourth Channel Authority, both of which are self-regulating. Within individual broadcasters, there are specialist staffs to ensure that programme-makers, before transmission, comply with external or in-house standards. To differentiate them from the outside regulators, therefore, they are described here as editors, although I try, when confusion could arise, to distinguish them again from those senior figures among programme-makers who are also called editors.

'Britain' covers four constituent members: England, Scotland, Wales, and Northern Ireland. Scotland was an independent kingdom until 1707 when, by the Act of Union, it was joined with England and Wales. When necessary to distinguish one of them from the others, it is named.

The functions of the main organizations which appear in the text are:

Federal Communications Commission (FCC)

Established by the US Communications Act, 1934, as the successor to the Federal Radio Commission. Consists of five Commissioners, no more than three drawn from the same party, nominated by the President and appointed by the Senate for five years. Its responsibilities extend beyond broadcasting to include telecommunications of all kinds. In broadcasting, the Commission awards licences to radio and television stations on the basis of 'public interest, content, and necessity', required, without definition, in the Act. Although it emphasized content regulation as a precondition of the renewal of licences, the political climate of the past two decades has diminished the Commission's energies in this direction, coupled with the increasing difficulties of overseeing the multiplicity of stations now licensed.

Corporation for Public Broadcasting (CPB)

Created by the Public Broadcasting Act, 1967, as a non-governmental, non-profit-making agency to foster and support a Public Broadcasting Service (television) and National Public Radio, allocating funds provided by Congress.

National Association of Broadcasters (NAB)

The trade association of terrestrial broadcasters in the United States.

British Broadcasting Corporation (BBC)

From 1927 onwards, the BBC has been wholly responsible for the selection, production, and transmission of programmes in radio and, later, television, under the supervision of a Board of Governors appointed by the Crown on the advice of the Government. The BBC's activities are defined by its Royal Charter and a licence issued by the Minister responsible for broadcasting. In 1997, the BBC's network of transmitters was sold to a commercial operator. Largely funded by a licence fee levied on all owners of television-receivers. Radio-receivers are no longer licensed, the BBC's radio services being supported out of the licence-revenue.

Independent Television Commission (ITC) and the Radio Authority

Formed in 1991 by dividing the former Independent Broadcasting Authority, these two bodies issue and regulate licences to commercial broadcasters, including the providers of satellite and cable services. Both are funded by their licensees.

Sianel Pedwar Cymru (S4C): the Welsh Fourth Television Channel

Launched in 1982, after considerable political pressure within Wales, the station broadcasts in the Welsh language for about thirty hours a week, mainly in peaktime. It takes the remainder of its output from the national Channel 4. Has a board of seven members appointed by the Government which provides an annual grant, with advertising revenue as a supplement.

Congress shall make no law respecting an establishment of religion, or prohibiting the free exercise thereof; or abridging the freedom of speech, or of the press, or the right of the people peaceably to assemble, and to petition the Government for a redress of grievance.

(First Amendment to the American Constitution)

Nothing in this Act shall be understood or construed to give the [Federal Communications] Commission the power of censorship over the radio communications or signals transmitted by any radio station and no regulation or condition . . . shall interfere with the right of free speech by means of radio communication.

(Section 326, Federal Communications Act, 1934)

It shall be the duty of the [Independent Television] Authority to satisfy themselves that, as far as possible, [in] the programmes broadcast . . . nothing is included . . . which offends against good taste and decency or is likely to encourage or incite to crime or to lead to disorder or be offensive to public feeling or which includes any offensive representation of or reference to a living person.

(Section 3 (1) (a), UK Television Act, 1954)

1

Starting Places

The Third Domain

Standards of taste and decency in any society do not exist in isolation from the prevailing morality in that society. In an authoritarian state, they are the product of the ruling orthodoxy as interpreted by those in power. Their expression in the media is an extension of the means of social control. In democracies of a pluralistic kind, however, as the United States and Britain have increasingly become, the issues are less clear-cut. At the turn of the century, a British lawyer, Lord Moulton, wrote:

There are three great domains of human conduct: the first is where our actions are limited or forbidden by law. Then there is the domain of free personal choice. But between these is a third domain, that in which there is neither law nor unfettered freedom. This is the domain of 'obedience to the unenforceable', where people do right although there is no one and nothing to make them do right except themselves.[1]

Writing nearly a hundred years ago, Lord Moulton was less conscious than we are now of the many influences which affect our actions. We are less our own free agents than he believed. Nevertheless, the distinction he drew between the three domains keeps its value. Indeed, the proper cultivation of the third domain may have grown in importance as, with more moral uncertainties than before, we have placed less trust in the law as an instrument of moral control.

Fifty years later, the comedienne Beatrice Lillie used to sing a cheerful song whose refrain was 'We are all rotten to the core, Maud.' In it, she took delight in the moral decay she purported to see all about her. We laughed

[1] An Address on 'Law and Manners', given at the Authors' Club, London, 4 Nov. 1912.

because we were merely flirting with the possibility that she was right and were reasonably sure that her perception was false. Since then, the laughter has become tinged with a certain uneasiness. 'You may call an Englishman stupid', it was once said, 'because he knows he is not. But beware of calling him immoral.' But we should also beware of exaggerating the extent of those moral uncertainties by confusing, as it is not difficult to do, a lack of manners in contemporary societies with an absence of morals.

In the past twenty years, both Britain and the United States have experienced changes in their prevailing ideologies: in the latter an intensification of its long-standing trust in the market, in the former an acceptance, still heavily qualified, of the benefits which the market can bring. The thinking which prompted the changes remains a powerful influence on the governments in both Washington and London. Indeed, the Oxford theologian Oliver O'Donovan believes that the changes we have observed in the past twenty years may be as much political and ideological as they are moral. One result, Professor O'Donovan suggested to me, has been to encourage us to think of society in Britain as more divided than it actually is:

since the startling revival of neo-liberalism in the 1970s which took everybody by surprise—I don't know anyone who expected that these old nineteenth-century doctrines would be taken out and dusted down and suddenly become reigning orthodoxy . . . I didn't expect it, thought they were all in the past. But . . . that sudden new neo-liberal line on everything . . . [has] had a terribly wide effect on the way things are organized, because of the total thorough-goingness of government, revolutionary government changes of thought. Plurality in society has become a necessary hypothesis to make the whole reorganization of society understandable . . . I take it that those who have advocated the massive introduction of choice, the pluralization of everything, think . . . it's positively sensible and has manifestly good effects. But the reason they think that, or at least a hypothesis for their being able to think that, is the notion that we all want something very, very different from one another . . . But it's not clear to me that society has changed just because the reigning doctrine about society has changed . . . We're very much the same kind of quiet-living, decent civilized people, lots of us as we were in 1970, it seems to me. The prejudices are the same, the suspicions are the same. It's just that we have to read ourselves now in terms of being a highly differentiated society because we are told we are.[2]

The reality, on both sides of the Atlantic, is that a considerable degree of consensus on some basic moral questions exists. To take a modern example, we have made a moral issue, although often heavily qualified by politics, about our exploitation of the environment. As Professor O'Donovan said in the same conversation, there is a close link between

[2] Regius Professor of Moral and Pastoral Theology. Personal interview, Oxford, 21 June 1996.

morality and anxiety, making us more moralistic according to the intensity of our concerns. We fear for the consequences of destroying our natural resources on our own generation and on the discharge of our responsibilities to the generations which follow us. We tend, therefore, to adopt uncritical attitudes without recognizing the complexities of achieving any practical solutions in which the global community can concur, all equally affected, but not all equally responsible. It is arguable that broadcasting, so readily and uncritically blamed for a decline in moral values, has contributed to our change of attitudes, heightening our consciousness of destructive actions throughout the world against wildlife habitats, rainforests, and tribal communities which, collectively or individually, have become the foci of our worries.

More traditionally, very few people would maintain that murder is anything other than evil, even though we are divided about the morality of exacting an eye for an eye and killing in our turn the perpetrator of murder. Nor is any real defence offered for child-abuse and rape. Indeed, public attitudes towards both have grown harder in recent years. Evidence of their pervasiveness has become more available and taboos on their discussion have become more difficult to maintain. The qualifications which used to be expressed by men about rape are heard less frequently than they were, certainly from judges. For social and biological reasons, incest remains a more powerful taboo in most societies, almost too strict for it to be talked about in broadcasting in anything other than a very rare documentary or an occasional news-item.

What characterizes those actions is that they all have victims whose suffering is visible. Robberies, too, have their victims, but, with some robberies, we begin to tread the edges of moral ambivalence. What was described to me, in another conversation I had while researching for this book, as the old arsenal of principles and values does not sit easily alongside the new dilemmas.[3] 'All property is theft' has relatively few defenders as a general principle, but some contemporary forms of theft are seen in less black-and-white terms. Stealing when there is compensation for the victim from an insurance company is not perceived as a crime in quite the same way as is robbery from a helpless old person. Cheating a large corporation, whether or not it is your own employer, is not condemned as automatically as a mugging. The element of individual suffering, so essential for sympathy and for sympathetic treatment in the media, is missing. Insurance companies, like big businesses of all kinds and large stores, are considered too impersonal to be injured by crimes of that kind. The cynical, and probably justified, assumption is that they will eventually pass on

---

[3] Richard Holloway, Bishop of Edinburgh. Personal interview, Edinburgh, 22 Aug. 1996.

any losses to their customers. Some branches of the media readily demonize large companies and corporations when individuals are in conflict with them, adding to the perception of such organizations, even when they are behaving responsibly, as ripe for the kind of revenge which thieving or a form of fraud may appear to exact.

So what has changed? Confidence in moral attitudes has weakened with the weakening of confidence in those who once asserted them and, where necessary, enforced them. Context has come to play a bigger part. In particular, the individual, conscious of fewer allegiances or obligations than before, makes more independent judgements. 'Nobody else was involved/hurt' has become a standard defence of other forms of behaviour which are not classed as criminal, even though, in the past, some of them may have been. To take an extreme example, attitudes to suicide have changed profoundly in the last fifty years or so. This has happened most notably in the case of dying patients who choose to take their lives with the object of ending their own suffering and relieving the distress of their dependants. From that, it is a short step to assisted suicide and euthanasia. Persuasive arguments exist for or against both, even though, in Lord Moulton's day, they would not have been countenanced. Abortion, while it remains abhorrent to large numbers of people, is acceptable to others no less honest in their opinions. The same is true of contraception.

The catalogue of causes for these changing attitudes, observed in the Western world over most of this century, is lengthy and often the reflection of personal prejudices. It includes improvements in education and a consequent reluctance to take very much on trust from previous sources of authority; a general decline in religious beliefs; a great reduction in levels of poverty; advances in medical science which, as well as making their own contribution to that decline, allow us to live longer; and, perhaps the most fundamental of all, the still-evolving changes brought about in the relationships between men and women for which women's greater economic independence and the liberating effects of the contraceptive pill are responsible.

Many people would add the media to the list. They point to the huge sums spent annually on broadcast advertising and are not always convinced by arguments that the purpose of such advertising is not to change behaviour, but simply to influence the choices consumers make, within legal and socially approved patterns of behaviour, between one product and another. They point to the apparent success of advertising campaigns directed at curbing drinking and driving. Many broadcasting practitioners, however, express a genuine belief that the media have played little or no part in initiating changes more profound than the replacement of one fashion by another. At one moment, flares are in, at the next they are out again.

Broadcasting's role in adding momentum to the pace of change is less doubtful. The rise in popular feeling in the United States against the continuation of the Vietnam War was not the deliberate creation of the media, but the media not only revealed its existence in different parts of the country, but also fuelled it with images and accounts of the war's realities, almost certainly quickening the pace at which hostility to American participation in the war grew.

The daily demands for material, fed by commercial pressures for sales and audiences, put a premium on the new and the changing. It is, moreover, in the nature of many programme-makers to wish to challenge old ideas and explore fresh ones. Some of them have a conscious wish to proselytize, even though the fallibility of the media in communicating messages unwanted by their readers or audiences is notorious. All broadcast programmes, however, when put forward as proposals for development, have to survive the scrutiny of managements often instinctively conservative and reluctant to court controversy, whether as a reflection of company policy or to maintain their own positions in the hierarchy.

It is no good trying to predict the extent to which these moral ambiguities, to which the majority of us are prey in one situation or another, will develop in the next fifty years. Almost every scientific or technological advance brings with it a fresh set of dilemmas and no accompanying set of solutions. The effect of these dilemmas, if they spread more widely, will make it even more difficult than now to traverse Lord Moulton's third domain, where refraining from action may be as important as engaging in it. The promptings of conscience, the equivalent of a hand on the sleeve and a murmured 'Yes, but . . . ', which provide that domain with its common currency are inseparable from the balance of democratic societies. The alternatives to maintaining a stable society by these means would be the extension of the rule of law within the first domain or the acceptance of the anarchy implicit in setting no bounds to the relativism of the second. The best hopes for a democratic society, and the institutions, like the broadcasters, which help to form it, can flourish only in the third.

The discussion of issues of taste and decency, which is the business of the book, necessarily calls for a lengthy prelude. In any country, the culture of broadcasting mirrors the society out of which it develops. In comparing American broadcasting with broadcasting in Britain, we have first to look at differences between those two societies which have influenced the growth of their broadcasting systems in one direction or another.

Differences

I had asked a friend for advice as I began working on this book. 'Don't let the language fool you,' he said. 'Take it from me, they're different.'

He was right, of course, about the differences. America is a true land mass, its east and west coasts almost as far apart as London and New York. Britain is a small island, the deepest inland-dwelling of its inhabitants never more than an hour or two from the surrounding sea. The citizens of Los Angeles are starting work when in Washington, at the other side of the country, its citizens are three hours closer to going home again. In Britain, people going to their shops or offices are likely to read the same headlines in identical morning papers, whether they live in the far north of the country or the far south. Only recently have Americans experienced newspapers with any serious pretensions to national distribution. Britons like to believe that Americans are enchanted by the new. They consider themselves generally more wary, sceptical of promises, a frequent response to novelty being a calm, 'I'm not bothered.' A Victorian Post Office official in London reportedly disparaged the telegraph, pointing to the abundant availability of messenger-boys to achieve the same purposes.

There are some 250 million Americans. When fully mustered, Britons number only a quarter of that. America is a country of restless immigrants, while a British politician's injunction to the workless to 'Get on their bikes' was thought a grave affront to the principle, not entirely worthless, that work should be brought to them. The British sometimes acknowledge that they too are a mongrel breed, but they are just as likely to be thinking of a mongrel's tenacity and fidelity as they are of its genetic make-up. Where in Britain is the counterpart to the experience of an acquaintance of mine, formerly British? Standing between a Croat and a Haitian, he was naturalized as an American in company with people from thirty-seven different nationalities. He had, in the process, given up being a subject and become a citizen, a change of role which is near the core of the differences between the two societies.

In broadcasting, the contrast is between a system which initially regarded broadcasting as an economic activity and a system which saw it primarily as a social and cultural activity. The diversity of terrestrial stations and of cable and satellite channels in the United States provides programmes and, in turn, revenues on a far larger scale than in Britain. However, the public sector of broadcasting, where British broadcasting really began, remains much larger in Britain than the combined resources of PBS and NPR which entered late and perennially under-resourced onto a stage dominated by commercial operators. The principle of public accountability is applied in Britain beyond the strict limits of the public sector. Official regulators exercise authority over the technical, commercial, and programme-making activities of television and radio companies, with an internal self-regulatory structure for the largest of the broadcasters, the BBC. Notches on a gun-barrel may be proof of either the skill of the marksman or the ease of his target, but, during the five decades in which commercial television has existed in Britain, the regulators' record in failing to renew licences bears comparison with that of the FCC in the seven decades of its existence.

The ideals of public service, independent of politics and commerce, have permeated British society for 150 years. Their extension in the late 1920s to broadcasting implanted them, first in the BBC and, thirty years later, in the structure and conduct of commercial broadcasting in Britain. The name of public service was given to a practice of broadcasting, accountable to Parliament, whose purpose was to give service, equally throughout the country, to the majority and as many of the minority interests of the audience as resources allowed. The achievement of universality, which has been almost complete for many years, is one explanation of the much slower rise of cable and satellite services in Britain, unlike the United States where scattered coverage and poor reception gave the promoters of the new services their most powerful sales argument.

The values of public service continue to filter through the British terrestrial system, their survival due to the continued existence of public and political support for the tradition, not only as it is expressed in broadcasting, but more widely, notably in upholding the principle of a National Health Service. It is the token of a sense of community. Not altogether surprisingly, few things said or done by Mrs Thatcher in her years as Prime Minister caused such outrage as the widespread suspicion that she really had said, 'There is no such thing as society.' Its survival in broadcasting also owes much to the presence within the managements of many of the commercial broadcasters of men and women brought up in the tradition. The values are present in the work of many programme-makers, particularly those who learnt their professional skills within the BBC. They belong to the generations, which existed in both Britain and the United States, for whom programmes came first. For them the word 'product' was a novelty to be regarded with suspicion less for itself than for those who introduced it into the industry.

With their successors brought up under the ascendancy of accountants, the future of the tradition is less certain. More than one of the Americans with whom I talked told me that the managers at corporate headquarters were now firmly in control, with programmes subject to the blind discipline of the bottom line. 'Broadcasting', said one of them, coining a phrase, 'cannot live by accountancy alone. When it is simply one profit-centre to be measured against others within the conglomerate portfolio, then its value within society is likely to be wrongly assessed.'

Apart from the differences briefly noted, there are at least two areas of particular importance in any comparison of the two societies and the broadcasting which they support: their differing attitudes towards free expression and commerce. And, in the light of our understanding of those differences, we need to explore the way in which the regulation of broadcasting developed.

Free Expression

The Status of Government

In 1776, the British colonies along the east coast of North America severed their constitutional ties with Britain. Following the Declaration of Independence, the former colonists became sovereign. Ceasing to be subjects of the Crown, they became instead citizens of the new United States, exercising the authority previously exercised from London by the King-in-Parliament. Under the new nation's Constitution, devised in 1787, legislature, executive, and judiciary, in conducting the business of the new nation, were to share power. None of them was to have superiority over the other two.

Britain's own constitutional position was unchanged by events across the Atlantic. The process continued by which, over the centuries, the powers of the monarch had been diminished: sometimes peacefully, sometimes abruptly, and, once, violently enough to bring about the execution of the King and the formation of a republican government under a Lord Protector. With the restoration of the monarchy after little more than ten years, the gradual transfer of powers was resumed. It led eventually to the present status of the monarch as a hereditary, non-political head of state, in contrast to the position of the elective presidency of the United States. In place of the equality of all citizens in the United States, the subjects of the Queen, as they remain, live, in effect, on the slopes of a pyramid, with authority exercised in her name by a Government ranked a little below the summit and accountable to Parliament. The creation of a Citizens' Charter by the last Conservative Government (1979–97) was seen by much of the British public as mere public relations, more form than substance, rather than as a signal of a significant change in their own constitutional position. Their scepticism was taken as a further sign of a decline in deference.

James Madison, the author of the First Amendment and later President of the United States, characterized the difference between the two systems of governance:

If we advert to the nature of Republican Government, we shall find that the censorial power is in the people over the Government, and not in the Government over the people.[4]

Madison's observation is at the heart of the different approaches in Britain and America to the regulation of their broadcasting industries.

Attitudes to Free Speech

On the American side, there is a profound commitment to free speech. The Bill of Rights, which in 1791 became an addition to the Constitution, is mainly concerned with 'Freedoms from . . .' rather than 'Rights to . . .', the approach which has found expression in some constitutions more recently drafted elsewhere in the world. The inclusion of freedom from government intervention in free speech as the first of the constitutional amendments contained in the Bill symbolizes the importance attached to it by the Founding Fathers.

As new means of distributing opinion have developed in the last 150 years, the scope of the First Amendment has stretched far beyond print. One of the Amendment's underlying purposes was to secure the integrity of the public debate which lay at the heart of republican government. When the debate is fettered, then the ability of the people to carry out their sovereign responsibility, as Madison had defined it, is compromised. A contemporary description of the First Amendment was given in a judgment by the US Supreme Court in 1994, when Justice Kennedy said:

At the heart of the First Amendment lies the principle that each person should decide for himself or herself the ideas and beliefs deserving of expression, consideration, and adherence. Our political system and cultural life rest upon this ideal. Government action that stifles speech on account of its message, or that requires the utterance of a particular message favoured by the Government, contravenes this essential right. Laws of this sort pose the inherent risk that the Government seeks not to advance a legitimate regulatory goal, but to suppress unpopular ideas or information or manipulate the public debate through coercion rather than persuasion.[5]

The judgment, on behalf of a majority of the Court, was given at the end of the a challenge by Turner Broadcasting to the legality of the 'must-carry' requirement imposed by the Federal Communications Commission on cable services. The distinction drawn by Congress between cable services and broadcast services is described more fully in the succeeding chapter.

---

[4] J. Madison, *Annals of Congress, 1794*.   [5] See ch. 2.

The extension of the First Amendment has stretched so far that, in the view of some critics, the Amendment has become a licence to make profits, not a measure to protect speech. It is time, some of them would go on to argue, for a revised version to be adopted in a form more suited to the circumstances of a modern, industrial, nation. I asked Henry Geller, General Counsel to the FCC in Washington between 1964 and 1970, who had expressed reservations about the workings of the First Amendment in modern conditions, whether he would have supported it, had he been one of the Founding Fathers:

Oh, yes, but I might have worded it differently. It just says 'should make no law', and, of course, that's crazy. You have to make a law, you can't shout 'Fire' in a crowded theatre, as Mr Holmes said, and others. Really, they've left it to the courts to carve it out. I think I would have considered it and tried to. . . . Once you do that, though, I admit I've embarked on a very, very, very difficult journey.[6]

Geoffrey Cowan, Dean of the Annenberg School of Communications in Los Angeles, doubted whether the First Amendment would have been adopted in the late twentieth century. However, after adding with a certain wryness, 'But you never know, sometimes the people do wise things,' he said:

However, I think the Court, in the way our system works, the Court can tread on the edges of these things. You have different judges interpreting even the First Amendment differently. In the Pentagon Papers case, you had [Justice] Hugo Black saying 'The Press can never be censored.' You had [Chief Justice] Warren Burger saying, 'You shouldn't be allowed to print it.' You had William Brennan saying, 'We should be allowed to print it, but there are narrow circumstances in which you wouldn't.' They were all interpreting the First Amendment and they do it with three different readings. So part of the genius of the American system is that it has the Constitution, but it has a Court which is more, maybe, in sync with, in tune with, the political differences to be able to mould them.[7]

Don West, then editor of *Broadcast and Cable* magazine, regarded as the platform of the broadcasting industry, agreed that the First Amendment could prove uncomfortable even for those who, like himself, were among its firmest supporters:

---

[6] Personal interview, Washington, 12 Feb. 1997.

[7] Personal interview, Los Angeles, 26 Feb. 1997. The Pentagon Papers was the name given in 1971 to a Defense Department study of the conduct of the Vietnamese War. It was highly critical of US military and diplomatic policy. The study acquired the name when it was passed to the *New York Times* which, against the wishes of the executive, planned publication. As the extract from the interview indicates, the Supreme Court, to which the executive took its case, upheld the right to publish, the margin being six justices in favour, three against.

I was watching Dave Letterman last night and he [was] taking for granted that the President had been having affairs. And I was offended by that and that somehow, because he was the President, he should be given more deference. Why should he speak of the President in that way? Why should he be the butt of jokes? But then I said, 'I'm a First Amendment absolutist, to the limit.' . . . You can't give the Government an inch because they will take a mile. I could not at all agree that the Government should have a hand in that. I [could] wish that he were governed by his audience or that he had better taste.[8]

The protection given by the First Amendment to free speech is, however, not absolute, although the limitations put on it from time to time by the courts continue to draw critical comments from those describing themselves, like Don West, as First Amendment absolutists. There is, for instance, a general doctrine of 'reasonable time, place and manner', of which Justice Wendell Holmes in the words quoted by Henry Geller provided the most celebrated example. Shouting 'Fire' when to do so could produce a disastrous panic is clearly unreasonable, as the justice went on to explain: 'The question in every case is whether the words used are in such circumstances as to create a clear and present danger that they will bring about the substantive evils which Congress has a right to prevent.'[9] He spoke at the time, in 1919, when the Supreme Court was beginning to be more frequently involved in free speech cases than before. In a later case, he was to add another memorable phrase to the litany of the First Amendment. He was addressing the arguments of those who, wholly convinced of the rightness of their ideas, would tolerate no opposition: 'the best test of truth is the power of thought to get itself accepted in the competition of the market, and that truth is the only ground upon which their wishes safely can be carried out.'[10]

Obscenity, which will be considered later, is unprotected, although the Supreme Court has worked its way through a series of decisions defining the conditions for exclusion. Commercial speech enjoys only qualified freedom, although the distinction is sometimes hard to make between advertising as a means of supplying information to the consumer and its use as advocacy for commercial gain.

For a time after its more frequent engagement with free speech issues began, the Supreme Court distinguished between 'high-level speech' and 'low-level' speech measured by the respective contributions they made to the public debate. In 1942, the Supreme Court placed in the minor category speech which might tend to incite an immediate breach of the peace: 'the lewd and obscene, the libellous, the insulting or "fighting"

---

[8] Personal interview, Washington, 11 Feb. 1997.
[9] *Schenck* v. *United States*, 249 US 47 (1919).
[10] *ARAMs* v. *United States*, 250 US 616 (1919).

words'.[11] Any value they had was, in the opinion of the Court, outweighed by the 'social interest in order and morality'.

The division of speech into high- and low-value provoked the criticism that the Court was obliged to make value judgements based on the content of the speech, something which was contrary to the First Amendment. This led to the evolution of the content-neutrality doctrine under which the Government could not discriminate between kinds of speech which were otherwise protected, because of any offence which they might cause. In a case in 1972, the Supreme Court concluded that there must be equality of status in the field of ideas.[12] The Government was not free to pick and choose between expressions of the good life.

From the starting-point of the preservation of the values of the republican debate, the interpretations determined by the Supreme Court were increasingly perceived to be moving on to the protection of individual self-expression. Critics of the way in which the Court's decisions have evolved had argued that they reflect a greater emphasis on rights rather than on the duties which should form part of the republican life, with the corollary, put forward by Robert Bork, unsuccessful in his candidature for the Supreme Court, that moral relativism must follow. He was particularly scornful of Justice Harlan's defence, with the words 'One man's vulgarity is another man's lyric', of an accused man's right to have the words 'Fuck the draft' written on the back of his shirt in a courthouse.[13]

In contrast, the British, although counting themselves free men and women, accept considerably greater degrees of restraint on free speech than would be tolerated in the United States. A small number of examples may illustrate the point. In America, not only public officials, but people falling within a very broad definition of public figures, can usually be regarded as fair game in the conduct of the robust public debate to which the country traditionally aspires. A far stricter law of defamation, for example, means that any similar debate in Britain is necessarily more constrained. Its effect has been magnified by the ability of those with matters to conceal to exploit other legal devices in threatening litigation to deflect unwanted enquiries from the media. Contempt of court, the Official Secrets Act, and rules on confidentiality may all be invoked. Most recently, new legislation directed at the prevention of 'stalking' has been invoked as a possible fresh means of discouraging investigative journalism.

Harold Evans, a former editor of the *Sunday Times* and *The Times* in

[11] *Chaplinsky* v. *New Hampshire*, 375 US 568, 572 (1942).

[12] *Police Dept. of the City of Chicago* v. *Mosley*, 405 US at 95–6.

[13] Robert Bork, *Slouching towards Gomorrah* (Regan Books/HarperCollins, New York, 1996), 98–9.

London and a powerful supporter of investigative journalism, has remained closely in touch with Britain. When I met him in the first weeks of 1997, he had been Publisher of Random House in New York for several years and has subsequently become Editorial Director of several publications including the *New York Daily News, U.S. News & World Report,* and the *Atlantic.* In 1995, lecturing in the city, he had recited, for the benefit of his American audience, some of the restraints under which the British journalist labours, acknowledging that he had had first-hand experience of some of them, notably in the *Sunday Times*'s campaign, while he was its editor, on behalf of the claim for compensation of children affected by the drug thalidomide. The British had, he said, always admired the Americans for their freedom, but now, he believed, things were changing. He noted in America a greater reluctance to insist on the investigation of the real sources of power in government and business, the infiltration of tabloid values into the serious Press and television, an obsession with sexual scandals, and a willingness, left and right, to accept the inhibitions imposed by political correctness. It was becoming possible to argue that the agenda for debate, as opposed to enquiry, in Britain was generally wider than it was in the States. He told me:

> I've been here for twelve years now and I am a little less euphoric than I was. I've noticed two things. One is that the range of opinion is very small. Despite the torrents of fact, there seems to be a more mob attitude to opinion. . . . In Europe, in France and Britain, there is less information, but a greater freedom of expression. Here there is much greater conformity and it is harder for people to break free.
>
> Q. Who imposes the uniformity?
> A. Oh, the Press and broadcasting. I've been reflecting on how it might arise. I thought it might arise from the need to live together in a very heterogeneous community scattered over large distances. . . . Americans have always had a much greater fear than anywhere else I know of dissenting voices. Even though America was born in dissent and dissent, in quotes, is still cherished . . . the Press and broadcasting seeking to win a mass audience present a kind of mass consensus. An insecure public, insecure about its own education, insecure about where it belongs in the vast diversity of the country, also seeks points of identity. Identifying with the common opinion gives identity. The people don't have the British attachment to places. The population is relentlessly migrant.[14]

Speaking in Oxford, not long after I had met him, he said: 'For all the size and vivacity [of the USA], there are proportionately fewer independent voices than in Britain.'[15]

Over questions of national security, the decision of the Supreme Court

[14] Personal interview, New York, 29 Jan. 1997.
[15] Speech given at Oxford University, partly reprinted in the *Guardian,* 2 June 1997.

in the Pentagon Papers case demonstrated that, despite the weight and urgency of US government opinion that vital national interests would be jeopardized by publication, in the United States the right to publish was paramount. The tragi-farce of the *Spycatcher* case, lasting for three years from 1985, proved that the opposite was true in Britain.[16] On that occasion, the British Government carried to extreme lengths its attempts to suppress the memoirs of one of its former secret agents. Many Americans were astonished by the obduracy of its persistence, having been free, long before the British themselves, to read the book which prompted the Government's action. It was during proceedings in an Australian court, about as close to the ends of the earth as it is possible to get from Britain, that the British Cabinet Secretary, forced onto the defensive, uttered the words 'economical with the truth'. The words have been attributed in the past to both St Thomas Aquinas and Edmund Burke, but, although not original, their appearance in that setting from that particular mouth ensured them renewed life in the vocabulary of evasive speech in which the British, in or out of government, are practised. The scope of the Official Secrets Act, which notoriously covered Civil Service canteen menus, has actually been extended in the past twenty years, with the removal of the right to plead a 'public interest' defence. No barricades went up in Britain against the change, but, it must be conceded, the British do not often display great fervour in defence of free speech.

A Freedom of Information Bill was included by New Labour in its 1997 election manifesto, but the timetable for its appearance remains to be confirmed. In the summer of 1998, reports from Whitehall indicated that civil servants were having difficulties in accommodating the realities of government operations and the necessary aspirations of such a Bill. The prospects of a rerun in Britain of the Pentagon Papers affair were hardly improved early in 1997 when a British newspaper handed back an embargoed government document which came into its possession. Not long afterwards, the incoming New Labour Government indicated that it would incorporate the European Declaration on Human Rights into British law, but how the Declaration marches with Britain's long history of an unwritten Constitution and parliamentary sovereignty will be a matter for prolonged debate. Starting with a clean slate, as the Founding Fathers did when they set down the American Constitution and the Bill of Rights, for all the difficulties they encountered, may appear easy by comparison.

---

[16] P. Wright, *Spycatcher* (Viking Penguin, New York, 1987). Further details can be found in Hugo Young's biography of Margaret Thatcher, *One of Us* (Macmillan, London, 1989).

Henry Geller expressed the general dismay of Americans when conscious of British attitudes to free expression:

I'm horrified by what you do in Britain. It's shocking.... The Official Secrets Act ... leaves ... no protection at all. I just cannot imagine the Nixon Government having that power.... I'm just horrified by it. I believe that one of the greatnesses of America, it's eroded a little bit, is the protection of the individual.[17]

The veneration for free expression in the United States can prompt a degree of surprise among Britons to match the degree of Geller's horror. The absence of the strict *sub judice* rules which, in Britain, heavily restrict reporting and comment before and during trials produces, in America, a kind of journalistic free-for-all in accusation and speculation, creating an impression of a disregard for the individual's right to a fair trial. It is true that, unlike his earlier criminal trial dominated by television, the civil trial of O. J. Simpson from which television cameras were absent restored some of the faith which had been lost in the American judicial process. The atmosphere surrounding the original trial, however, had been simply one example of the dramatization of American justice, with real-life lawyers competing in theatricality for celebrity status and leaving observers on the other side of the Atlantic, as well as many people in North America itself, with concerns for the future of justice itself.

Allied to the spirit of the First Amendment is a widely shared suspicion in the United States of the motives of authority, particularly marked when directed against the Government in Washington. Many Americans, while stopping short of active hostility, display a suspicion which borders on it. The British find that surprising, having been accustomed, however grudgingly, to treating their governments as being on their side, ultimately at least. Their mood may be changing as scepticism about Parliament and other institutions grows. Some at least of a change of mood may be attributed to the eighteen years of dominance by a single party after 1979 and the public's disenchantment with the conduct of certain of its members in the later years. As this book will show, there is evidence that a large majority of Britons continue to expect governments to play a more interventionist role, in particular, in broadcasting, than many Americans would find comfortable or, indeed, could regard as constitutional. The stress which Americans generally place on individualism and their opposition to the surrender of decisions to other people has no close parallel in Britain.

[17] Personal interview, Washington, 12 Feb. 1997.

Commerce

A second, highly influential, difference in the evolution of the two broadcasting systems lies in the national attitudes towards commerce. The Americans, with their belief in individualism and little faith in Government, took to heart Benjamin Franklin's statement that no nation was ever ruined by trade.[18] They have put their trust in commerce and the moderating effects of the market-place. The British have displayed, in contrast, a wariness towards admitting commercial values into their institutions, sceptical about the unqualified benefits the market is claimed to deliver. The roots of their wariness can be found in a set of values heavily promoted among the middle and upper classes in the nineteenth century and later. In that period, these values were drummed into the heads of the future leaders of all the most important areas of British national life. Young people who had the choice were not encouraged to make their living in industry or in trade. With few exceptions, schools and colleges put a premium on the arts to the neglect of engineering and science. The large number of lawyers in the former British colonial territories compared with the small number of engineers is continuing evidence of the earlier imbalance which has yet to be fully corrected.

British society remains hierarchical, although less rigidly than was true up to 1939. Possession of land is still an important criterion for social position, although its political significance has very largely disappeared and may, if the House of Lords is reformed or abolished, disappear completely. Entrepreneurialism and risk-taking have only recently become respectable, but bankruptcy remains stigmatized in Britain, even though such incidents are of little account in the United States and close to a way of life in Australia. Britons still have an expectation of probity in financial affairs which has outlasted their moral indignation at sexual misconduct. It leads them to wonder at the tolerance given in the United States to apparently widespread financial malpractice. Although the winner of a large lottery prize is regarded as the beneficiary of a happy accident, the British have yet to be reconciled to the high earnings of managers in industry and financial services. They are not convinced that these are only the rewards of the economic vitality which has so enriched America.

I discussed the difference in attitudes with Jean Boddewyn, Professor of International Business at Baruch College in New York. Boddewyn is a Belgian-American and saw the contrast as existing as strongly between America and Europe as between America and Britain. Europeans liked to consider themselves as less materialistic than Americans, but Boddewyn

---

[18] Benjamin Franklin, *Essay: Principles of Trade*, in *Works of Franklin*, ed. Jared Sparks, vol. ii (T. MacCoun, Chicago, 1882), 401.

believed that, while Americans were materialistic about use, Europeans were materialistic about ownership and wealth because those were the roots of the class systems still strong in Europe. Americans, he said, wanted to know a person's income, because that was what gave him or her status. The British, as Europeans, wanted to know what the person's father did. There might be a few people in America who would look down on the *nouveau riche*, but basically, he said, it was income which positioned an individual. Though there were now tables of the wealthiest men and women in the United States, it was not the wealth which impressed most people, but the belief that it allowed them to stand a lot, to give a lot, and to exercise political influence. 'When I hear that Americans are materialistic, as if Europeans were spiritualistic, I don't buy that. I come from Europe and I know how it goes.'[19]

In the following chapter, we shall consider how the differences between the two societies, particularly over free expression and commerce, have been reflected in the evolution of their respective broadcasting systems.

[19] Personal interview, New York, 28 Jan. 1997.

2

Developing Regulation

Asa Briggs, in the first volume of his *History of Broadcasting in the United Kingdom*, records that early reactions to the possibilities of broadcasting were mixed. Some were adverse, with complaints about the vulnerability of confidential signals to eavesdroppers and the disadvantages of interference by one signal with others.[1] But there was a slow realization that broadcasting held out the promise of very much more. While the growing amount of amateur activity ceased in Britain when war broke out in 1914, with American amateurs experiencing similar treatment three years later, thinking about the wider prospects for radio was not suspended. Briggs quotes two prescient statements about the future of the medium.[2] The first was by David Sarnoff, one of the eventual founders of the Radio Corporation of America. He forecast a range of programme material broadcast from what he called 'A Radio Music Box'. The other appeared in the 1918 edition of the *Yearbook of Wireless Telegraphy and Telephony*. It came from Arthur Burrows, later to be the first Director of Programmes for the British Broadcasting Company, forerunner of the Corporation. Not only did Burrows foresee the variety of programmes envisaged by Sarnoff, but he suggested that advertisements could be placed in the intervals between programmes. His imagination did not, however, advance further than suggesting they might be for soap or tomato ketchup.

It was against a background of such visions and the work done in wartime on its technical development that, once the Armistice had been signed, the two governments began to consider what should be done with

[1] A. Briggs, *History of Broadcasting in the United Kingdom*, 5 vols. (Oxford University Press, London, 1961–95), i. 34.
[2] Ibid. 39–41.

radio. Government involvement was inevitable: not only had much of the pioneering technical work been done by the military in the two countries, but, by international agreement, governments controlled the frequencies which the new services would require. The pre-war anxieties about interference had not diminished and, therefore, control was needed if signals from different stations were to be kept clear of one another. The extent to which there was an early failure to achieve this in the United States led to bitter disputes before it was remedied. If frequencies were considered public assets, then their use in the public interest must be ensured. The question then faced by the two governments was how that was to be done.

In the opening years of the 1920s, there was a measure of agreement, surprising in the light of subsequent events, among the voices raised in Britain and the United States by people concerned about the future. There was talk of broadcasting as a trust. Leonard Goldensohn, the founder of the third American network, ABC, spoke of broadcasting as more than a business. 'It is a trust,' he said.[3] Sarnoff's view of how broadcasting might be used was sufficiently uncommercial for him to continue for several years to think in terms of support coming from endowments of the kind given to libraries and museums.[4] He spoke of broadcasting as a public service, with the tasks of entertaining, informing, and educating the public, words that could, and did, regularly enter the debate in Britain. His design for a governing body for the new public service broadcasting company to carry out the task bore some similarity to the formula adopted in Britain for the British Broadcasting Corporation. Its activities would be controlled by a board on which would serve distinguished figures from public life.

But in 1922, when Sarnoff set out these thoughts, the Corporation was still some distance away. Before then, created in the same year, there was to be a British Broadcasting Company, a commercial organization formed by a group of receiver manufacturers. To the justifiable assertion that it was a monopoly, the official response was that the company was open to any receiver manufacturer who wished to join in. It was funded by a royalty on the sale of receivers and the proceeds of a licence fee set and collected by the Post Office. Under the terms of its operating licence, a ceiling of 7.5 per cent was placed on dividends paid by the company.

In the United States, stations were being licensed by the Department of Commerce under the Radio Licensing Act of 1912. Any American citizen

[3] R. Clurman, *To the End of Time: The Seduction and Conquest of a Media Empire* (Simon & Schuster, New York, 1992), 309. Quoted by L. Bogart, *The Media System and the Public Interest* (Oxford University Press, Oxford, 1955), 55.

[4] Briggs, *History of Broadcasting*, i. 44.

could apply for a licence, as could any company incorporated in an American state. Herbert Hoover, who was Secretary of Commerce for many of the formative years of radio, had the power to allocate one of a limited number of wavelengths available for broadcasting and to set time-limits for its use by the licensee. However, the courts told him, when a challenge was raised to one of his decisions, that he had no power to refuse anyone a licence. Hoover, who expressed a genuine interest in the broader possibilities of the medium and even spoke of a public trust as Sarnoff and others had done, had to contend with a situation which threatened to get out of control. Station fought with station over the use of shared frequencies or operated at higher than the authorized power with the intention of swamping out rival signals. Complaints about interference from neighbouring transmitters flowed in to anyone prepared to receive them.

In response, as an attempt to promote discipline, Hoover convened a series of radio conferences. A scheme was created in 1923 under which stations were divided into three tiers, the most substantial, in the top tier, receiving more favourable treatment in the allocation of frequencies, with guarantees against interference, and broadcasting hours. Educational stations, which had been among the earliest pioneers and reflected a particular view of the role radio should play, were ranked in the third and lowest tier.[5] They lacked the powerful friends who might have shifted the balance of the argument more in their favour and away from business interests. Four years later, in 1927, Congress approved the establishment of a Federal Radio Commission in the continuing effort to ensure an orderly development for the medium.

The Radio Act of that year required the Commissioners, who took over the granting of licences from the Commerce Department, to have in mind 'the public interest, convenience and necessity'. The words had reportedly been taken, by a piece of legislative serendipity or a draftsman's instinct for economy, from legislation devised in the previous century for utility companies. At first sight, an analogy between the roles of broadcasting companies and companies operating such utilities as water and electricity was not altogether far-fetched. It was drawn by people, including Hoover himself, who saw the social and cultural possibilities of radio as a medium of enlightenment to which all the citizens of the United States should have access, as they had access to electricity and cooking-gas. The parallel, however, carries less conviction when drawn between broadcasting services and, for example, the running of public transportation. No explanation

[5] R. W. McChesney, *Telecommunications, Mass Media and Democracy: The Battle for Control of US Broadcasting, 1928–1935* (Oxford University Press, London, 1993).

was offered for the words of the prescription themselves. The interpretation of 'public interest, convenience, and necessity' was left to the Commissioners and their successors, the members of the Federal Communications Commission, who replaced them in 1934 under a new Communications Act.

In Britain too, allied to distaste for what was reported to be happening to broadcasting in the United States with confusion over frequency-use and talk of increasingly strident advertising, there was support for the promise of enlightenment held out by radio. The moral impulse for 'improvement', especially of the less privileged sections of society, which had resulted during the Victorian era in a large number of public works, was still strong in the 1920s. It has been pointed out that the foundation of the BBC as a public corporation was itself the product of the tradition responsible for the establishment of libraries and museums, as well as for the concept of public service with high ideals which had been reflected, for example, in the reform of the Civil Service.[6] Although not free from self-interest, those who developed that earlier tradition recognized Matthew Arnold's arguments for the spreading of culture as a means of tempering society and forging a sense of unity. The Christian tone of their aspirations is reflected in the quotation from the Epistle to the Philippians which was placed above the entrance hall in Broadcasting House, London: 'Whatsoever things are true, whatsoever things are honest . . . think on these things.'[7] It was a calculated reminder of that purpose to all those who worked in the building or visited it. That its aspirations were enduring is demonstrated by a memorandum written towards the end of the Second World War about one of the BBC's two radio networks: 'so designed that it will steadily, but imperceptibly raise the standards of taste, entertainment, outlook, and citizenship.'[8]

The sense of patronage which that sentence conveys contrasts markedly with the emphasis of the final words of the programme policy statement provided by the Independent Broadcasting Authority for the fourth British television channel at its launch in 1980. The Authority expected that, no less than the three existing channels, the new service would add to the enlargement of the public's knowledge and experience, so making 'a real contribution to the society of which broadcasters and non-broadcasters alike form part'.[9]

The Corporation, to replace the existing commercial company, came

---

[6] P. Whannel and D. Cardiff, *A Social History of British Broadcasting*, vol. i (Blackwells, Oxford, 1991), 9.

[7] Philippians 4: 8. Briggs, *History of Broadcasting*, ii. 459.

[8] Briggs, *History of Broadcasting*, iv. 63.

[9] Policy statement given by the IBA to the Board of Channel 4 on its incorporation in 1980.

about as the result of a recommendation, published in 1926, the year before the Radio Act became law in the United States, from a Government Committee in Britain, chaired by the Earl of Crawford. The revenues from the licence fee which had largely financed the old Company would now be diverted to the new body. There would be no advertising, a position which has been maintained, despite challenges more or less overt, throughout the BBC's existence.

In accepting the recommendation, the Government met with general approbation, among the limited number of those whose views were held to be important, that Britain would be preserved from sliding into a commercial morass. The governing body of the new Corporation, five people appointed by the Crown on the advice of the Prime Minister, were to be regarded, in the words of the Crawford Committee, as trustees of the national interest in broadcasting. When the Government was asked why a Corporation, which would have a Royal Charter, had been preferred to a company or a statutory body, the response was that the former would be too like just another company while the latter would seem too like a government department. Expressed simply, a Charter allows its possessor to do anything the Charter does not expressly forbid, provided it is 'incidental or conducive to' the objects and powers of the chartered body. In that, it is the precise opposite of a statute which limits the freedom of a statutory body to the objects specified in it. The distancing of the Government from the detailed business of broadcasting, which the Crawford Committee had recommended, relieved Ministers of any responsibility for answering questions in Parliament on day-to-day issues of programme-content.

The preamble to the Royal Charter referred to the value of broadcasting as 'the means of disseminating information, education, and entertainment'. Like the Federal Radio Commission and its successor, the present-day Federal Communications Commission, the BBC was given no more formal indication of how it was to interpret its basic duty. The Governors were to be responsible for each link of the broadcasting chain, from the making of the programmes in the BBC's own studios by their own staff to the final act of transmission by the BBC's own transmitters. How these increasingly complex things were to be done was left, it was understood, to the Board.

The flavour of British society at that time was not to be lost for another three decades, as an incident which occurred in 1958 demonstrated. The then-Director General of the BBC, Sir Ian Jacob, in a memorandum to the Board of Governors opposing the broadcasting by the BBC of horse-race starting prices, warned that it could lose the BBC the support of 'those people whose good opinion we should seek to justify'.[10] It was only shortly after the Director General had written his memorandum that 'Those people', from whose ranks many Governors had been drawn, were freshly labelled in the public imagination as 'The Establishment'.[11] It was not difficult from outside its ranks to see 'The Establishment' as a sinister force: its members linked by family, education, or occupation, communicating with one another in signs and language whose true meanings were concealed from the very much larger number of non-members. It is a matter of debate how far the image matched the reality, but the wide currency given to the phrase at the turn of the 1960s and afterwards suggests that it struck a responsive chord at a moment of impending change.

Forty years later, the Chairman of the BBC, Christopher Bland, when he was told the story of the Director General's advice, observed:

One of the great revolutions that John Birt [the Director General] has instigated and encouraged here is focusing the BBC on its audience, on the wider needs of all its audience. Both in general and also in specific terms, it makes a very conscientious and quite efficient attempt to serve the needs of all its wide range of licence-fee-payers in different ways. I think it is now regarded as its primary responsibility . . . The idea that we exist really to please a thousand people within a few miles of [Broadcasting House] no longer runs.[12]

However, should the first Governors have lapsed in any of their duties, not least those connected with the maintenance of taste and decency, then they would have been recalled to it by Sir John Reith. Formerly the General Manager of the displaced Company, he was now the BBC's first Director General. Reith was a Scot, a son of the Manse, who professed a stern form of Christianity. He possessed a decisive personality which, allied to the lofty physique which encouraged Winston Churchill to call him his 'wuthering height', enabled him to drive forward his moral ambitions. Under him, the BBC's standards in each one of the fields in which he interested himself were to be of the highest. They had been so at the Company, where, in January 1923, it was laid down that: 'All entertainers must give a guarantee that . . . they will not say or sing anything of a vulgar character.' With one of the earliest references to one of the key elements in the continuing debate about standards, the presence of children in the audience, the instruction continued: 'With approximately two million people, including children, listening, it is obvious that all matter must be entirely above reproach.'[13]

---

[10] BBC archives, G5/58.

[11] Used by Henry Fairlie in 'BBC: Voice of the Establishment', *Encounter*, 13/2 (Aug. 1959).

[12] Personal interview, London, 6 May 1997.

[13] BBC archives, R34/292/1.

John Reith saw no shame in the paternalism of the tradition he pursued. It represented, indeed, a positive duty, for which he might have been chosen, to set out for the BBC's audience a rich assortment of programmes from which it might make its choice. Dismissing the idea that the business of broadcasting was to give the public what it wanted, he argued that the logical end of that approach was a persistent underestimating of public tastes. He was later to state openly his conviction that it was justifiable to use what he called 'the brute force of the monopoly' to uplift the audience. In the invocation of his name, which continues half a century after he left the BBC, he has been like a flown god to whose shrine devotees return in the hope, or possibly the fear, that he may not have finally departed. It was he who imbued the new medium in Britain with a moral purpose which survived his departure and received a further lease of life from the prestige which the BBC enjoyed during and for a few years after the Second World War.

Today, when 'moral purpose' smacks too much of a past with more convictions, it may be more appropriate to write of a moral sense guiding those who take editorial decisions, whether it is expressed in a definition of standards which one would want 'observed in one's home', to quote a definition offered to me in New York, or something reflecting a more conscious working-out of the relationship between values and the standards which are derived from them. However, as much as anyone, Reith's is the reason why it is possible to ask questions about the place of morality in the business of broadcasting and the responsibilities which may fall, as a consequence, on governments and on the broadcasters as well as on programme-makers.

My own view was that Reith's presence at the BBC, with his strong Christian beliefs, was, with hindsight, a happy accident for the quality of British broadcasting. It was, however, challenged from a wider perspective by Professor Duncan Forrester, of the Department of Christian Ethics and Practical Theology in the University of Edinburgh:

I don't think it [the Christian emphasis of the BBC] was as closely tied to the personality of Lord Reith as you suggest, because I think he crystallized the spirit of that age. If you look somewhat later, at the 1944 Education Act, it had a very similar understanding of the national education system and it again was Christian-based and promoting values which were founded on Christian, unashamedly Christian, premises. So I think there has been a massive and pervasive [process of] secularization since then which has not only questioned a Christian basis, but also led to a great deal of pervasive value-relativism and uncertainty. The other process is, I think, largely distinct from that. It is the movement from public service to markets ... from the public interest and the BBC being a teaching body for the whole British people to consumer sovereignty, with consumers and advertisers ultimately having control of content or what is assumed to be consumers' wishes. And this goes very well with an increasingly strong reaction against any kind of paternalism.[14]

The Television Act, 1954, which broke the BBC's television monopoly after twenty-seven years, by creating an alternative television service funded commercially, laid down, however, that the programmes of the new service should: 'maintain a proper balance in their subject-matter and a high general standard of quality'.[15]

Allowing for reasonable criticisms of the BBC's shortcomings, this was a fair summary of the policy which the BBC had tried to carry out in the years of the monopoly. The 1954 Act, however, was to be followed over the next forty years by a series of Broadcasting Acts which were to become more detailed in the prescription of programme content. In the new Act, the rubric of information, education, and entertainment was taken up and repeated in a slightly changed order, although no priority was given to one element over the others. The members of the new ITA were to be appointed by the Minister responsible for broadcasting, a form of appointment appropriate to a statutory body rather than a public corporation. They were taken to be, like the Board of Governors of the BBC, trustees of the national interest in broadcasting. Unlike the Governors, however, they would employ no programme-makers and own no studios, but they were to be co-publishers of the programmes supplied by companies to whom they would grant limited-term franchises. The programmes would be broadcast over a new network of transmitters, operated by the Authority and again planned to give universal coverage in the tradition of public service. The Authority would franchise companies to broadcast programmes and commercials in one or other of a series of regions into which the country was divided. In exchange, the franchisees would pay a rental varying in each region according to its expected level of advertising.

The Act required the Authority to ensure that, as far as possible, nothing offensive to good taste and decency should be included in the programmes of the service which the new authority was to oversee. As we have seen, no similar requirement had been laid upon the BBC. The inclusion of the taste and decency clause, called 'a silly clause in a silly Bill . . . trusting the Authority and then tying its hands' by Labour opponents of commercial television, reflected parliamentary and public concerns about the possible impact of a commercially run service on standards in broadcasting. The clause, the text of which appears at the start of this book, was to survive into several further pieces of broadcasting legislation, although the

---

[14] Personal interview, Edinburgh, 10 June 1996.
[15] *Hansard*, 27 May 1954, cols. 714–17, committee stage of the Television Bill.

proscription of offensive representations or references to living persons was withdrawn.

The atmosphere surrounding the debate in 1953 and 1954 before the passage of the Bill recalled Lord Macaulay's saying that there was no spectacle more ridiculous than the British public in one of its periodical fits of morality. Hyperbole was everywhere. It was crowned by Lord Reith, as he had become, who compared the coming of commercial television to the Black Death, the medieval plague which laid Europe waste (although he failed to remark that one of its more benign consequences was the improved lot of those peasants who survived its ravages).

When, in the early 1960s, there was pressure for the BBC to be put under the same obligations towards taste and decency as the commercial companies, the Corporation resisted strongly. It argued that the Government ought not to become concerned with defining standards which, by nature, were constantly evolving and that, while the presence of the clause in the statute strengthened the hands of a regulatory body like the ITA in dealing with its franchisees, the same specificity applied to the BBC amounted to a derogation from the Governors' powers. Eventually, despite the rearguard actions of Hugh Greene, then Director General, and others, the Chairman of the BBC, in 1964, reluctantly conceded. He did so in the form of his reaffirmation, in a letter to the Postmaster General, of the BBC's duty to ensure high editorial standards and, as far as possible, avoid offence in matters of taste and decency. The phraseology was very similar to that of the clause with which the Television Act bound the Independent Television Authority, but the fact that the letter was, in the end, volunteered by the BBC was held sufficient to maintain the Corporation's independence from government interference. Subsequently, the undertaking has been built into the BBC's governing instruments.

The effect of putting down such a marker was to create a battlefield for the future on which various causes would be fought for, not all of them with much to do with broadcasting. The BBC archives contain the reactions of one of the BBC's defeated negotiators. Quoting Shakespeare's *King John*, he noted, 'How oft the sight of means to do ill makes ill deeds done.'[16]

The original ITA has gone through several changes in its history. There was an early challenge, prompted by the BBC, to the use of the word 'Independent' in its title. Did it not imply that the BBC was, by contrast, not independent? In the knowledge that the label would be perceived unfavourably by many people, critics asked why it should it not be called what it was, that was, a service funded commercially? But the defenders of

---

[16] BBC archives, T16/594.

'Independent' could point to the steps taken to safeguard programmes from the commercial influences which were causing such anxieties: for example, the regulator's oversight of programmes and the rigid separation of commercials from the rest of the output. The word remained.

The Authority's name was changed to the Independent Broadcasting Authority in 1972 when it added commercial local radio to its responsibilities. As the IBA, it was responsible in 1982 for launching Channel 4, as a wholly owned subsidiary. The funding of the new channel, by subscriptions, so-called, from the ITV companies in return for the right to sell the channel's advertising time, preserved the principle of no competition between broadcasters for the same source of revenue.

Then, in 1991, following the Broadcasting Act, 1990, and retitled Independent Television Commission to symbolize a changed role, it took over the regulation of cable services from the Cable Authority. The Authority was abolished after a short-lived and ineffectual existence, having failed to provide the Government's inflated expectations of the new technology with any real substance. Responsibilities for commercial satellite broadcasting were also entrusted to the ITC, although, as with its cable licensees, satellite licences carried no public service obligations, a fact which greatly concerned the Commission's terrestrial licensees who complained that their ability to compete on even terms had been handicapped. To complete the pattern of changes under the 1990 Act, the IBA's former responsibilities for radio passed to a new regulator, the Radio Authority, authorized to create the first commercial radio networks in Britain alongside its existing local stations.

Underlying these changes, included in the Broadcasting Act, 1990, and mandating competition for revenue for the first time in the history of British broadcasting, was the wish of the Government to institute regulation 'with a light touch'. In its view, the role of the IBA, as the co-publisher of the programmes it transmitted, was too interventionist, denying the freedom of its franchisees, the programme-making companies, by its powers to call in advance for entire schedules and individual programme scripts. In future, its successors, the ITC and the Radio Authority, would act only in retrospect, with new powers to enforce the terms of the licences they issued: affecting technical standards, advertising practices, and programme matters. In making this profound change in the role of the IBA, the Government allowed its philosophy of economic freedom to triumph over an instinctive wish, manifest in other directions, to dominate free expression.

Halfway through the previous franchise period, the IBA had issued reports on the companies' performances, detailing strengths and weaknesses in their programme outputs. In the new circumstances of retrospective authority, the ITC issues its reports annually. Michael Grade, Chief Executive of Channel 4 until the early summer of 1997, in expressing resentment at the tone of that year's reports, exposed one of the dilemmas of any form of content regulation:

Frankly, I don't [care] what [the ITC] think about my programmes. Their job is to see whether or not we have fulfilled the letter of the licence. Whether they liked [this] series or they liked this or that show is irrelevant. The only thing they have to look at is, 'Did you meet the terms of your licence?' The rest of it is entirely subjective, from people who have, in my view, no locus in deciding what they like and who cares? Who is it? They liked this, they didn't like that . . . who? [Which of them] didn't like this? Can I meet the person who didn't like this programme? I don't [care] what they think about my programmes.[17]

The FCC, on present evidence, has been unable, or unwilling if its fiercer critics are to be believed, even to conduct on any regular basis the kind of simple head-counting of stations' output which would fulfil Grade's view of the ITC's responsibilities. But quotas, which have been suggested as a means of steering companies' outputs in approved directions, have no automatic association with quality. A series of thirteen bad or indifferent programmes may count towards filling a quota without any benefit to the audience. The question, therefore, is whether any worthwhile regulation of output in the public interest can be immune from issues of quality once the initial choice of licensee has been made, taking into account any undertakings about content which the licensee has given. And that carries with it the further question of whose notions of quality should prevail, even if the question remains somewhat easier to answer in Britain than it has traditionally been in the United States.

The question was extensively trawled in the United States shortly after the end of the Second World War. When programming in the years after the Second World War was under heavy criticism for its quality, the FCC attempted to measure the performance of the radio companies against the criterion of the public interest set down for licensing by the Communications Act. Letting the companies condemn themselves out of their own mouths, the Commission set out a record of promises made at the time of application for a licence alongside a record of the programmes actually transmitted. Although paying tribute to the qualities of some programmes, the resulting report, known as the Blue Book from the colour of its binding, made clear the extent to which many of the companies were in default of the obligations they had undertaken. Moreover, numbers of them compounded the offence by breaching the guidelines of their own industry association, the National Association of Broadcasters.

[17] Personal interview, London, 30 Apr. 1997.

That the FCC should tackle programming issues came as an outrage to many members of the NAB. The First Amendment and the provision against censorship in the Communications Act were invoked as protection from the criticisms the FCC had made. In a later age, the Blue Book would have been spin-doctored out of existence by its enemies, but the result of the attacks on it in the spring of 1946 were no less effective. The FCC initially showed fight, but it was put on the defensive, not least by the opposition it had stirred up among Congressmen with either commercial or political stakes in radio stations. Eventually the Commission lost its stomach for the battle it had entered with so much bravura. In cataloguing the companies' failures, the FCC had set out a definition of what the public interest in broadcasting might be. Its implementation, however, would remain sporadic at best. Following the attempts made in the 1990 Children's Television Act to raise standards in children's programmes, even casual scrutiny of companies' output indicated the continued presence of the semantic tricks in the deployment of categories and content made familiar in the days of the Blue Book. The jury remains out on whether significantly better progress has been made following yet further attempts made after the Presidential Summit in 1996 on Children's Television to strengthen the regulatory grasp.

New technologies have presented fresh opportunities and brought new entrants to the industry. The British regulatory system has undergone several institutional changes in the years following the launching of Independent Television in 1954. The FCC, however, has remained the sole regulator of both television and radio in the United States. There have, however, been profound changes in the nature of its administrative responsibilities. Under the Reagan administration, there was an important shift in official attitudes towards the role played by the Commission, coloured by changes in attitudes towards commerce. Tracy Westen, President of the Center for Governmental Studies in Los Angeles, illustrated the change by quoting the words, 'What is good for General Motors is good for America', which, when first spoken by the company's President in 1953, attracted unfavourable comments. By the time of Reagan's presidency, said Westen, they had become acceptable.[18] Deregulation was the watchword, with any intervention in the operation of the free market heavily disapproved of. The result was that the limited oversight of content which had been characteristic of the Commission in earlier years declined still further.

From the principle of 'public interest, convenience and necessity', embodied in the 1927 Radio Act and repeated in the 1934 Communications Act, had emerged the notion of broadcast licensees as public trustees. In

---

[18] Personal interview, Los Angeles, 25 Feb. 1997.

return for their licences and access to scarce frequencies, they accepted an obligation to honour certain public service undertakings. These undertakings have included the service of local needs, the provision of informational and political broadcasts, and the service of children with educational and informational programmes. Because cable services do not make any call on publicly owned frequencies, they are under no similar obligations, but are subject to must-carry requirements.

It was the must-carry requirements which were under challenge in the case of *Turner Broadcasting* v. *the FCC,* quoted in Chapter 1. In order to protect off-air broadcasters from undue competition from an increasingly powerful cable sector, Congress had included provision for 'must-carry' in the Cable Television Consumer Protection and Competition Act, 1992. Varying as the number of channels on offer by the individual cable operator varied, a proportion of the channels had to be given over to the relaying of local programmes of different kinds. Turner's challenge, under the First Amendment, failed since, in the opinion of the majority of the Supreme Court, the requirements, imposed under the Act by the FCC, did not interfere with the content of the operator's remaining channels. As a result, the provision was content-neutral, to do with the manner rather than the matter of the message carried, and therefore not subject to the 'strict scrutiny' of the First Amendment, but to the lesser 'intermediate scrutiny' applicable where no interference with the cable operator's message was involved.

However, the trustee principle has been invoked once more by Congress in the case of direct broadcasting by satellite (DBS) and, as a result of a provision in the 1996 Telecommunications Act, will continue to be applied to off-air broadcasting in its digitalized future form. Like analogue broadcasting with which we have been familiar, digital broadcasting makes use of publicly owned frequencies, with a demand from broadcasters for their use which outstrips their availability. In a development of the public trustee principle, on which frequency-allocation had previously taken place, President Clinton, in his 1998 State of the Union address, stressed the importance of securing from the broadcasters a return for the channels they had been allocated at no charge for digitalized services. The President's letter to the Chairman of the FCC made particular reference to the provision of free or discounted airtime for campaign advertising as a means of strengthening democracy. Citing an increase in campaign advertising costs from $70 million in 1970 to $400 million in 1996, the President looked for rapid action. In a complementary move, an advisory group, led by the Vice-President, has been charged with formulating public interest requirements to be demanded of the providers of digital broadcasting and is in process of doing so.

In the closing chapter of this book, mention is made of an alternative proposal under which at least some public service requirements would be commuted for a levy paid by the broadcasters to be spent either on new channels run non-commercially or by Public Broadcasting to fulfil public interest goals.

Both British patterns of regulation and those in the United States have employed regulation with the positive objective of maintaining the range of programming on offer to their audiences. Each country, however, has a distinct approach to the regulation of content which has led the British to support a much greater degree of intervention in the detail of programmes, as subsequent chapters will describe.

3

Taste and Decency

That's not to say that every broadcaster . . . has exactly the same standards at all times and in all places.

(Lawrence Grossman, former President of PBS, 1997)

In the first of the two previous chapters, we looked at the historical and cultural differences which characterize the societies in which American and British broadcasters, and their programme-makers, work. In the second, we considered the distinctive approaches which those differences have produced in the broadcasting structures which the two societies have each established. One approach is deeply rooted in commerce and suspicions of government. The other reflects suspicions of commerce with its policies, including those affecting programmes, prescribed by government with evidence of continuing public support. Before considering the ways in which these approaches are reflected in the regulation of the issues which they create from day to day, we should look at the meaning of taste and decency.

Concepts of Taste and Decency

At Large

Like sex and violence, taste and decency do each other a disservice when they appear linked together as a single phenomenon. The law distinguishes them. It knows no offence of bad taste. Taste is ephemeral, a matter more of manners and fashion, by nature capable of rapid change. On the other hand, an issue of decency touches on something more profound and permanent, a recognition of common humanity, the preservation of individual human dignity through the regard owed by one human being to another. A sense of decency, giving us an understanding of the moral worth of an action, provides the rules by which most of us, in every society, try to live. Sometimes it is enforced by law, as in cases of indecency, as we have noted, and some kinds of obscenity, but, echoing Lord Moulton, it is for the most part unenforceable. What determines the moral worth of an action can vary according to the society or era in which it takes place. The values of Christianity vary from the values of Aristotle, but they reflect what C. S. Lewis has called traditional morality:

neither Christian nor Pagan, neither Eastern nor Western, neither ancient nor modern, but general. . . . in a certain sense, it is no more possible to invent a new ethics than it is to set a new sun in the sky. Some precept from traditional morality always has to be assumed.[1]

Good taste has an elusive quality, easier to recognize by its absence than its presence. We are not all capable of defining its elements and, if we were, we would be unlikely to agree what they were or even if they were there at all. Milos Forman's film *The People vs. Larry Flynt*, a vivid illustration of the protection which the First Amendment is capable of providing for the most extreme forms of free expression, contains a reminder of the old tag: 'Never argue about taste and, above all, never litigate.' When we praise 'good taste', we may do so with a certain unease, suspecting the possibility that some original, rough, vitality has been squeezed out of whatever it is we are praising.

Bad taste is often better company. Basil Fawlty, the hotel-keeper in the television series *Fawlty Towers*, is funny because we know that, in real life, hotel-keepers generally behave rather differently towards their guests. But if we have stayed in enough hotels, most of us are aware of having glimpsed Fawlty's shadow once or twice, as well as experiencing within ourselves feelings very like Fawlty's own that Hell is other people. Bad taste, defying the canons of good taste, can be a source of pleasure, provided that we, and its perpetrators, know what the canons are. Without such knowledge, the alternative is a kind of loutishness. However, as Martha Bayles has pointed out in an account of the present struggle between popular and elite culture, loutishness is now often knowingly aspired to as a weapon in the struggle by supporters of the former.[2]

The distinction between taste and decency can be illustrated by considering the treatment of death in different communities. Respect for the

---

[1] C. S. Lewis, *The Seeing Eye* (Ballantine Books, New York, 1992), 71, 72.

[2] M. Bayles, *Ain't That a Shame? Censorship and the Culture of Transgression* (Institute of US Studies, University of London, 1996).

dead and for the business of mourning is common to most societies. The need for rituals to help the process of coming to terms with the emotions that surround the loss of a close family member is almost universally recognized. So too are the significance of the final hours and the actual moment of passing. All these attitudes are reflections of that fundamental morality which seeks to protect the dignity of the individual. But, within that tradition, there are numerous examples of behaviour surrounding death which differ between cultures and from generation to generation. The Chinese habit of wearing white as mourning-dress contrasts starkly with the black clothing characteristic of the last rites in many Western countries. Then, to take a further example, there are the loud public lamentations which accompany Muslim funerals, occasions when, in the West, expressions of emotion would be muted as part of a particular kind of solemnity.

Obscenity

In Britain, broadcasting has been subject since 1980 to the provisions of the Obscene Publications Act, 1959, but, to date, no prosecutions under the Act have been brought against any broadcaster. The Christian pressure groups which helped to persuade the Government to extend the Act to broadcasting almost certainly entertained higher expectations of successful prosecutions than either the terms of the Act or the history of its use in the courts suggested. The lack of subsequent prosecutions against broadcasters is sometimes cited as evidence of the effectiveness of the self-regulation of the broadcasters as well as of the regulatory processes. But it is also in line with the inaction of the prosecuting authorities towards other forms of publication of similar material. A prime reason for that reluctance has been the difficulty of finding contemporary juries prepared to convict. Where once jurors were anxious, whatever their private standards of morality may have been, to appear to uphold a strict interpretation of public propriety, the opposite has become true as jurors fear being tagged as censorious.

Under the Act, the test of obscenity is whether the material complained of, taken as a whole, tends to deprave or corrupt those who are likely to read, see, or hear it. 'Corrupt' has been interpreted in the courts as 'likely to lead to serious damage', exceeding mere disgust or revulsion. In recent years, evidence of literary merit offered by responsible critics has been an additional defence open to publishers and writers.

In the United States, obscenity lies outside the protection of the First Amendment, although a series of cases before the Supreme Court over a period of years honed the test to be met if a prosecution were to be successful. In *Roth* v. *United States* (1957), it was held that three conditions had to be established: the dominant theme of the material taken as a whole appealed to a prurient interest in sex; the material was patently offensive because it affronted contemporary community standards relating to the description or representation of sexual matters; and the material was utterly without redeeming social importance.[3] The third condition was subsequently modified in 1966 when the Supreme Court considered the eighteenth-century English novel *The Memoirs of Fanny Hill*. It had been banned in Massachusetts. The closing words of the third condition gave way to 'utterly without redeeming social value'.[4] However, the impossibility of proving the absence of social value led to the abandonment of this criterion. In 1973, in *Miller* v. *California*, Chief Justice Warren Burger produced a further version on behalf of the Supreme Court. It was 'whether the work, taken as a whole, lacks serious literary, artistic, political or social value'.[5]

Indecency in Britain is not associated with harm, but with causing offence to public feelings. It was an issue in a trial involving the Independent Broadcasting Authority in 1973, when the Authority was challenged over the transmission of a documentary about Andy Warhol. While it was recognized by the Authority that words and images in the programme did raise issues of taste and decency, its members believed that the serious nature of the programme justified their inclusion. There were several steps in the hearing of the case. It had been launched on the initiative of a private individual, but, although he was eventually ruled to have no standing in the matter, it was pursued as a matter of public interest by the Attorney-General. The Authority's decision, based on its members' view that the programme did not offend against taste and decency, was eventually upheld. The Court, while not necessarily agreeing with that view, recognized that the Authority had behaved reasonably and according to law in reaching it. The actual transmission took place a little over two months late.[6] A post-broadcast poll showed that more than 80 per cent of those members of the audience who were questioned considered it a fuss about nothing, a fairly common reaction in the aftermath of public controversies often gleefully stoked up by the popular Press eager to embarrass the broadcasters. Echoing the characteristic language of tabloid headlines, such events were described

[3] *Roth* v. *United States*, 354 US 476 (1957).

[4] *A Book named John Cleland's 'Memoirs of a Woman of Pleasure'* v. *the Attorney-General of Massachusetts*, 383 US 413 (1966).

[5] *Miller* v. *California*, 413 US 15 (1973).

[6] For a fuller account, see J. Potter, *Independent Television in Britain*, vol. iii (Macmillan, London, 1989), 124–30.

by one senior television executive, having experienced many of them, as 'stormovers'.[7]

Indecency was again at issue in the American case of 'The Seven Dirty Words' (*FCC* v. *Pacifica Foundation*, 1978). A radio station had broadcast in the daytime a monologue containing indecent language. In response to a complaint from a listener, the FCC forbade the future transmission of the words at times when large numbers of children could be expected to be in the audience. The Supreme Court upheld the ban. In its proscription, the FCC describes as indecent 'language or material that depicts or describes, in terms patently offensive as measured by contemporary community standards for the broadcast medium, sexual or excretory activities or organs'. The FCC has shown itself to be relatively tenacious in its pursuit of indecent language on radio, imposing fines totalling $2 million over a period of years on stations carrying the satirist presenter Howard Stern.

In Broadcasting

Audiences

Newspapers, magazines, and books have to be bought or borrowed. So do video-recordings. Cinemas and theatres have to be visited. Broadcasting, however, is there in the home. The decision to install a television set is taken almost casually nowadays, as natural an action as putting in electricity. In the United States, the law provides that broadcasting should not be treated as a utility, but the physical similarities between piping in programmes by cable and connecting up with the public water supply underlines the irony of borrowing many years ago the 'public interest, convenience and necessity' prescription from utilities legislation.

Once, for most households, the receiver stood in the room most closely identified with relaxation and the gathering of the family. Its physical position in the household gave it a kind of authority. Advertisers often posed the happy family gathered in front of the set listening-in in an earlier age or viewing a little later: *paterfamilias* in his chair, children beside him, another child perhaps on its grandmother's knee, and Mother, usually on her feet, posed in the kitchen door as she prepares for another act of service to the others as evidence of a well-cemented group. It was also the perfect setting for the creation of the embarrassment which, because family conventions have been transgressed, stimulates protests to the broadcasters, even if the underlying cause of some complaints lies elsewhere. Some complainants disguise their own feelings by claiming to be lodging protests on

---

[7] Sir Jeremy Isaacs, the first Chief Executive of Channel 4.

behalf of third parties, for example children or old people, considered unable to speak for themselves. Others, however, are motivated by what they regard as a duty to others supposedly more vulnerable.

Then, as the number of sets owned by each family began to grow, radio and, subsequently, television were dispersed into other rooms. In many households, listening and viewing stopped being group experiences mediated by a sharing of individual responses to what was being broadcast. Instead, they turned into individual encounters. The family became spread out through the house: men viewing sport in the living-room, women carrying a transistor-set and listening to radio wherever they were, children watching television in their bedrooms. It is harder to feel embarrassed on one's own and even harder to go to the lengths of complaining to the broadcaster, so the element of embarrassment grew less, although it still remains a powerful motive for numbers of complaints in Britain.

Whatever the changing circumstances of listening or viewing, broadcasting has been there in the home for much of this century, ready at the touch of a button, and even without stirring from an armchair, to provide a range of visual and aural experiences, for all practical purposes, limitless. Until the coming of the Internet, broadcast programmes had a more immediate and pervasive access to the home than any other form of media. Now that the Internet has arrived, its contents under no effective form of regulation, the concerns familiar for many years in the debate about standards in broadcasting are being expressed all over again, focused, once more, on the dangers it presents for young people.

'They have parents, don't they?'

As with the cinema, whose introduction ushered in years of controversy about its effects on the young, so with radio and television. Both the United States and Britain have largely come to terms with the first two, although anxieties are still expressed about the alleged debasement of values by popular radio: by the lyrics of pop music or the crude outspokenness of some presenters. Fears about television's effects continue. Among the charges are that watching television, particularly programmes intended for adults, will encourage children into delinquency, from petty acts of theft to extreme acts of violence. It will destroy their respect for all kinds of authority and make them harder to control at school, in the home, or on the streets. It will endorse the use of language which their parents do not want them to use, at least in the hearing of the parents or the parents' friends. It confronts them with adult dilemmas with which they lack the knowledge and the experience to deal. In short, children, because of television, are considered by many people to be growing up too fast.

The amount of time spent by children in front of the screen, it is argued, when compared with time spent in school or in other activities, like reading, at home must inevitably exercise an influence, for better or for worse, on their development. With the medium increasingly influenced by commercial considerations, children are learning the values of the marketplace, conditioned before they are citizens to become consumers. As George Gerbner has pointed out:

For the first time in human history, most of the stories about people, life and values are not told by parents, schools, and churches, or others in the community who have something to tell, but by distant conglomerates who have something to sell.[8]

The evidence, though considerable in volume, to support the fears of television's harmful effects on children remains more cumulative than demonstrable in instances of immediate cause-and-effect. The attempts of politicians to make a direct connection between crime and television programmes have rarely seemed convincing. After the murder of the 2-year-old Jamie Bulger by two 10-year-olds in Liverpool, one of the few recent events to create a deeply shared sense of national shock in Britain, it was asserted that the manner of the child's death on a railway line had been copied from a horror video, *Child's Play III*. However, there was no incident in the video which could have prompted an imitative action of that sort, nor, indeed, any proof that either of the two boys had actually seen it. But critics point, with varying degrees of accuracy, to rising levels of crime among children and young people in both societies, to increased divorce rates, a debasement of family life and the values associated with it, and the decline in the quality of life which accompanies them.

'They have parents, don't they?' The response of some broadcasters that any responsibility for the consequences of children's viewing must rest with parents is, to their critics, irresponsible. Some parents or others in charge of children may be uncaring, but often they may have no choice about being absent at some time. Bad housing may leave parents and others with no choice but to keep small children in the same room as themselves until the end of viewing for the day. In all these cases, children are potentially vulnerable. But, as broadcasters have countered, with large numbers of British viewers regularly agreeing with them, television cannot be tailored to the unassessable needs of children. Growing up is a constant process of coming to terms with a whole lot of things of which some

[8] G. Gerbner, 'The Hidden Side of Television Violence', chapter in *Invisible Crises*, Critical Studies in Communication and in the Cultural Industries (Westview Press, Boulder, Colo., 1996).

aspects of television, but by no means all, are only one. Why should only the bad be assumed to rub off on the child-audience? Are children not being used as a screen behind which politicians are moving to a different goal, an exercise of greater control over the medium? Isn't recourse to the protection of children the last refuge of the demagogue, as someone suggested? Stuart Fischoff, a writer and psychologist in Los Angeles, compared the politicians' situation to that of a man, knowing he has lost a key in the yard, looking for it indoors because it is too dark to look outside.[9]

The Adult Audience

From the earliest days of broadcasting, children have been considered to be the section of the population most at risk from its effects, whatever they may be. But, within the adult part of the population, there are individual groups who may be considered vulnerable in one way or another. Women are sometimes said to be the largest of them, regularly exploited and stereotyped. But many women reject this view as patronizing. However, there are, as well, racial and religious minorities, people with disabilities, and the aged, who may be thought of as vulnerable to harm whenever what distinguishes them from the rest of the population is exploited: the frailties of old age or disability, the practices associated with a different set of beliefs from those held by a majority, or a different skin-colour. The profound issues they raise are of decency rather than taste.

And, finally, there is a much larger group, a majority perhaps, capable of being offended by breaches in their perception of popular morality. Lawrence Grossman brought in a rather different emphasis. He talked of the dishonouring of certain standards by a broadcaster as a violation of the relationship between the broadcaster and the audience. Alan Yentob, of the BBC, gave that relationship the name of a contract. The registering of possible offence is the starting-point for anyone overseeing issues of taste and decency. It is for them to decide whether there are other interests to be served which may legitimately outweigh the significance of the offence or harm a programme may cause. In doing so, they have to have in mind that what may be offensive in itself will, from time to time, have to be seen or heard by the audience, but in forms which do not amplify it. It is sometimes potentially more offensive to seek to disguise the full measure of offence than to let it be seen for what it is. No less than sensationalizing their treatment, attempts to sanitize the horrors of either the present or the past may distort the truth and deny justice to their victims. Responsible broadcasting owes a place to the dead from Buchenwald or Rwanda.

[9] Personal interview, Los Angeles, 14 Nov. 1996.

The Scope of Taste and Decency

When he wished to dismiss potential objectors to a proposed episode of the police-series *Cagney and Lacey* dealing with an abortion clinic, the producer referred to the 'nine little old biddies', who would write to the network's head office.[10] It was a patronizing description of his fellow-citizens in the exercise of their democratic right, but it conveys the stereotype so often identified with taste and decency. The narrow preoccupation of the law with their sexual aspects, combined with the fact that the words, bracketed together, have become shorthand for that kind of prissiness, tends to conceal the fact that issues of taste and decency in broadcasting stretch far beyond the boundaries of sex.

News

Events which are tasteless or outrage decency occur throughout the world daily. The resulting news-items are not, as some journalists would have it, the product of an unstoppable force of nature, but an artefact heavily influenced by the audience to which it is addressed. There is an inevitable process of selection and compression, necessary for reasons of time and comprehension. Programme editors can and do, therefore, choose different ways to communicate the nature of those events. Commercial pressures to compel attention by entertaining even at the grimmest moments, summed up in the news editor's phrase, 'If it bleeds, it leads,' are increasing rather than diminishing in their impact on editors' approach.

Editorial skills can ensure that audiences receive a sense of the magnitude of suffering in a famine in Africa or floods in Bangladesh without lingering on the orphaned or the dying in a way which itself becomes an outrage against dignity. They can retain the original horror of a disaster, the outrage to dignity represented in the aftermath of an explosion or an air-crash, so that the audience shares in the experience. On the rare occasions when news events can be covered live, the visual and spoken narrative has to be shaped to communicate it effectively.

In the act of mediating between the event and its appearance on the screen, the programme-maker can make a difference between the audience's comprehension of the event and a dulling revulsion. The same skills can be used, however, simply to commodify the event, reducing it, without feeling, to the predictable elements of such events: the rescue crews, the ambulances, the walking injured, the scattered luggage, the tormented relatives. In short, imposing all the paraphernalia of a well-dressed

---

[10] K. C. Montgomery, *Target: Prime Time*, Communications and Society (Oxford University Press, New York, 1989), 210.

disaster-movie set on the desperate confusion of actual tragedies. The British series *Drop the Dead Donkey*, satirizing a modern television news-room, included among its characters a reporter who carried a small teddy-bear to drop into shot on such occasions.

In 1996, when sixteen small children and their teacher were murdered by a gunman in a Scottish school, the BBC decided to limit its coverage. The decision was influenced by what the BBC considered the public mood to be in a moment of national grief. American newsmen asked the BBC afterwards about the absence of images of bereaved parents. I understood that there would be great reluctance in the United States for such decisions to be left to the judgement of others. It was partly the result of competition between newsrooms, but as one American put it:

The interesting issue is that, if the British population found out that the BBC made a judgement to show restraint on account of their sensitivities, there would proba-bly be great support. . . . Despite what Americans say, I think that if they found out, their reaction would be 'censorship.'[11]

Language

Questions of taste occur regularly in the use in programmes of profanities or other words whose appearance gives offence to some people. In Britain, complaints about allegedly 'bad' language are raised by the public with the broadcasters more frequently than complaints about any other taste and decency issue. Related to language capable of giving offence is the question of respecting religious sensibilities which may be a matter of lan-guage or of images. The law of blasphemy exists in Britain only to protect the Anglican religion, a relic of the days when state and state religion were interdependent and an attack on the established faith could be construed as seditious. Today, when many people have no knowledge of what may give offence to any faith, broadcasters will inevitably find themselves drawn into criticisms which, in one sense, are of nobody's making.

Stereotyping

This is another area which gives rise to objections, whether it is of race or religion, gender, age, or sexual preference. The stereotyping of disabilities has become a significant issue in recent years. The casual application of 'schizoid' to indecisive or irresolute behaviour has drawn protests in Britain from schizophrenia sufferers or their relatives. So has the apparently casual treatment of such distressing, if little-publicized, conditions as agoraphobia. In all such cases, the programme-maker

---

[11] Conversation in Los Angeles on 15 Nov. 1996.

and the broadcaster have to balance respect for the sufferers against the prevailing conventions of everyday speech. An over-rigid emphasis on either is capable of blunting the communication which is his or her primary aim.

Privacy

There are dilemmas of a different kind in the area of privacy. The lives of most people, throughout their existence, are of little public interest. But sometimes, more often accidentally than deliberately, they move or are moved into the glare of media attention. The reasons are frequently tragic and, as was so cruelly demonstrated in 1997 by the massacre of tourists at Luxor and the subsequent confusion over the whereabouts of some victims' remains, so can the consequences be. If people are not themselves victims, then they are the relatives or friends of people who are. The extent to which the media are then entitled to expose their suffering raises important questions of privacy. There can be no hard-and-fast rules except the exercise of a proper degree of restraint which stops short of exploitation. But that too is a matter of interpretation.

Some people in such circumstances find them easier to bear by nursing their own distress, saying little or nothing to anyone outside their immediate circles. Others, however, find relief in sharing it. That appears to have been true of the Aberfan disaster in Wales in 1964, another tragedy involving schoolchildren and their teachers. A spoil-tip from the local coalmine collapsed one morning, largely burying the school. The rescue operation lasted for many hours, watched by the children's relatives and others from the local village community. Television covered the event constantly, despite the opposition of the Chairman of the National Coal Board who wanted no coverage of major disasters. It seemed that television had caught the national mood better than the Chairman whose Board was responsible for the tip.

People are, however, often asked to decide the course they want to follow when they are at their most vulnerable. They may effectively not be given a choice. A woman who had lost a child in the destruction of Pan-Am 103 was shown rolling in anguish on the floor at the airport where she had received the news. She was later reported to have said that she wished she had not been exposed in that way at a moment of extreme vulnerability.

But, away from tragedies, there are issues of individual privacy which may arise out of scandals of different kinds or out of successes for which no publicity is wanted. The right not to be communicated with or about is hardly less important than the right to communicate.

Schedules, Standards, and Expectations

There are three factors which, with others, influence the nature of programmes we watch or hear and have a bearing on the way we respond. They are the schedules in which the programmes are placed, the standards which they observe, and, finally, the expectations which the audience itself brings to watching or listening.

No programme service can exist without a schedule, an ordering of the material it is transmitting, whether its output is a mixture of programmes, as on the great American and British networks, or is consistently specialized, always appealing to a particular set of interests, whether they are relatively wide, such as various forms of sport or cookery, or narrow, such as rose-growing. The audience turns to a service of the second kind in the knowledge of its largely unvarying nature. Advertisers using such a service, if it is commercially run, can be confident about the sort of audience their commercials will be reaching. Network schedules are more complex, nets with which the broadcaster snares the audiences he or she is seeking: the commercial broadcaster in order to deliver them in the right combination of numbers and demographics to the advertisers on whom the company's financial success depends, the public broadcaster to fulfil the goals which have been set by those who finance her or him. Those goals, serving one interpretation of the public interest, are traditionally summarized as entertainment, information, and education.

Scheduling is a mixture of instinct, knowledge born of experience and research, and good luck. It is a craft rather than the art or science it is sometimes called, although it contains a mysterious instinct which links it to art and a reliance on the experiential which characterizes scientific enquiry. Like all crafts, it can be practised better by some than by others. Committees make poor schedulers. They add compromises of their own to those which even the lone scheduler has to make between aspirations and availability. However, even the most inspired individual scheduler rarely retains his or her pre-eminence for very long. The luck which they need to combine with their own instincts of what will draw the audience, their nose for the successful formula, has a way of running out.

Good luck will deal the scheduler a strong hand of programmes which can be deployed to advantage. (When it is being particularly generous, it will give rival channels a hand of weak programmes.) Bad luck will deliver programmes whose inherent weakness cannot be disguised for long by even the most cunning manipulation of the schedule. The fortunes of networks are cyclical, waxing for a time because of good management and a flair for detecting the right talent and material, then waning because the

43

successful touch has been lost: there may have been an over-reliance on tired formulae, a reluctance to believe that a promising idea will ever come good, a corporate loss of nerve, or the creaming-off of too much profit with an accompanying failure to invest. It takes time to turn a faltering schedule around, time to find or originate new programmes and then bring them forward to swing the audience back in the scheduler's favour.

Research will tell the scheduler about demographics and about the programme ingredients which, in various combinations, may have worked before, but, despite the now common reliance on focus groups, it cannot guarantee success for future programmes, including those which are clones of past successes.

Experience and instinct go hand in hand, providing the scheduler with a sense of the standards appropriate to his or her audience. A schedule intended for a younger audience will observe different standards from one addressed to an audience of older people and those who watch it or listen to it will expect it to do so.

Standards are declared in codes or guidelines, which provide clues to the way in which they should be applied. But if they become not clues, but directions to be followed more closely whatever the context of the programme, they turn into prescriptions and, as the Pilkington Report on British Broadcasting, published in 1962, commented: 'Good broadcasting is a practice, not a prescription.'[12]

Finally, to expectations: audiences bring different expectations to different programmes, more complex than the difference of one kind of programme from another, but derived from differing times of day, differing channels, differing artists, and differing weights of seriousness of purpose and context.

Scheduling

For only the briefest moment, at the very beginning of its existence, is the schedule of a major channel without a history. When that moment has gone, it becomes the prisoner of its past. It acquires landmarks: the regular programmes which fix its character in the minds of the audience, the compulsive events in an annual calendar, the individual time-slots which, it is hoped, will imprint themselves firmly enough on its viewers or listeners to persuade them to make firm commitments to view or listen. It acquires a style of presentation and an attitude in the way it addresses its audience. It wants to cultivate a sense of agreeable anticipation among those who watch or listen, even though that may make change, when it becomes desirable, more difficult. Christine Hikawa, Vice-President of ABC's Stan-

[12] Cmnd. 1753 (1962), *Report of the Committee on Broadcasting, 1960.*

dards and Practices Department, said: 'I think the experience is that if you change or surprise the audience, they get mad at you. . . . I've never had the experience where [the schedulers] suddenly want to make a radical change.'[13]

Scheduling in Commercial Services

A commercial service, in competition with others, has to begin with the commercial consequences of its decisions. The livelihood of the service depends on ensuring that advertisers are delivered audiences of the right size and demographic composition. It may no longer be the twenty million people whom the advertisers wished to reach thirty years ago. The market has changed. When, in Britain at the start of the 1980s, Channel 4 was being planned as a service with an innovatory remit, it was argued that the minority audiences it was intended to serve could never yield the revenue the channel would need. With little compromise to its original objectives, the channel nevertheless succeeded in achieving profitability. With what some critics have considered more serious compromise, higher levels of profitability were reached, high enough to provoke talk of privatization, turning a company with no shareholders to consider into one in which profits and dividends would compete for the board's attention with the range and quality of programming.

The new compulsion is to reach a smaller number with the particular tastes and interests the advertiser needs for his or her product. To respond to the advertisers' messages, the audience has to be in a receptive frame of mind. A programme generating a gloomy, introspective, mood among those who see or hear it will make them less disposed to buy the goods associated with it. Happiness and contentment are the all-important ingredients, to be offered whenever possible, if necessary conferred on events despite themselves. Todd Gitlin, in his book *Inside Prime Time*, writes of commercial television offering a window on the world through which Americans look before withdrawing into their own, real, worlds.[14] Others suggested that American television offered its public a vision of society as they would like it to be, its values lagging behind the changes in the wider society. Michael Grade, as a Briton who has worked in the States, put it in this way:

The primary purpose of American television is purely to entertain, to divert people, and to take them out of themselves. . . . It's a commodity, you watch it, you have got to give people instant gratification which means instant, excellent, entertainment which they do so well and the competition is so fierce, the market is so big

[13] Personal interview, New York, 14 Jan. 1997.
[14] T. Gitlin, *Inside Prime Time* (rev. edn. Routledge, London, 1994).

that, in the end all you get is entertainment. . . . It's all designed to make you feel good. It's not a function of regulation. It's just the function of the market.[15]

The commercial television broadcasters in Britain, free from financial competition for almost thirty years after they began operations in 1955, were constrained in their pursuit of audiences by the terms of their contracts with the regulator, the ITA. There were minimum requirements for certain kinds of programming and government limitations on hours of broadcasting (an arrangement favouring the BBC whose income, unlike its expenditure, was unaffected by longer hours). There was also the powerful example of the BBC which, however enthusiastically the new commercial channel was welcomed by large numbers of the audience, the public did not wish to see abandoned. As Michael Grade, who has alternated between commercial television and the BBC, was to say many years later, when he had returned to the former, the Corporation was 'there to keep us honest'. Not all his colleagues agreed with him, but many of the audience would recognize what he was saying.

The coming of increased competition was officially recognized in the Broadcasting Act, 1990. It contained a substantial acknowledgement, hardly conceded before, of broadcasting as an economic activity, partly the fallout from an inquiry, chaired by an economist a few years earlier, into the funding of the BBC. Disappointing government expectations, the inquiry reported against imposing advertising on the BBC, arguing that the effect would be to draw off revenues from commercial television and so reduce, in the Committee's words, 'consumer choice and welfare'.[16] But perhaps the most striking outcome of the Committee's report was the challenge it delivered to the traditional perception of broadcasting in Britain as a social and cultural activity by giving currency to the idea that its prime function was economic. It was an idea which, a few years later, was to enjoy its high summer. Although, as we noted in Chapter 2, the future regulation of commercial broadcasting was to have a 'light touch' in the interests of economic freedom, the television companies forming the network on Channel 3 continued to have public service obligations imposed on their programming. Cable and satellite services had no similar restrictions. It amounted, as their spokespersons protested, to tying their hands behind their backs as they entered the new competitive arena.

One consequence of the new regime has been a closer degree of collaboration between the broadcaster and advertisers. Marcus Plantin, Director of the ITV Network from 1992 to 1997, said that this was made

[15] Personal interview, London, 30 May 1997.
[16] Cmnd. 9824 (1986), *Report of the Committee on Financing the BBC*.

inevitable once ITV's advertising monopoly was broken. He believed that the retention of former programme-makers within the senior ranks of the ITV companies had been a significant factor in maintaining a balanced schedule in peaktime, with serious material not being driven out to the fringes. Although in planning the network he had no dealings with the ITC as the regulator, the individual companies making programmes for the network had their contractual commitments to fulfil.[17]

Scheduling in Public Services

The BBC, from its inception as a public corporation in 1927, was charged with providing a comprehensive service of programmes, initially in radio and then, from 1936, in both radio and television. As it added new channels, its goal was to increase the coverage it could give to a widening range of tastes and interests. Had finances and frequencies allowed, then it would have sought to match in programming the universality which it attained in transmitter coverage. When its monopoly of television was broken in 1955, the competing commercial channel was established to provide a service 'in addition to' that provided by the BBC. In 1972, a small number of local commercial radio stations was established, breaking the BBC's monopoly of radio, with three national commercial networks to follow in the 1990s. None of these new services was ever considered to be a replacement for anything in the range of national, regional, and local television or radio programmes being supplied by the BBC. That remains the position at the end of the 1990s, although financial constraints are affecting the BBC's ability to maintain the range.

In the United States, Public Broadcasting was created late in the day in order to fill in the gaps left by the failures of the market-place. The service has been consistently short of money and under constant pressure from its ideological opponents in and out of Congress, one of whom described Public Broadcasting to me as broadcasting's 'soup-kitchen'.[18] It has, in consequence, been denied the ability which the BBC has had from its earliest days to reach the majority audience with programmes of popular appeal. As a result, both National Public Radio and, to a greater extent, Public Television (PBS) exist on the edges of the market, attracting much loyalty from small sections of the population, but not making their mark with the mass public.

Publicly funded channels, despite their financial independence, nevertheless have to observe some of the same disciplines as their commercial rivals. The public broadcaster's continued access to public funds usually

[17] Personal interview, London, 14 Apr. 1997.
[18] Conversation in Banff, Canada, May 1982.

depends upon demonstrating sufficient appeal to sufficient numbers of the audience that the political will to maintain them in business does not weaken. Both processes are bound by audience availability, increasing the importance of those times of the day when the largest numbers of people are free to watch. The public broadcaster's approach to scheduling will not, therefore, be very different from that of a commercial rival, though with the need to reconcile the demands of the minority audience with those of the majority. The public broadcaster's scheduling is likely to reflect the strengths and weaknesses of its competitor's schedule when each is trying to draw audiences away from the other. The strength of the BBC's position for so long in British broadcasting had, as we have seen, consequences for the nature and quality of all British broadcasting. With increased competition, however, the retention of that distinctiveness becomes harder and, to the extent that its effects have been beneficial for the general range and quality of programming, its influence becomes weaker.

The BBC's schedulers have had the advantage of far greater resources than PBS and NPR can deploy in the United States. They have the further advantages of enjoying public support on a far greater scale than their American counterparts and of stronger political backing in all the main parties. The truth of the last point was demonstrated in the lengthy debate about the future of the BBC before the granting of a new Charter was agreed in 1995.

Standards: Codes and Guidelines

The National Association of Broadcasters in the United States produced a code for radio and, later, a code for television. The Code, as the product of the Association in its role as the trade organization of the broadcasting industry, was criticized as contrary to anti-trust legislation. Eventually, a legal action was brought in 1979 against the Association by the US Department of Justice. The department's action was founded on the view that the effect of the Code's limitations on the use and amount of advertising time was artificially to increase the price of advertising. The District Court in Washington proceeded on the specific point of the restriction against advertising more than one product in any commercial less than sixty seconds in duration. Other aspects of the action were not pursued. When it finally succeeded in 1982, the action led to the abolition by the NAB of the advertising code and, later, the provisions of the code affecting programmes.

The twenty-second edition of the Code, published in 1981, after the Justice Department had begun its action, states its purpose as:

The purpose of this Code is co-operatively to maintain a level of television programming which gives full consideration to the educational, informational, cultural, economic, moral and entertainment needs of the American people to the end that more and more people will be better served.[19]

It called for responsibly exercised artistic freedom and an understanding of all the segments of the communities the broadcasters are serving. It urges that sensationalism, shock, and exploitation are all to be avoided and special responsibilities towards children observed. The programme provisions require the social and human consequences of criminal activities to be made clear, with no demonstrations of criminal techniques. There are provisions for the presentation of balanced news services, for religious programmes, and the handling of controversial public issues.

Individual American broadcasters have their own codes for internal circulation, as do the commercial companies in Britain. Those I have seen tend to be more terse than the British versions, with fewer of the arguments for this requirement or that set out. The BBC, the Welsh Fourth Channel, and the two commercial broadcasting regulators in Britain all have sets of guidelines which are available to the public.

The former IBA, which was co-publisher with its franchisees of their programmes, wrote its codes in a non-mandatory style, but its successors, the ITC and the Radio Authority, have published their own programme codes as a combination of the mandatory and the advisory, distinguishing the former by printing the mandatory phrases in heavier type. The change reflects the more legalistic relationship between the regulators and their licensees brought about by the 1990 Broadcasting Act which replaced, as technology and economics had made inevitable, the closer, arguably cosier, relationships characterizing commercial broadcasting since its first appearance in the mid-1950s.

The ITC's Code acknowledges that, as views and attitudes change, it cannot be the last word on the matters it covers, recognizing too that it cannot be comprehensive. On violence, for example, it declares: 'The Code cannot provide universal rules. The programme-maker must carry responsibility for his or her own decision. In so sensitive an area risks require special justification. If in doubt cut.'[20] That 'If in doubt, cut' has survived for many years in successive versions of the code for commercial broadcasters. It should be seen in context with the doctrine of 'reference upward'. Section 1.14 of the Code states: 'Where a producer

---

[19] National Association of Broadcasters, *The Television Code* (22nd edn. Washington, 1981).
[20] Independent Television Commission, *The ITC Programme Code* (London, 1995).

has any doubt about the suitability of material covered in this Code, he or she must refer upward to the most senior programme executive . . . for advice or approval.'[21]

'Reference upward' has been close to the core of maintaining standards in British broadcasting for many years. Ultimately, if the situation demands it, a question can be referred all the way to the top of the broadcaster's management structure. Like all such systems, its weakness lies in the now-increasing possibility, as attitudes within society change, that a producer will not understand that he has a question to refer. The BBC, which once reflected a kind of cultural homogeneity, has found itself particularly vulnerable to the effect of changed patterns of employment. Production staff now come and go with a regularity that contrasts with days when it was said that to unseat an Anglican bishop was rather easier than to secure the dismissal of a BBC employee. As with other broadcasters, differences in attitudes between generations are underlined when a largely youthful corps of programme-makers is serving audiences generally rather older. In the BBC's case, the spreading of institutional values, once a prime responsibility of the BBC's Training School, has become proportionately more difficult.

Factors in Setting Standards

Codes and guidelines exist to set down the limits which programme-makers should observe, but, inevitably in the nature of the industry, they must be interpreted case by case. In the more legalistic framework within which British commercial television has operated since 1990, staff in Compliance Departments or their equivalents are engaged in ensuring that the requirements of the regulators, set out in their licences, are met. In the BBC, responsibility rests with production departments, subject to any necessary checks where the material in a programme appears to demand it. Among those consulted is Phil Harding, Controller, Editorial Policy, who told me that, in such situations, he thinks first of the audience:

When I'm making those judgements, in the end I'm very conscious of the fact that I'm not exercising my judgements. I'm very conscious that I'm trying to exercise judgements on behalf of the audience or audiences. . . . And when I do that, I really do try to visualize—I can't quite explain how I do this—I really do try to visualize the audience. I actually do, in my head, try to conjure up real people and think what real people's reaction to that would be. I don't actually mean defined characters, but people you've met over a period of time, people you've met in public meetings.[22]

[21] Independent Television Commission, *The ITC Programme Code* (London, 1995).
[22] Personal interview, London, 17 Apr. 1997.

The network news divisions in the United States have their own editors to apply judgements when questions arise. For the entertainment output of the networks, the work is done by the Standards and Practices Departments based in New York or in Los Angeles. I spoke to Christine Hikawa, at ABC, about this:

Q. Would you say that it really is . . . it is a commercial imperative which for most of the time drives your decisions? I'm not asking that in a pejorative way, but . . . because it won't play with the advertiser, because [the advertisers think] it won't play with the audience?

A. A lot of time the advertisers use the audience really, I mean, that is what the advertisers are basing their standards on. We do it a lot on audience research. I feel that, after ten years in this job, when I see something I know that . . . I know how far to go before it will offend people, I know that we are going to get complaints about something so you do develop a sense, partly from hearing from people.[23]

I asked another Standards and Practices executive to explain what would warrant setting aside a network company's paramount interest in sales. I understood that there would have to be a special agenda which would include those occasions on which the company was attempting to serve a social purpose. The presentation of a drama on a particularly sensitive social issue might provide an example or the showing of *Schindler's List*. To run commercials with Spielberg's Holocaust film would be unacceptably insensitive to many of those watching, while the controversial drama could have been expected to draw only a reduced audience.

The work of the departments begins at the earliest stage of development. Stuart Fischoff provided me with his perspective as a writer and critic:

Real conflict can only happen between peers, between equals. Since there are not equals in that context . . . you have a writer who is working with a producer or a development person at a network and you have the network people above him or her. What there is is tension, but there is no real conflict because the writer knows that if they don't like him, they can just toss him out. So in that sense there is no real conflict. Implicit in what I'm saying is the fact that in most instances what the networks want, the networks get. . . . Most of what you see on television is essentially the assemblage of body parts, a Frankenstein. Whatever the writer's vision was at the beginning, rarely do we see that followed through. . . . What's interesting about television is that people are always saying that everyone is simply a barbarian at the gate. They're simply in it for its commercial value. They don't care about this, they don't care about that. This is a very blatant untruth. Particularly when it comes to writers . . . writers get into the business of writing because they want to write, they have a point of view, they have a voice they want to express. When

[23] Personal interview, New York, 14 Jan. 1997.

people who write create a series, an idea for a series, they usually have an artistic, an aesthetic, social, political, message or premiss. . . . It's usually one compromise, one change after another.[24]

Although certain standards are absolute in both the United States and Britain, others may vary for a number of reasons, often linked to the expectations, the last of the three factors which, with schedules and standards, influence the programmes set before the audience.

Time of Day

The time of transmission is an important element in reaching decisions about when and what to schedule. Two examples may illustrate the point. Swearwords, as the first of them, will cause less offence to many people at some times of the day than at others, although there are some viewers and listeners who will never be reconciled to their appearance. The use of swearwords, especially at times when children are likely to be viewing, is objectionable to many people, whether they are parents or not. The degree of offence, however, which attaches to individual words changes with the passing of time, just as the weight of offence can vary from one part of a country to another.

In the second example, decisions about degrees of sexual explicitness also depend on the issue of timing. In American network television, the rules are much stricter than they are in Britain once the 9.00 p.m. Watershed (see pp. 66–7) has passed. Simulated sexual intercourse, although relatively rare on British television, is more frequently seen there than it is in the United States. The same is true of full frontal nudity. I asked Phil Harding whether it was harder to take decisions about sexual explicitness than about degrees of violence, partly because the public is less ambiguous in its attitudes towards violence and saying, 'That's enough' should be correspondingly easier than drawing a line on sex.

One would never attempt to draw these comparisons out because violence and sexuality are equally important, but in the end violence is about pain, and ultimately, loss of life, which must be some sort of absolute. Sexuality, unless it's about sadism or sado-masochism, is not about that, although clearly its consequences again can be very serious. No, I don't think I would find decisions about the one more difficult than about the other. I do think that I do take a more serious view of screen violence than of screen sexuality and I think that attitudes towards screen sexuality have liberalized in the last three or four years. I also think it's easier to meet concerns and get things right with sexuality by scheduling than it is about violence.[25]

[24] Personal interview, Los Angeles, 14 Nov. 1996.
[25] Personal interview, London, 17 Apr. 1997.

Choice of Channel

Audiences at the end of the 1990s are highly mobile. The invention of the zapper, combined with the variety of material offered by multi-channel broadcasting, has meant that they are constantly migrating from one service to another, pausing here, rushing past there, until they strike something which holds their attention for longer. Channels want to assert their identities by such means as on-screen logos, but also by defining more clearly the nature of their product.

Like other members of Standards and Practices Departments in the United States or the men and women making judgements of the same kind for British commercial broadcasters, Chris Hikawa acts only for her own company. David Lloyd, however, working for the Radio Authority in Britain, like other regulators with responsibilities across a large number of licensed companies, has increasingly to take into account the nature of each individual company with the particular audience it is normally serving. The growing number of niche stations did not, he said, mean that the general climate was growing more permissive. One station had a young listenership heavily critical of anything smacking of sexism. Commercial radio in Britain, he said, contained less bad language than any form of television simply because it did less drama and the public generally favoured politeness in exchanges between presenters and their audiences. Shock-jocks had not prospered in Britain.[26]

Within the BBC, providing two television channels, several radio networks, and many local radio stations, the decisions have also to reflect the different nature of each outlet. The audiences for the two older channels, BBC1 and ITV, are more conservative, while audiences watching BBC2 or Channel 4 are more receptive to experiment and innovation, charges actually laid on Channel 4 by its parliamentary remit. Channel 5 is still too new to determine whether the bid it made initially for a young audience will be sufficient to sustain it economically or if a new strategy will be needed for its survival.

Alan Yentob, Director of Television at the BBC, described the thought processes:

[The BBC] does produce material which is strong and marginal and possibly the kind of material which requires . . . has quality about it and is not simply gratuitous. For instance, it surprised me that we were able to put out a film of David Lynch's on BBC2. At the point when I first saw it, I didn't know that we could. But if you create an environment in which the material can be looked at intelligently, if the film has qualities and is a film of some ambition and it finds the right place in the schedule, then we find we can do it. And it doesn't have to attract the kind of

[26] Personal interview, London, 30 Apr. 1997.

audience who are simply out there looking for cheap thrills on the BBC . . . the whole point of having several channels is . . . the message that BBC2 sends is that it has earned the right to put out this kind of material, but it might be slightly shocking to some viewers, while wholly appropriate to a part of society, quite a substantial part of society, some two-to-three million people. . . . Films which appear on BBC2 uncut will very often be cut on BBC1. Again, one of the advantages of having two channels is that we believe that what is acceptable and permissible and, in fact, demanded on BBC2 is not something that would be tolerated by the audience's expectation level on BBC1.[27]

Familiarity with Artists or Material

Audiences build up expectations about individual artists or particular programmes. They develop an understanding of the particular conventions employed in a detective series, recognizing the limits which are observed in the incidence, for example, of violence or sexual explicitness. If those limits are breached without warning, then offence is likely to be caused. A British police series once showed one of the central characters, a senior policeman, beating up a suspect in a cell. What was at issue for the viewers who subsequently complained was not the ferocity of the attack, which was relatively mild, but the perpetrator of it. He had stepped beyond limits which had been identified from the character's behaviour in previous episodes, so jolting the audience's expectations. The same degree of violence administered by a different character would, almost certainly, not have aroused the same response.

There are comedians who can succeed with material which, if handled by other comedians, would cause great offence. It can be explained by an extra layer of charm, a pretence of shamelessness, or a better sense of timing, hinting at the point of a line and allowing the audience to reach it before the final words have been spoken. A frank use of bad taste can also override objections, although the British appear more tolerant of it than the American networks. *Absolutely Fabulous*, a comedy series in which the two central characters, two women in the fashion world, drank and took drugs, failed to find a network placing in the States, even in an American version, despite its popularity and apparent acceptability in Britain.

Topical References

Entertainment programmes take their place in schedules which also report the day's events, national and local. The possibility of causing offence by insensitive scheduling is, therefore, a real one. In the USA each programme, from its inception, is monitored by a member of the company's

---

[27] Personal interview, London, 30 Apr. 1997.

Standards and Practices Department. A similar watch is maintained in Britain within the different structures of the British commercial companies, the BBC, and S4C. Up to the time of transmission, therefore, programmes are monitored in case any late-breaking news raises doubts about their suitability for being shown that day. On the day of an aircraft disaster, for instance, it may not be judged appropriate to screen a film which has recognizable parallels, tragic or farcical, with the event if the public mood is thought to have been sufficiently affected. Another programme may be substituted or, in the event of very major disasters, a whole evening's schedule or more may need to be changed. On the night of President Kennedy's assassination in 1963, at the BBC there was an intense argument, on rather different grounds, about whether to transmit, for the sake of the child-audience, a scheduled comedy which had nothing to do with the events in Dallas. The outcome of the decision, to maintain the transmission, is of less relevance than the fact that, whatever it was, it could expect to be criticized by 50 per cent of the audience.

The Regulators' Role

The broadcasters must make judgements about content in advance of transmission. The regulators in Britain at the ITC and the Radio Authority, and in the United States at the FCC, make their judgements after the programme has been broadcast. The commercial regulators in Britain, although they have the power to fine offending companies, will normally caution companies as a first step. The Radio Authority, for example, imposed a fine of £20,000 for a third offence by one of its licensees, a reflection of the comparatively low level of earnings by the British radio companies. By contrast, the ITC fined one of its licensees the sum of half a million pounds for an offence to do with product-placement, that is, the forbidden practice of so placing a commercial product in shot that it would serve to promote it as if it were an advertisement.

With a proliferation of stations, the problems of monitoring their outputs on a regular basis become very great and there is, in consequence, a greater reliance on complaints from the audience. Since complaints of that kind represent a self-selected group of the audience, it is important that they do not assume too great an influence on the regulators' attitudes, especially in the areas of taste and decency.

The principle of fining for editorial errors, where it exists, needs very cautious handling. The original editorial judgement and the regulator's subsequent disagreement with it is usually a matter of opinion. In the case of rap lyrics, for example, which may fall foul of a regulator, it is likely that men and women from one culture are passing judgement on another of which they can know little. In such circumstances, they can only invoke their own understanding of popular morality. Their situation is further complicated by the deliberate use made of language by one generation or culture to offend members of another. There is, of course, a difference between an occasional error in judgement and a persistent series of errors for which some penalty has to be exacted from the licence-holder under the terms of his or her licence. But marking a difference of opinion with a penalty needs to have a particular justification stronger than a mere assertion of authority.

Until the spring of 1997, there were two statutory bodies concerned with the maintenance of standards in British programmes. They were the Broadcasting Complaints Commission, which dealt with fairness and privacy, and the Broadcasting Standards Council, dealing with the portrayal of violence, sexual conduct, and matters of taste and decency. The Council was also given research responsibilities, essential to strengthen the credentials of its findings. Both bodies handled complaints falling within their remits from the public.

The confusion generated by the existence of two bodies led to the Government's decision to merge them in a single Broadcasting Standards Commission. The Commissioners, now totalling thirteen, personally consider, with the help of a small staff, the complaints sent to them. A lay view is therefore brought to bear on the editorial judgements which caused the complainants to write. Much of the business with the audience is conducted in correspondence, but hearings are also held, particularly in cases of alleged breaches of fairness and privacy when facts, rather than opinions, are in contention. When the Commission has reached its conclusions, on the basis of evidence from the complainant and the broadcaster, it has powers to require the broadcaster to publish them on air or in the Press. Possible conflicts with the duties of the BBC Governors and the members of the commercial regulatory bodies prevent the Commission from applying further sanctions, but, in a modest way and at low cost to the complainant, it provides a form of independent redress for the audience. Its independent standing increased the value of its research projects into such issues as the portrayal of sex in programmes, public attitudes to bad language, and the treatment of survivors in disaster. Further support for its independent standing was provided by the Commission's funding, a mixture of government finance and a compulsory levy on broadcasters.

This chapter has necessarily covered a good deal of ground not directly connected with the main subject of the book. It does, however, supply the context within which the decisions to be discussed in subsequent chapters are taken. However, sheer quality may be the justification, on some occasions, for setting aside the constraints which the observance of standards imply. So may the sheer necessity of faithfully reflecting the world in fact and fiction: the prime duty of broadcasting, I believe, in any democratic society. If that duty is done, offence and outrage cannot be avoided. As the World Council of Churches observed of television many years ago, a service which never gives offence is itself offensive.

4

The Particular Case of Children

Introduction

Many people's concerns about television's impact upon children begin with the medium's supposed ability to teach and, by teaching indiscriminately right things and wrong, to do children harm. Television is present in the home, watched for many hours a day by adults and, for even longer, by children. More and more children live in households where there are sets in different rooms and many children now have their own set in their own room. Even before they walk, children sit in front of the set, often with the most limited supervision or no supervision at all, television serving as a baby-minder. However, what may seem irresponsibility on the part of parents who take the baby-minder's goodwill on trust may not be the result of choice, but, in modern circumstances, of necessity.

I have deliberately avoided the use of the words 'power' and 'influence'. In many conversations about television's role in society, the words are used as if they were interchangeable. More strongly than radio, television possesses the capacity to alter the public agenda by focusing upon a single issue or on a single group of people, but whether that is 'power' or 'influence' is a matter for individual judgements. However, with the scattering of the audience to a much larger number of outlets than before, that capacity is liable to be diminished. In the sense of being able to compel people to do anything they do not wish to do, television has no 'power', but it shares with almost anything else we encounter during the day a capacity to influence us. Newspapers, books, the conversation of friends, all of them may colour our thoughts, alter our perspectives, confuse situations for us or clarify them. We tell our children stories, give them books to read, or take them to see films because we think they will be influenced for the better. We ourselves do not, indeed, read books or go to the cinema determined to resist every influence, of whatever kind, they may try to exert on us. If we do, we might as well leave the book unread or the film unwatched unless we regard it simply, in the words of the English novelist Rose Macaulay, as a way of killing time for those who like time dead.

Perhaps, as a result of such exposure, we will do or believe whatever it is, if it is anything at all, that the newspaper, book, or film sought to persuade us to do or believe. On the other hand, we may not and opt instead for the very opposite. Whatever we decide, we shall have made our choice as adults. Children, however, with their inexperience and lack of knowledge, are less equipped to deal with the arguments, which may often be unstated, against one thing and in favour of another. They do not automatically pick up the signals provided by costume, manner, or speech about the nature of one character or another in a drama or in a studio discussion. They are less able, therefore, to choose.

In infancy, children watch a series of images of which they either make no narrative sense or evolve a storyline of their own with little connection to the original. Progressing from that state, they remain incapable for a time of distinguishing fact from fiction, fantasy from realism. When they are apparently paying little attention to a programme whose content holds no interest for them, they may nevertheless see or hear things in passing which influence them. A partial understanding of the context may provide a garbled version of its reality. *The Snowman* is a much-loved cartoon shown regularly at Christmas-time in Britain. It tells how a snowman from the garden, coming to life, takes a little boy to visit a kind of snowmen's Valhalla, flying with him through the air there and back. It did, however, make at least one child, mysteriously afraid of snow, fearful that all snowmen were liable to carry children away, including the snowman built for her in her own garden.

Even if we take the view that only a small proportion of the total audience is, in some more serious way, at risk from television, in the sense that what they see or hear may harm them or lead them to harm others, our worries remain, not much diminished. In the dysfunctional marks of society around us, we think we may be seeing evidence of what television is doing. It is tempting to do so even when we acknowledge, as the majority of people do, the existence of many alternative causes. We want television to ensure that the values which we most esteem are passed on to a new generation and, in order to accomplish that, we want the programmes seen by children to reflect those values in forms which children will comprehend.

What Children Watch

Children watch three distinct kinds of programme, even though the words 'Children's Television' may be used interchangeably to describe programmes made in order to instruct children, following in a formal and systematic way a particular pattern of study, as well as programmes made to entertain children outside school, though often having characteristics of an educative or informative kind. These two categories are described below, with a description of the very much larger third category, the programmes primarily intended for adults, but watched for much of the time in great numbers by children of all age-ranges.

Educational Programmes

These are programmes made for watching or listening to in schools as part of the children's education. Their target-audience may include early teenagers who would not wish to be thought of any longer as children. The programmes' main purpose is to provide support for the teacher in the classroom. Printed back-up material is often made available to teachers for prior study and the enrichment of subsequent discussions in the classroom. Pictures of distant places, diagrammatic explanations of complex problems, the illustration of art-treasures, and, where funds are available, specially produced drama are all likely to be in the annual output. When educational programming is highly developed, individual series may be planned in conjunction with either national or local educational authorities and with an eye to the set texts of major public examinations. Broadcasting is one of the cheapest means of spreading information to large numbers of people and such collaboration makes it possible for schools to make the best use of the material it supplies in sustaining the curriculum.

In Britain, these programmes continue to be transmitted on the main terrestrial channels during twenty-five weeks each year. Increasing use is being made of the early morning hours to download material for schools to record and use as it suits their own timetables.

In the United States, there has been long-standing dissatisfaction with the lack of any serious contribution by the broadcasters to children's educational and informational needs. The Children's Television Act, 1990, was an attempt to remedy this by imposing a requirement on broadcasters to demonstrate to the FCC, as a condition of licence renewal, that they were meeting these goals for children between 2 and 16. But it was clear soon afterwards that the words 'education and information' were being imaginatively interpreted. As an example, *The Flintstones*, a comic cartoon series about a Stone Age family, was being put forward as a programme whose educational properties could be weighed in the broadcaster's favour.

In the summer of 1996, President Clinton convened a White House Summit on Children's Television. The discussion struck at least one of those present as fresh, concerned not as so often in the past with television's responsibility for this or that ill within society, but, instead, with the positive contributions which the medium might make to the moulding of a culture fit for children to grow up in.[1] It was agreed that stricter rules of interpretation should be applied to the demands of the 1990 Act. A few weeks later, the FCC was to publish new regulations, announced at the Summit. They laid down that a minimum of three hours a week of core educational programming was required for automatic licence renewal, combined with effective promotion and clear labelling. Scheduling at accessible times, that is, between 7.00 a.m. and 10.00 p.m. rather than before dawn, was also called for. The Commission stated its aim of improving the level of accountability by broadcasters to their communities. The rules took effect on 1 September 1997. How successful this can be in altering the culture which has previously denied children this kind of output can only be judged in the longer term.

Children's Programmes

Because of the limited appeal of radio to the child-audience, the second category of children's programmes is largely confined to television, which has greater appeal for the child-audience. It covers the programmes specifically produced for children when they are at home: at the weekend, in the early morning and late afternoon, and during vacation times. Although they are directed in Britain at children between the pre-school years and the age of 13, the cut-off point is lower than it would have been a few years ago, reflecting the more rapid maturity of modern children, in which television itself has played a part. Children have become more familiar with the conventions and pace of adult programmes, the increased use, for example, of a more disjunctive style of narration, making them impatient with the values of many programmes intended for them or with anything which seems, too transparently, to be talking down to them. This fact has recently been acknowledged by the coining of the expression 'tweenies' for the upper end of the 'child-audience' between 10 and 16, recognizing that it has interests of its own which are inadequately served. Reportedly, some 57 per cent of the tweenies are regular viewers of *Friends*.

---

[1] Report in *Connect*, 13 (Fall 1996) (Center for Media Literacy, Los Angeles).

Anna Home, then Head of Children's Television for the BBC in Britain, acknowledged in 1997 that some older children would watch the programmes aimed at 12- and 13-year-olds, although they would be reluctant to admit to doing so. Her primary object was to entertain, but her aim was to educate through entertainment.[2] The output for which she was responsible included a high proportion of material specially made for the child-audience. Nickelodeon, one of the most successful of the children's cable channels in the States and Britain, is also responsible for many original productions. Geraldine Laybourne, its President, told the World Summit on Children's Television in Melbourne in 1995 that, when the company realized the poverty of programmes generally on offer to the child-audience, to bring about a more diverse output, it saw no alternative to going into production itself.[3] PBS, despite almost continuous financial constraints, has been responsible in the States over many years for maintaining a range of programmes of high quality made specially for children. Other channels intended for children have tended to concentrate on entertainment, little of it original and including a lot of cartoons of mixed quality. In their drive to provide entertainment, they often lack the element of 'roughage' which many children enjoy as part of the diet, a reflection of the excitement of discovery and learning which, for some children at least, forms part of the process of growing up.

A clear dilemma for broadcasters in providing programmes for children lies in maintaining the following of the child-audience without provoking complaints from parents about unsuitable material. The BBC's Director General, Sir John Birt, expressed the problem in these terms:

One of the difficulties, to be candid, is that today's children are very, very different from yesterday's. To some extent we may be treating large numbers of children as they used to be rather than as they are. I have no doubt at all that today's 12-, 13-, 14-year-old is an altogether more knowing person than he or she would have been twenty or thirty years ago. It is a difficult issue for broadcasters. We know, in our children's programmes, that if you treat them as if they were darling little things, they don't watch what you put out. Unless you recognize their interests and the validity of their expression, they will ignore you. I think one of the toughest tests for the BBC is how we can engage our children whilst continuing our proper role of expanding their horizons and exposing them to material which they are not going to get in other places. And that is a testing task.[4]

Anna Home described how the dilemma outlined by Birt affected her choice of programmes. There was, she said, a constant attempt to serve two

[2] Personal interview, London, 15 Apr. 1997.
[3] World Summit on Children and Television, organized by the Australian Children's Television Foundation, Melbourne, 12–17 Mar. 1995.
[4] Personal interview, London, 21 Apr. 1997.

masters: the parents who paid the licence fee and the children who wished to maintain their street-cred. Attitudes among parents inevitably differed. Some wrote to thank her for keeping their children informed, others blamed her for destroying their innocence. However, she felt that if children grew up believing the world to be a beautiful blue-skied place, they were in for a shock. Holding the balance provided the most difficult part of her job.

She offered an illustration of the problems she had to confront. Many parents have either forgotten their own experiences of childhood humour, do not wish to be reminded of them, or believe that television should pursue a more obviously tasteful line in its choice of programmes for children to set them an example. The BBC had shown in children's time a film in which schoolboys were competing in peeing over a high wall. The winner emerged in the best traditions of David and Goliath. The child-audience approved of the film, numerous parents did not. The Australians, who made it, could not understand why the British were so tight-lipped about it. To judge from the puritanism which prevails in much network television in the United States, it seems unlikely that the film would easily find an outlet on an American network. When a clip from the film was shown at the Children's Summit, it was generally applauded by delegates from the West as sufficiently light-hearted to deflect offence. However, a sharp denunciation of it from an Asian delegate drew a round of applause from the remaining Asian delegates. It was, he said, in bad taste and therefore, for him and his colleagues, subverted the moral values which broadcasters were expected to uphold.

The moral problems confronting children are regularly presented in a number of drama series and serials in Britain by both the BBC and Independent Television. The latter has produced such series as *Press Gang*, built around a school newspaper and the team of children who produce it, and *Children's Ward*. Probably the best known of all is the BBC's *Grange Hill*, which, set in a London secondary school, has been running for many years and has by now appealed to several generations of older children. Like some of the Schools programmes, they have been criticized for their choice of such themes as child-abuse, Aids, and teenage pregnancies, regardless of the way in which the stories told have been resolved. Some plots have been built around sexual themes, but they have also dealt with other issues, such as the concealment of theft or bullying, which are of interest to children at school. Home is clear that the moral values portrayed in programmes for children should be conservative or, in her word, traditional. Right must be clearly defined, as wrong must be, with none of the ambiguities commonplace in material for adults.

BBC Children's Television has, for many years, presented a daily round-up of news. Editorial control of *Newsround* is the responsibility of the Children's Department and not of the News Division. Starting from a selection of items thought to be of interest to children, the choice has now moved to the presentation from a child's point of view of items which may include some of the most demanding stories of the week. The Aids epidemic and two of the worst outrages perpetrated against children, the murder of Jamie Bulger and the shooting of sixteen children and their teacher at a Scottish primary school, were all treated: the Bulger case only after the trial was over, while the other two stories were handled according to the conventions made familiar by the programme to the child-audience over many years.

Adult Programmes: Responsibilities

The final category of programmes watched or heard by children consists of those programmes primarily intended during the remaining hours of the day for adults. They are principally television programmes. Children's listening to radio is confined very largely to music, although critical British parents, nostalgic for the pleasures of their own childhoods, argue that children's appetites for speech on radio have languished for want of feeding. The apparent lack of interest among children in speech programmes and the individual nature of most adult radio listening are the reasons why the television Watershed (see pp. 66–7) has no parallel in British radio services.

However, it cannot be assumed by the broadcasters that when children are present in the radio audience there need be no concern for them. In the spring of 1997, the BBC dismissed Chris Evans, the very popular presenter of a breakfast programme on Radio 1, the channel attracting the largest radio audience in Britain. Evans, a highly accomplished professional, had built up in television and on radio a strong appeal to a large audience of young adults either living or aspiring to live a lifestyle at odds with their elders', particularly as far as sexual freedoms go. It was the strength of that appeal which persuaded the BBC, in order to reverse falling audience ratings, to give him the popular morning slot on Radio 1. He did the job of restoring the numbers of listeners very effectively, not least with the children who had followed him from his breakfast-time television programme.

Although he played no part in it, the decision to dismiss Evans was one of which the Chairman of the BBC, Sir Christopher Bland, personally approved.

A. He and I parted company when I was driving my son, who was then 12, to school. We had Radio 1 on and he turned to me and said, Dad, what's oral sex?'

That is not the sort of question I want to be asked at that time of the morning because someone has decided to air it on Radio 1. That was a clear line which he overstepped. . . . And then he overstepped another and he went. So that is, as it were. . . . I had no doubt at that point that he had gone too far. We also, I think, have had the view for some time, on both the BBC and ITV, that certain things on certain channels at certain times of the day are permissible, are acceptable, but inadequately signposted and too early are not [permissible].

Q. What are you fearful of? Are you fearful of the embarrassment, the kind of embarrassment you were caused or because of actual effects? Are you protecting familial harmony or are you taking it more seriously because you feel this is not the way it should be done?

A. I think more seriously. It is not the way it should be done. It plainly is not. And it is not for an entertainer to decide when I want to talk to my son about oral sex. If I choose never to, that is my privilege. If he chooses to ask me, it is not because Chris Evans in the morning has told him to. I think it's broader than that, I wasn't embarrassed by it at all. I was made furious by it.[5]

The effect of Evans's departure was, reportedly, a fall of more than a million in the listening figures for Radio 1.

In Chapter 3, we considered the factors which influence the standards to be observed by a particular programme, including the time of day, the channel, and the performers involved. The resulting standards reflect the editor's estimate of the audience's likely expectations. In the case of Evans's morning appearances, there was a sharper difference than usual between the expectations of different sections of the audience. To the majority of those listening to him, his material caused little offence. As time has passed, so attitudes towards the discussion of sex have become more tolerant and therefore the degree of sexual explicitness in programmes has been increased. At a different time of day, when the audience contained fewer children, it is reasonable to suppose that the material would have been considered acceptable. But in the morning, the BBC decided, it must apply a different criterion, one reflecting the significant presence within the overall audience of children, an echo of the FCC's ruling over the 'Seven Dirty Words'. For the BBC, the range of topics and their treatment were unsuitable. It was the children who made the difference and who continue, especially in television, to make the difference until the middle of the evening.

Research in both Britain and the United States has shown that very young children are watching television until at least eight or nine o'clock in the evening, with significant numbers of them and of their older brothers and sisters staying up even later. Older children, in particular, are more

[5] Personal interview, London, 6 May 1997.

65

likely than not to have access in their own rooms to television-receivers and, in many cases, video-recorders as well, enabling them to watch programmes transmitted even later, despite their parents' wishes or without their parents' knowledge. Children, whatever order their parents may try to impose on their viewing, find little difficulty in watching in their friends' houses programmes which their parents have barred. They are also capable of mastering in very little time any kind of blocking device so far available on domestic receivers.

As we noted in Chapter 3, there is little support for restricting television at all times to a point where it is invariably suitable for children, but the choice of programmes in the early to mid-evening can often create conflicts between the interests of the adult audience, for whom the programmes are primarily intended, and the interests of children. Some programmes are capable, according to their critics, of harming children by relaying the wrong values. If not inciting children to violence, they may suggest to children that violence is an acceptable way of resolving conflicts. They may familiarize children with the kind of language their parents do not want them to use, or confront them with adult sexual situations, including divorce and violence, for which children are not prepared. There are parents who say that, while they have no objection to the treatment of such themes, it is often the way in which they are treated which is unsuitable for children and may cause them harm.

These anxieties are found on both sides of the Atlantic. The British tried to resolve them by adopting the 9.00 p.m. Watershed. It made its appearance in the final decade before the climacteric period in the early 1960s for both British and American broadcasting. In Britain, paternalism, a little less securely than before, was still in the saddle. Only a short time before, the Government had agreed to the abolition of the so-called Toddlers' Truce, an hour in the early evening when there was no television broadcasting. The truce was intended to allow parents to put their children to bed undistracted by the rival claims of bathtime and the screen. It demonstrated a wholesome, if misplaced, faith in the disciplined conduct of British households, to say nothing about the universality of British plumbing.

John Birt, the BBC's Director General, explains the Watershed's relatively robust survival forty years later:

I start from the position that we should not, at times when children might view in large numbers, and particularly before the 9.00 p.m. Watershed, broadcast programmes which would embarrass the family viewing together. Grandparents, parents, and children ought to be able to sit down and watch programmes without being affronted or embarrassed and without parents having to explain notions which a young mind need not yet have to grapple with or understand. This is not to say we cannot have the odd double entendre before nine o'clock, but, by and large, it is still a test which we hold dear.[6]

In America, the closest parallel was the creation in the mid-1970s by the broadcasting industry of the 'Family Hour'. Between 7.00 p.m. and 9.00 p.m. there was a self-imposed ban on programmes considered unsuitable for viewing by the family audience. The introduction of the ban was the culmination of pressures on the broadcasters which had been given quickened momentum by the publication of the Surgeon-General's Report in 1972. The Report accepted the existence of a link between screen violence and aggressive behaviour among children. Congress added its weight, as did the FCC, and the industry's declaration followed. The 'Family Hour' proved short-lived. Challenged by the Writers' Guild as an interference in their rights to free expression during prime time, it was held by a federal court judge sitting in California to be unconstitutional. The grounds for the decision were that the FCC had applied inadmissible pressures on the broadcasters. By the end of 1980, the Hour had been abandoned.

I asked Michael Grade, at the time he was still Chief Executive of Channel 4, what obligation was owed by the broadcasters to the child-audience watching after the passing of the 9.00 p.m. Watershed. Not every parent, I said, is in a position to take the child away from a television set which may be in the family's only room. When he replied 'None,' I asked him about a responsibility towards those children who were neglected by parents either uncaring or absent. He again replied 'None,' adding that the majority of complaints came from parents who were embarrassed.

I don't believe that television influences people. I just don't believe it. Because if it were that influential, there's so much of the Good on television. In every cop-show the baddies always lose, the moral values are there. Why aren't they influential? I just don't believe it. Certainly in trivial issues like fashion, but that's fashion. It's got nothing to do with right and wrong. And if television is so powerful, why don't party political broadcasts work? So I don't believe that children, I don't believe that anybody is influenced to behave in a particular way by television.[7]

Stuart Fischoff, writer and psychologist, believes that responsibility for resolving the conflict should be borne by parents.

The whole problem with television is trying to get parents to parent. It isn't really a problem with television. The reason that you have Governors and politicians demagoguing about it is that they know they can't get parents to parent, but they can get political hay out of bashing television. And this is the grand hypocrisy of Western civilization. . . . So it looks as though television is a cause when it's actually only an effect, the consequence of parental neglect. . . . And in some sense the

---

[6] Personal interview, London, 21 Apr. 1997.
[7] Personal interview, London, 30 Apr. 1997.

entertainment people are right in their indignation about hypocrisy. But on the other hand, they are also not taking their responsibility for how powerful is the medium they have developed. It's doing a lot of negative things. So they are also hiding behind the First Amendment as politicians are hiding behind children. Everybody is running for cover and engaging in demagoguery for the sake of not having their own ox gored.[8]

Television Programmes: Children and Sex

Many of the older children in Britain who watched the drama series designed for them and described earlier will also watch programmes intended for the next age-group. The American series *Beverley Hills 90210* or the series *Heartbreak High*, made in Australia, concern themselves more fully with the emotional problems which accompany early sexual relationships. They are usually screened in the early evening, the time when their target-audiences are most likely to be available to watch. Their timing inevitably raises questions among parents about the suitability of their relative sexual frankness for the younger children who may also watch them, attracted perhaps by their apparently greater sophistication. Much of that sophistication is expressed in talk, some of which may be expected to go over the heads of the younger members of the audience. More generally, on both British and American networks physical expressions of sex, going beyond kissing and mild caresses, are kept to a later time.

At the end of 1996, the Kaiser Family Foundation and Children Now, based in Oakland, California, produced the results of a survey of the sexual messages contained in television programmes transmitted during the former Family Hour, the period between 8.00 p.m. and 9.00 p.m. on the networks, an hour earlier for local stations.[9] A great deal of talk about sexual activity was revealed, measured as 3.1 such incidents on average in every one of the hours monitored during the month reviewed. By comparison, sexual activity was much lower, limited to kissing and caressing, with a still more limited incidence of simulated intercourse. There was a partial comparison with findings from programmes transmitted in 1976 and 1986, one episode only of each programme shown in the Family Hour as against three episodes in the survey of 1996 programmes. The percentage of programmes with some sexual content rose from 43 per cent in 1976 to 75 per cent in 1996.

The survey noted that, in the years between 1976 and 1996, reality programmes, such as *Cops*, became a regular ingredient in the Family Hour,

[8] Personal interview, Los Angeles, 14 Nov. 1996.
[9] *Sexual Messages on Family Hour Television: Content and Context*, A three part study by the Kaiser Family Foundation and Children Now (Oakland, Calif., 1996).

although their incidence was low (16 per cent of all programmes in 1996). Unsurprisingly, the amount of sexual talk or behaviour in reality programming, much of which is shot in public places or during encounters between the police and criminals or their victims, was found to be low. The overall increase in sexual talk and behaviour recorded in the survey can, therefore, be attributed to the sitcoms and dramas which occupy most of the Hour. As noted in the next chapter, research in Britain has found that the greater proportion of sexual behaviour portrayed on television occurs between people in an established relationship, although it is a married relationship only in a minority of cases. The American survey, while indicating that the nature of much of the sexual behaviour was mild, drew attention to the near-absence from the programmes of messages about the risks and responsibilities associated with sexual behaviour.

The children whose attitudes to these programmes were also surveyed were between 8 and 13 years old. The reaction of their parents ranged from shock at the amount of sexual material screened in the Family Hour through surprise at children's apparent familiarity with the innuendoes and jokes it contained to gratitude, finally, at the opportunity they were given by some of the programmes to initiate important discussions with their children.

The findings were subsequently the subject of a long article in the *New York Times* which concentrated on the pervasiveness of sexual references in, and on the general mediocrity of, material obliged to rely heavily on 'nudge-and-winks'.[10] Issues of programme quality, however, often tend to be of secondary importance to those who are principally troubled by the supposed omnipresence of sexual themes and by what they consider irregular sexual behaviour which might set poor examples to children and young people.

In the area of sexual behaviour, as in many others where the standards of an earlier time are invoked as a reproach to the current generation, television, whatever the source of its funding, has to confront a dilemma. It is that the medium cannot be too far removed, either forward or backwards, from popular morality as represented by popular behaviour. In many parts of both the United States and Britain, people do choose, without any association of guilt, to live together without marriage. There is no such thing as 'television' which can decide to make up its independent mind either to encourage or discourage this trend. In any case, the unreliability of television as the means of delivering an unwelcome message is well established. While an individual channel might sustain itself successfully by pursuing a policy of upholding marriage and celebrating the family values

---

[10] *New York Times*, 26 Jan. 1997, section 2, p. 41.

which accompany it, it is unlikely to attract the general viewer with no specific commitment to that policy. It may, or may not, be in the national interest or even the public interest that couples, by being joined together in a legal or a spiritual union, make a contribution to the stability of society. That is no longer, if it ever was, a proper concern of the broadcasters in a democratic, pluralist, society. By contrast, the broadcasters' obligations towards decency are no less present in their treatment of sexual issues before a child-audience than before an audience consisting almost entirely of adults.

News Programmes

Although many children do not watch news programmes, the content of both national and local news programmes scheduled around 6.00 p.m. is likely to include coverage which could exceed the boundaries some parents would think it right to set to their children's knowledge. British television normally draws a distinction between what may be shown in an early-evening bulletin and what may be shown later. Images which might be thought capable of disturbing children in the audience may be withheld from early bulletins, although spoken accounts of the news-item may be broadcast. In doing this, they seem to be following the evidence in research described in Chapter 7.

Children and Advertising

As they watch programmes, both those designed for them and those designed for adult audiences, children see a great many commercials. They are a particular cause of concern to many parents on both sides of the Atlantic. Although the FCC attempted to deregulate children's advertising, Congress passed legislation in 1990 which imposed limits of twelve minutes an hour during the week and ten-and-a-half minutes at weekends. In Britain, the Independent Television Commission regulates the amount of advertising time permitted in each hour. No time-limit is applied specifically to children's programmes, but programmes for children lasting less than half an hour may not be interrupted by commercials.

In the opening paragraphs of its Children's Advertising Guidelines, NBC acknowledges that advertisers have a special responsibility to protect children from exploitation. The Guidelines indicate the nature of some parental anxieties by setting down the obligations imposed on advertisers: no glamorization or exaggeration of a product, no peer pressure nor pressure on parents, no antisocial behaviour, no abuse of children's familiarity with artists or celebrities. There are restrictions on the advertising of certain products within or adjacent to children's programmes. Among these are feature films. While trailers for 'G'-rated films may be shown in or around children's programmes, those for 'PG'-rated films have to be the subject of specific clearance before they can be screened in the same time-periods. Higher rated films are not allowed to be trailed within them.

The Children's Advertising Review Unit (CARU), part of the Council of Better Business Bureaus, is concerned with questions of truth and accuracy in national advertising directed in all media at children. While issues of taste and decency are negotiated between the advertiser and the broadcaster in accordance with the principles set out in the latter's guidelines, the Unit is also concerned with what it terms 'appropriateness', that is, such questions as pro-social behaviour, safety, and positive role-modelling, all of which may touch on aspects of either taste or decency. It operates as part of the self-regulatory system established in 1971 by the advertising community. CARU was formed three years later to meet the special circumstances of child-directed advertising. Its Director, Elizabeth Lascoutx, emphasized that it has no concern with programming issues, such as the V-chip, and is not a children's advocacy group. It performs a dual role, combining the protection of children with the protection of the rights of advertisers. It encourages advertisers to develop the spreading of educational messages to children in the spirit of the Children's Television Act, 1990.

CARU may raise complaints as a result of its own monitoring or on the basis of information received from a consumer or a rival manufacturer or service-provider. In treating complaints, it observes six principles. The first two principles deal with the avoidance of the exploitation of children, the third and fourth with the need for truthfulness and the encouragement of positive social behaviour, while the fifth reminds advertisers of the need to include minority groups and avoid stereotypes. The last of the principles states:

Although many influences affect a child's performance and social development, it remains the prime responsibility of the parents to provide guidance for children. Advertisers should contribute to this parent–child relationship in a constructive manner.[11]

I asked Lascoutx what periods of the day she regarded as children's time.

We now take the position that, since there are now 24-hour children's channels . . . Nickelodeon, 24 hours that is basically targeted for children. Nickelodeon has now put in a young children's block at eight o'clock in the evening, so we think advertisers can't really hide behind the 'Well, it's not between two and five in the afternoon' any more. So our position is that during programming likely to draw a

[11] *Self-Regulatory Guidelines for Children's Advertising* (4th edn. Council of Better Business Bureaus Inc., Children's Review Unit, New York, 1991).

substantial child-audience and with a product that is likely to appeal to a child, we consider it child-directed and the advertising which fills that slot must be appropriate. So while most of our monitoring is of so-called kids' time, six till nine in the morning and two to five in the afternoon, we will look at anything which looks like kids' advertising.[12]

CARU monitors about 2,000 commercials a month. This activity provides the majority of the complaints with which the Unit deals. Its role is to engage in discussions with the advertisers in order to bring a commercial into line with CARU's guidelines. Lascoutx said that, when an advertiser agrees to change or withdraw an advertisement, action can be taken as soon as seven days after the original monitoring took place. While some advertisers are already familiar with CARU's role and may be represented on its advisory board, others, however, are not and may have to be persuaded to cooperate in the handling of a complaint.

If CARU's discussions are inconclusive, then there is provision for an appeal, never invoked so far, to the National Advertising Review Board. The Unit's conclusions are published regularly, opening with a summary of the complaint, the response made by the advertiser, and the decision reached. Where an appeal is being lodged, that too will feature in the statement. The same bulletins contain a monthly summary of the Unit's overall activity, from the total of advertisements monitored to the cases settled by withdrawal or modification and any submissions to CARU for advice prior to the transmission of a commercial. A reserve power exists to refer cases of non-compliance to an appropriate government agency, but in the Unit's twenty-four years of operation there have been only four references to either the FCC or the Federal Trade Commission.

I asked Lascoutx what penalties were attached if an advertiser was held to be at fault. Publication, she answered, was the only threat that the Unit had:

You know, the threat of bad publicity. People don't like it because it's distributed to the advertising community, a lot of the academic community and the regulatory community. And the Press. [Companies] don't need that, they don't want it.[13]

Frank Willis, Director of Advertising and Sponsorship at the ITC in London, said:

There aren't really taste and decency issues to do with products for children. There are things that go wrong, but they are not usually in the taste and decency area. I think those selling to children are aware of the sensitivities and they don't want to get across the parents.[14]

---

[12] Personal interview, New York, 6 Feb. 1997.   [13] Ibid.
[14] Personal interview, London, 8 May 1997.

He showed me a commercial in which a figure, described by Willis as 'nerdish', appeared, wearing a cycle-helmet. Parents complained that their children gave up wearing their own helmets because the figure in the commercial was so unattractive a role-model.

We did a back-of-the-envelope calculation and worked out the probability how many children would have not to wear their safety-helmets for there to be a fatal accident. The necessary shift in behaviour was not all that great, given the number of accidents there are and the number of children there are.[15]

On the evidence of the figures, a new commercial was made and, as a happy outcome, helmets went back on throughout the country.

The ITC applies differing restrictions throughout the day on the kind of products which may be advertised at particular times. The first of them is the area immediately adjacent to children's programmes. In the case of services appealing exclusively to child-audiences, this will cover the entire output. The ITC's Advertising Guidance Note quotes recent research which indicates that children may be more responsive to commercials transmitted adjacent to programmes they feel are theirs, that is, are specially directed to them. Willis explained the practical implications of this research on commercials within the zone, that 'immediately adjacent to programmes of particular appeal to the under-18s':

So if you're seeing a product and [with it are] Nike shoes, and a record, the Spice Girls [in their heyday] and Diet Coke, and you get a lager as well, the whole is adding up to a sort of shorthand description of what is a trendy lifestyle for a 16-year-old these days. Particularly if the programme is all about 15- and 16-year-old Australian kids and it's a programme which you all flop in front of as soon as you get home from school.[16]

The third area covers more generally the period up to 7.30 p.m. when, with children between the ages of 3 and 7 in the audience, treatments which are potentially frightening or distressing to them should be avoided. Because evidence of distress cannot always be anticipated, the Commission may decide to impose a restriction after a campaign has begun.

The fourth area extends up to the Watershed itself at 9.00 p.m. Willis pointed out that the Watershed's existence imposes a heavy commercial penalty because it prevents the spreading of campaign costs between cheaper daytime hours and peaktime. Because people start to go to bed at half-past ten, there is, effectively, only ninety minutes of programming in which certain commercials can be placed. Willis said:

[15] Ibid.
[16] Ibid.

A lot of the arguments are about that. Sometimes things will be cleared by arrangement, but sometimes the commercial is made and has to suffer on a take-it-or-leave-it basis. An example of where the Watershed is quite often invoked occurs when one of the tabloids has yet another Sex Supplement and what you see is . . . the ad will show a couple in a state of undress, rolling round in an interior and you don't actually see, as it were, anything that you shouldn't see. Otherwise apart from that, you could be looking at a soft-core movie. This will be advertising some extremely boring and anodyne pull-out supplement on how to improve your sex-life or what goes on behind suburban front-doors or whatever it is. And those tend to run post-nine because they always elicit offence.[17]

There is a fifth area which limits certain advertising to a very late placing. Willis cited the example of a gay chat-line, something totally unacceptable as the subject of an advertisement until the recent past, but now allowed to appear after 11.00 p.m. when the audience is increasingly made up of younger adults.

The question of children's vulnerability to commercials recurs in demands for a ban before the Watershed on the advertising of any products inherently unsuitable for them. Alcohol is already banned, but the health food lobby demands a ban on the advertising of confectionery. Willis described the lengths to which the ITC goes in its attempts to regulate commercials in the interests of young people:

And the adolescents are often watching things like *Home and Away* [an Australian soap] which don't count as children's programmes, but which we feel strongly should not be carrying alcohol. So we have a rather more complicated index-based system.[18]

He explained that, under the system, the number of young people within the sensitive age-group who were watching was compared with their percentage within the population. If the percentage watching were significantly higher, then certain products would be banned from advertising in or around that programme. Willis did not pretend that the banned commercials could not be watched at other times, but then they would appear in a context which did not suggest that the programmes, and therefore also the advertising, were targeted specifically at young people.

Abandoned in the Wasteland

One of the most comprehensive assaults to be launched in recent times on the treatment of children by American television was contained in *Aban-*

---

[17] Personal interview, London, 8 May 1997.   [18] Ibid.

doned in the Wasteland, a book first published in 1995.[19] It took its title from the denunciation in 1961 of all broadcasting standards in the States made by the then-Chairman of the FCC, Newton Minow. American broadcasting, he said, was one vast wasteland. Although the introduction of cable and satellite services has brought a wider choice to the audience, causing Minow to withdraw a little from the comprehensiveness of his original criticism, the word 'wasteland' has preserved its sting over nearly forty years. It was the natural choice for a title when Minow wrote the book with his co-author, Craig L. LaMay.

Towards the book's close, Minow and LaMay set out three goals for public policy towards children. The first of them reads:

It should meet the child's needs to be prepared for life as a productive citizen. Television, the nation's most powerful teacher, should be a conduit for the generational transmission of democratic values and the values of simple decency.[20]

I am sceptical, for the reasons in the opening paragraphs of this chapter, whether television can do much directly to prepare children for life as productive citizens. Although I understand the ambition better if it is interpreted in terms of the republican responsibilities which rest on every American citizen, I still doubt whether, outside the framework of identifiably didactic programmes directed to schools, children respond readily to anything overtly purposeful. The values of democracy, including the value of simple decency, stand a better chance of being understood through the more allusive channels of fiction and certain kinds of narrative documentary.

That is why it is important in shaping policies for children's programmes in both countries to provide the financial and other resources needed to ensure a diversity of output. Under competitive pressures, children's programmes have been consistently vulnerable. Children's needs require protection, not least from the rival claims on sources of funding made by programmes for adult audiences which hold out the promise to commercial broadcasters of increased advertising revenues. It is not sufficient to say that, among the latter, there are many which entertain, inform, and educate children as much as they do adults.

The Future Protection of Children

The second goal set by Minow and LaMay is the protection of children from violence and other programme material to which parents may

[19] N. N. Minow and C. L. LaMay, *Abandoned in the Wasteland* (Hill & Wang, New York, 1996).
[20] Ibid. 153.

object. They cite the V-chip as a technological means of providing security for the child on the Information Highway as infant chairs and seat-belts provide it on an actual journey. The V-chip, with the V standing for violence, originated in Canada. There, concerns about violent tele-vision, available without restriction in most of Canada from stations across the 49th parallel, have been running strongly for a long time. According to Keith Spicer, former Chair of the Canadian Radio/Television and Telecommunications Commission (CRTC), the Canadian antipathy to violence is deep-seated, the product of history and geography. The ideal Canadian image, he suggested, was of an unarmed Mountie disarm-ing a criminal.[21] The V-chip would enable parents to eliminate not only violence, but any material which, on the evidence of advance information and the labelling of programmes, they considered unsuitable for their children. It has the disadvantage of all informational devices that its effectiveness depends on the preparedness of its users to make use of the information available to them. The same is true of the British 'Watershed' described earlier in this chapter, although it does not require the user to programme any technical device. Experience suggests that those already concerned to care for their children's viewing will be the ones to make use of the device, in whatever form it is eventually marketed. At the time of writing, although some of the early optimism about the promise of the V-chip has been qualified in the face of technical difficulties and the disadvantage noted above, nevertheless the coolness towards the device exhibited by British broadcasters and the British Government has not been shared in a number of other countries.

More information about forthcoming programmes is now available to American audiences following the introduction of a rating system for programmes containing sexual, violent, or indecent material. Under the Telecommunications Act, 1996, the FCC was given the right to establish such a system, but its exercise of the right was deferred for twelve months. In that time, the industry was to devise a system of its own. If it failed to do so, then the FCC would, under certain conditions, be able to institute a system of its own, although the chances were that such a system would founder in the face of First Amendment challenges.

Under the system, devised, after prolonged travail, by a committee under the chairmanship of Jack Valenti, President of the Motion Pictures Producers Association, small symbols appear briefly in one corner of the screen at the start of network television programmes to indicate

---

[21] Personal interview, Paris, 29 May 1997.

their nature. Like classifications in the cinema, the symbols are age-related. The requirement laid upon Valenti's committee was that the system should be compatible with the operation of the V-chip when it became a standard piece of equipment, prescribed by law from early in 1998, on all television sets with a screen-width of thirteen inches or more.

Although some parents indicated that the new system was of real help to them, others were less grateful. Not only were the symbols, which are also published in *TV Guide*, the principal weekly listings magazine, hardly more than brief flashes at the start of a programme, but age-limits in themselves were considered by some critics to be of little value in indicating the nature of the content determining them. Individual children vary in the rate at which they mature and parents argue that they should be given more detailed information on which to base decisions about what their children are allowed to watch. Some would welcome an indication of the reasons for awarding a particular classification, even so terse a clue as an initial 'V' or 'S'. But, the counter-argument runs, an initial tells the parent nothing about the nature of, for example, the violence which a programme contains.

Moreover, the decisions on classification are not taken collectively, but are the responsibility of the individual broadcaster. In the first weeks of the system's operation, disparities were quickly noted between the networks in their estimation of where on the six-point rating scale particular programmes should be located. A different approach, being developed by the World Wide Web consortium and known as 'Platform for Internet Content Selection' (PICS), may have later applications for television services. It would enable subscribers to limit the material they receive to an agreed set of categories or individual items. So a believer in a particular religious faith could arrange for the material which he or she might expect to find distasteful or offensive to be filtered out in advance. Alternatively, he or she might opt for particular items, with everything else withheld. In theory, the number of options is unlimited, provided there are enough subscribers to justify the costs of operation for one particular sets of interests or another. It avoids any chilling effect which might be attached to indiscriminate labelling of the kind now practised.

Labelling, although extensively practised by other means, such as the Watershed, has never taken any significant graphic form in Britain. Although some companies have experimented—using, for instance, the symbol of a dagger for a violent programme—the imprecision of a single symbol has seemed too unsatisfactory for further exploitation. One alternative, the creation of sufficient symbols to distinguish between the many different levels and forms of violence, rapidly becomes impractical. If applied to the programming of a blocking device, such as the V-chip, it could become too time-consuming for all but the most dedicated users to persist with its use. Knives, for example, have a particular horror for many people, fully exploited by some directors, but underplayed by others. To distinguish between degrees or methods of violence or sexual explicitness, which logically would be desirable, would be costly on the regular basis which would be essential for an effective system.

Several years ago, one of the British Independent Television companies and, later, Channel 4 experimented with the use of a red triangle to indicate a programme of an adult kind. The triangle was shown continuously in one corner of the screen. The experiment was ended when it appeared that the symbol was attracting younger viewers rather than enabling their parents to direct them away from the programme marked. However, evidence gathered more recently in America and published in 1998 has indicated that the use of symbols can contribute to a reduction in the audience of the numbers of younger viewers watching a marked programme.[22] One network executive has claimed that advisories or warnings may cost networks up to a million dollars in advertising. Advertisers have apparently registered the likelihood that they could be influenced in their time-buying decisions by a rating system.[23] That carries with it the possibility of commercial pressures on the broadcasters to temper their classification decisions in response. Programme-makers, in turn, fear that this may have consequences in the support they receive from the broadcasters for more mature material, for example, the serious popular drama series running in mid-evening.

Learning about the Media

The third of the goals set down by Minow and LaMay is the provision of better opportunities for parents to understand the nature of the medium. Their call underlines the lack of facilities in schools and elsewhere for teaching media awareness. When I was in Los Angeles gathering material for this book, I spent an evening at the Center for Media Literacy with a small class of adults under instruction by the Center's Director, Elizabeth Thoman. It was a valuable experience if only because it drove home how limited also are the opportunities for parents and others with responsibilities for children to appreciate the advantages, as well as the limitations, of the media. In an age when, with images of all kinds abounding, the unco-

---

[22] J. Hamilton, *Channeling Violence: The Economic Market for Violent Television Programming* (Princeton University Press, Princeton, 1998).
[23] Article in *LA Weekly*, 10 Jan. 1997.

ordinated flow of messages from the Internet, as well as pervasive talk about the merits of the Superhighway, the media are dominant, it is surprising that we apparently take such little trouble to prepare our children, and ourselves, to normalize them as a part of their lives in the present and future.

5
Sex: Since the Sixties

In *Soap* (1977), women sat around a table talking about sexuality and their enjoyment of orgasms. And the first reaction was 'edit it out'. And someone said, 'Men sit around the table talking about sex, don't they?' So we said, 'Yes.' 'Well, why can't women sit around tables talking about sex?' And we said, 'You're right.'

(Alfred Schneider, former Vice-President of Policy and Standards,
ABC, 1997)

To every new generation, sex comes as a revelation which it firmly believes to be unique. The claim to uniqueness of the revelation to the 1960s generation could be more justifiable than most, at least for the extent of its reverberations. The English poet Philip Larkin wrote that sexual intercourse began for him in 1963. It was the year, as Larkin put it, which fell between the trial at the Old Bailey of *Lady Chatterley's Lover* under the Obscene Publications Act, 1959, and the appearance of the Beatles' first LP, two events connected with the revelation which had their own particular consequences for literature and music, as well as in much wider circles. It was a time of awakening, of a changing of attitudes in Britain and the United States more profound than any which had occurred for a long time before.

British broadcasting was also in a process of change in the 1960s. To read the report of the Pilkington Committee, published in 1962, the furore about sexual explicitness on television which was to develop not long afterwards would appear to have been largely unexpected.[1] The word 'sex' did not appear at all in the Committee's appraisal of BBC Television's

---

[1] Cmnd. 1753 (1962), *Report of the Committee on Broadcasting, 1960*.

output. There were references to moral standards which were probably intended to include the portrayal of sex, but the Committee directed particularly critical attention, not at sex on the screen, but at the greed which quiz-shows on the new commercial channel were thought to encourage.

The BBC defended to the Committee a series of Sunday-night plays which had, by its own admission, contained an undue emphasis on the 'sordid and sleazy', owing to a failure to provide, as originally planned, a balancing number of comedies. The Committee accepted the BBC's concept of a duty to produce 'kitchen-sink' drama if it were a significant element in current dramatic writing. The Corporation could not discourage such writing. It should, however, according to the Committee, be scheduled in the light of the BBC's obligations to serve a wide range of tastes and interests. The Independent Television Authority, when questioned by the Committee, had defended the right to broadcast kitchen-sink plays on the same grounds as the BBC had advanced. However, it conceded that there had been too many of them and, when it had said so to its franchisees, the numbers had been reduced.

One of the companies' major successes had been a series called *Armchair Theatre*, which had drawn on the rich flowering of dramatic writing which was then enriching American television. Sydney Newman, the Canadian who was the driving force behind *Armchair Theatre*, transferred in 1962 to the BBC, taking with him for further development his belief in 'agitational contemporaneity'. As the BBC's Head of Drama, he was at the centre of the controversy in which the BBC was shortly to be embroiled.

When the Pilkington Report appeared, the BBC, with Sir Hugh Greene as the successor to Ian Jacob as Director General, was fighting back against its commercial rivals. After several years on the defensive, it had campaigned vigorously for its own cause while Pilkington and his colleagues were deliberating. And it had not been above conducting some black propaganda against rivals whose commitment to commerce, it suggested, was possibly greater than their commitment to broadcasting. Greene professed particular scorn for the 'discovery', though the fact had never been concealed, that one of the main shareholders in an ITV company was also interested in running laundries. That, he considered, was no sort of proper activity for anyone associated with the business of broadcasting.

In the aftermath of the Report, the Government awarded the BBC the second channel it had been seeking, while the independent sector, licking its wounds after Pilkington's strictures on its alleged lack of serious programmes and general triviality, was coming to terms with a closer regulatory control over content.[2] There was also a sense of political change in the air, with the Conservative Government, in office since 1951, showing signs of exhaustion.

With confidence renewed in a changing climate, programme-makers in BBC Television were encouraged to push out the boundaries. The response from most of its audience was favourable. Criticisms grew, however, among a section of the audience which disapproved of the liberalism of the new regime, a manifestation, as they considered it, of the permissive society.

One of the areas on which the critics concentrated was the output of television drama, particularly its single plays. They contained, said the critics, too much sex. The values of family life were being eroded. That there was a good deal of sex about generally, and more talk about sex, and that the values of family life were undergoing change were all undeniable. What was less certain than the BBC's critics believed was that the BBC was the engine of change rather than, according to the choice of metaphor, its mirror or its transmitter, reporter, or missionary.

Although, more than thirty years later, the campaign against the representation of sex on television goes on in Britain, it does so in a more muted form. The level of tolerance has risen among the audience, although misjudgements in scheduling decisions can provoke angry responses, particularly from parents. I asked Clare Mulholland, Deputy Chief Executive of the Independent Television Commission until the end of 1997, what explained the growth of tolerance in public attitudes towards sexual material on television, even among people not themselves disposed to watch it.

I think several things happened over the period. Sex education in schools, the women's movement, a whole different attitude to male and female relationships, more confidence among women at one stage too, without feeling exploited by sexual portrayal. I think it became acceptable to show that women were willing partners, not just in romance, but in the enjoyment of sex.[3]

However, she considered that the single most influential event in altering attitudes had been the onset of the Aids epidemic in the mid-1980s. It led, among other things, to a unique collaboration between the BBC and Independent Television in jointly scheduling a week of special programmes about the disease. One programme, placed in the early evening to draw an audience of young people, demonstrated the fitting of a condom, a piece of unprecedented frankness justified on the grounds

[2] For a fuller account of ITV's reaction, see B. Sendall, *Independent Television in Britain*, vol. ii (Macmillan, London, 1983), pt. II, *passim*.

[3] Personal interview, London, 12 May 1997.

that the situation created by the appearance of Aids was itself without precedent.

What changed the vocabulary, it changed the vocabulary of images, was the whole 'Aids' week and the programmes associated with that. They simply took on the discussion of sexuality, sexual techniques, references to condoms, all that it brought with it. The exploration, the separation of sexual behaviour from morality and proper concerns about responsibilities in relationships. I think that just blasted the subject open. To me, it was a complete revolution . . . And I think, after that, perhaps . . . I don't know, I can't speak of what happened within families, but my impression is that because of the scare of Aids . . . we were all deeply alarmed and concerned and anxious to harness broadcasting to this effort. Which, as I say, looks with hindsight more sinister. I do think it made the dialogue between young people and parents easier, it cut across generations, because people talked about the subject. I just believe that in a lot of ways a lot of barriers suddenly came down very, very fast.[4]

Mulholland's reservations about the week of joint programming, which can be criticized as an attempt at social engineering dubious even in a major crisis, have to be set against an air of something approaching panic. The Government's irresolution in determining policy arose not least from the distaste for the subject felt at its most senior levels. It was evident in an initial advertising campaign, on television as elsewhere, remarkable for an obliqueness which bordered on incomprehensibility. This official hesitation was a contributor to the feeling among broadcasters that something had to be done. To set aside the normal conventions of competition between the two branches of the duopoly, as it was then, was thought to send a powerful signal to the audience about the urgency of the situation as it then appeared. It is hard to believe that such an act of collaboration would be repeated in the diverse circumstances of broadcasting a dozen years later.

The appearance of Aids brought about changes in television advertising policy in Britain. Frank Willis, Director of Advertising and Sponsorship at the Independent Television Commission, said:

When the Government was actually saying 'Use a condom', that changed the whole debate. And for us to be banning the advertising of branded condoms or any sort of condoms because people might feel offended was going to seem so backward that that policy was just swept aside.[5]

One contraceptive company rapidly established itself as the market-leader and, after an initial challenge, its rivals faded away. Since then, Willis continued:

[4] Ibid.
[5] Personal interview, London, 8 May 1997.

there has virtually been no branded condom advertising. But it's all permissible. We had just long enough . . . to experience some of the difficulties of condoms, because one of the guidelines says that [advertising] must not encourage promiscuity. Does this mean that you can only show or refer to condoms in a matrimonial setting? Because that would have been absurd, given the reasons for allowing condom advertising in the first place. But if you then show it in a positive way with people loading up 'just in case I get lucky tonight at the party', it would be very hard to say that you were not at least condoning promiscuity. So it took several hours [to achieve a] compromise where you referred to it outside any context or where it was in the context of what appeared to be a settled relationship. And it was left to the Government to do the 'scare' advertising. Because the condom people did not want to sell it as an emergency, as a 'scare' product. They wanted people to have a positive view of the product and to associate it with a positive and enjoyable activity which they hoped people would indulge in as much as possible because the more they indulged in it, the more condoms they would sell. So the Government could talk about the terrible consequences of going to bed with someone you didn't know. We had to position [the condom advertising] somewhere in between. So it was quite demanding at times, to know where to draw the line, but we didn't get huge amounts of complaints. Because of the Aids background.[6]

With the ban on the advertising of contraceptives on the American networks, I have sometimes been surprised to see commercials in the United States for products which seem as personal as contraceptives, although not raising the ethical issues which surround the use of the latter. They included advertisements for what the NBC Standards and Practices Department, in its code on Advertising Standards, calls 'catamenial devices', known in Britain, however, as 'sanitary protection'. Their introduction into British television caused considerable controversy, partly because of fundamental objections to the presence of such advertisements at all, regarded as an invasion of privacy, and partly because of embarrassment created within the watching family group. Although television advertising lies outside the remit of the British Advertising Standards Authority, the Authority's Director General, Matti Alderson, acknowledges that its potential for raising embarrassment is greater than that of poster-sites or other forms of targeted advertising:

In fact, a lot of people do feel embarrassment and I do think that perhaps it is a more contained embarrassment when you are talking about television. Because you are all sitting in the room together and then the san-pro advertisement comes on and Granny is harumphing and the youngsters are looking pink. Whereas posters, you pass them, and newspapers and magazines, you close them and they are not quite such a shared experience as watching TV.[7]

[6] Personal interview, London, 8 May 1997.
[7] Personal interview, London, 22 May 1997.

Frank Willis said:

That particular debate is closed now . . . not going to be turned backwards and I think there would be a great outcry if it was. A good example of the polarization of the debate was when there was a famous commercial [which] got an awful lot of complaints, more complaints than any other similar commercial ever. And it did so not because it was markedly more explicit than other san-pro commercials had been in terms of its product demonstration . . . but why it was so intrusive [was that the presenter was] more or less leaning out of the television herself and saying more or less, 'Don't you hide there, we're going to talk about sanitary protection. You jolly well listen.' So it was impossible to avoid and the sort of expression which spontaneously came up in some of the complaints was, 'You know, it didn't give you anywhere to hide.' In some family situations where people are more reserved about these things, the thing is just ignored and is not talked about. If referred to, it passes, and if the child asks a question, it is gracefully deflected and we move on. But [here] it was so impossible to ignore and that, I think, energized people. The absorbency test was one thing and the manner was another.[8]

From July, 1998, recognizing changed attitudes and the offence caused to some viewers, by the bunching of san-pro commercials after 9.00 p.m. the ITC applied restrictions around children's programmes appealing to the under-tens.

The portrayal of sex on television has never created the same intense furore in Britain that it has in the United States. Not only is the yoking together of religious and political interests on the right of American politics without a significant British parallel, but puritanism exercises a less influential presence in Britain than it does in America. As Tracy Westen put it to me:

I think we have it upside down. We tolerate watching someone be shot on television, but we don't tolerate watching someone be romantically sexual. . . . But I think it can be explained by American history which is a combination of puritanism and the exploitation of the frontier.[9]

Moreover, the threat of sanctions by advertisers against the commercial television companies, which has been exploited by some religious groups in the United States, carries little weight in Britain. The BBC's funding gives it, as it was intended to do, immunity from such threats while, with a tighter regulatory regime, a sharper division exists within commercial television between advertising and programmes. It is difficult, for instance, to imagine a British parallel to the call by a religious movement in the United States in the summer of 1997 for a boycott of the Disney Corporation for its disregard of family values.

8 Personal interview, London, 8 May 1997.
9 Personal interview, Los Angeles, 25 Feb. 1997.

The Particular Case of Abortion

Nowhere is the argument more vehement than over the issue of abortion. The most intense example in the US occurred in the early 1970s over an episode of the sitcom *Maude*. The series was the offspring of *All in the Family*, which, following the model of an outspoken British series, *Till Death Us do Part*, made a parade of the outrageous prejudices of its central character, Archie Bunker, heir to the traditions of the central British figure, Alf Garnett. *All in the Family* and the programmes it spawned reflected the migration to comedy of some of the serious issues previously dealt with in drama. The intention in both the British and the American versions of the programme was to pillory the sentiments mouthed by the principal characters, but some evidence later suggested that their satirical intention had been missed by sections of the audience. They regarded the programmes as endorsements of the prejudices rather than the reverse.

Maude, with its liberal-minded heroine, appeared in the autumn of 1972. Two of its episodes told the story of Maude's abortion and her husband's vasectomy, the first of which eventually took place, the latter did not. The genesis of the plot lay in the attempts by a body called the Population Institute, based in Washington, to carry media opinion with it in its campaign against uncontrolled population growth. The Institute proved to be beating a drum to whose sound much of the entertainment industry was ready to respond, with some of the industry's most important figures agreeing to give time to the issues the Institute was raising.

The controversy aroused before transmission by the decision to show the two episodes was mild in comparison with the storm which followed it and the storm raised by the decision eight months later to repeat the two episodes as part of a summer rerun of the whole series. Many of the objectors rejected the treatment of serious subjects as material for comedy and protested at the 8.00 p.m. timing chosen for the episodes. The Catholic Church demanded equal time, asking for either two further episodes which would put the arguments against abortion or two other programmes transmitted in the *Maude* slot. When CBS, the broadcaster, refused, the Church went to the FCC for a decision under the Fairness Doctrine.[10]

[10] Under the Fairness Doctrine, announced by the FCC in 1949, licensees were forbidden to editorialize or allow those who bought time to do so. They were obliged to reflect different shades of opinion when broadcasting on controversial issues. It was meant to protect the public's right to hear a variety of opinions, but was attacked by the broadcasters as an abridgement of their right to free expression. In 1987, the FCC withdrew the requirement. Its removal disadvantaged minorities who had used its existence as leverage to have their views broadcast.

At that time, in 1972, the Fairness Doctrine had not applied to entertainment programmes. Its use had been confined to political programmes to ensure that a balanced set of opinions was presented. It therefore took time for the Commission to reach a conclusion. There could be no question that *Maude* had dealt with issues, in abortion and vasectomy, on which clear divisions of opinion existed. In June 1973 the Commission gave its conclusions, acknowledging that the obligation towards fairness was also to be observed in entertainment programmes. As with other categories, fairness did not have to be achieved in an individual programme. Accordingly, the complaints about *Maude* were not upheld.

CBS decided, in the spring of 1973, not to repeat the two contentious episodes in the summer rerun of the series. However, on hearing the news, the Population Institute persuaded the broadcaster to reverse its decision. Although the intention to repeat the episodes emerged late in the day, it was not late enough to avert a major attempt by the opponents of abortion, led by the Catholic Church, to persuade the broadcasters to back down. Several affiliate stations, taking the local temperature, declined to show the episodes and advertisers melted away, influenced by the prospect of courting unpopularity for their association with the programmes and, a more worldly reason, by the reduced audience to which they would be played. When the episodes went out, they did so to a mixed chorus of further protests and praise for the broadcaster's staunchness in the face of moral and commercial pressures.

According to Kathryn C. Montgomery, from whose *Target: Prime Time* this summary has been drawn, his experiences with *Maude* persuaded Norman Lear, the producer, that advocacy groups had to be dealt with in a more organized way than the running battle over *Maude*.[11] It was a time when not only groups representing moral positions, particularly over questions of sex, were becoming active; ethnic and cultural minorities were also seeking more considered treatment by television. The steps which Lear took are not of immediate concern for this book, but they were a response to the appearance in the early 1970s of new forces in America with a particular interest in influencing editorial decisions about programme content.

A decade later, CBS became involved in another debate about the portrayal of abortion. In this case, the New York police series *Cagney and Lacey* wished to produce an episode built around an abortion clinic. The FCC's Fairness Doctrine, which was to remain in force until 1987, even though allowing balance to be achieved over more than one programme, had

[11] K. C. Montgomery, *Target: Prime Time* (Oxford University Press, New York, 1989), ch. 3.

proved administratively difficult for the broadcasters. They had eventually chosen the alternative of securing balance within an individual programme. As a result, there were lengthy arguments between the producer, Barney Rosenzweig, and the broadcaster's Standards and Practices Department in order to ensure balance. Alerted to the broadcaster's scheduling plans, the opposition, with the Catholic Church in the van, sought to talk CBS out of showing the programme. But their attempts failed.

In neither of the two American examples was there a question of the explicit portrayal of an abortion. But it was the explicit nature of certain images which brought a British pro-life group into conflict with the broadcasters during the general election campaign of 1997. Under British electoral law, any group putting up a minimum of fifty candidates is entitled to a limited amount of free television airtime. The Pro-Life Alliance, having produced the qualifying number of candidates, proposed to support their arguments with clips from an American video, *Hard Truth*. These were said to show body-parts from aborted foetuses. The BBC and the Independent Television companies declined to show some of the illustrations and the broadcast went out only after editing had taken place. The Independent Television Commission, with no powers to preview, concurred subsequently in the decisions which the companies had taken.

The Portrayal of Sexual Activity

Two main issues give rise to concerns on both sides of the Atlantic. The first is the actual representation of sexual activity in programmes. The second is the discussion of sex or topics related to sex in ways or in settings considered by some of the audience to subvert the traditional values of family life. Since many children watch adult programmes, the contention is that they will receive a debased view of sex.

To portray any significant degree of sexual activity, beginning at an amorous kiss, is, for some sections of the audience, an intrusion into something essentially private. Older Muslims who have settled in Britain, for example, are often deeply disquieted at the appearance on the television screen of behaviour which would not be regarded by most Britons as improper even in the street. To progress from that to the simulation of sexual intercourse, which is all the law allows in either country, is to follow a path every stage of which marks, for one section of the audience after another, a boundary of which editors and regulators must take account. The problems are primarily matters of taste, governed by all the considerations, noted elsewhere, of scheduling and the provision of advance information to shape expectations. But each boundary marks, for some viewers, the point at which what begins as a question of taste gives way to one of decency, the moment at which the dignity of the individuals concerned, whether as actors in a drama or a sitcom or as members of the audience, becomes vulnerable.

The operation of the 9.00 p.m. Watershed in Britain means that, while sex is spoken of with considerable freedom in the soaps and in the drama or sitcoms which follow them, there is very little sexual behaviour beyond kissing before that time. Couples are seen about to get into bed together, or very little later, well before the moment when, in old Hollywood films, the waves began crashing onto the shore or trains vanished into tunnels. Or, post-coitally, a couple may be seen in bed. No simulation of the sex act, however, is shown in the pre-Watershed period. After 9.00 p.m., it appears with increasing realism, although legally required to remain only a simulation. Even simulated, however, it can create difficulties for those making judgements about its acceptability, whether as regulators outside or editors inside the broadcasting organizations.

The Broadcasting Standards Council, which, in 1988, was given an advisory role in British broadcasting, took the decision that it should make no distinction, in setting limits, between the portrayals of heterosexual and homosexual relations. In either case, there would be individuals who, having been warned of a programme's content, would decline to watch. Provided that there had been adequate advance information, there could be no justification for any discrimination if the acts themselves were legal. In considering sequences of sexual activity, whether heterosexual or homosexual, about which it had received complaints from the audience, the Council's greatest difficulty was often to decide the duration for which it was appropriate for a sequence to run. There is clearly a length at which it may become too extended to be justified in its particular context, growing closer to voyeurism: in other words crossing the boundary into the area of decency which no pretension to artistic integrity could warrant. But there are, no less clearly, inevitable differences between different groups of people as well as between individual directors or writers over the point at which enough may be considered to be enough.

Evidence that treatment and context, as well as the expectations of which John Birt and others had spoken, are crucial to the reaction of the audience was provided in a scene from Alan Bleasdale's drama series *GBH*. Written for Channel 4, it was a picturesque account of a political opportunist, wily and charming. One sequence showed a woman addressing her lover's penis. In its place in the series and on that channel, it provoled little comment from the audience, although it was of a candour unacceptable in the past.

Nudity

That frankness has not been extended as far on network television in the United States. Indeed, nudity, even that of children, can give rise to difficulties for the broadcasters. Christine Hikawa recalled:

actually it was a very strange cultural experience for me. I'm Japanese-American, I was born here, but my grandparents came from Japan and nudity is not a big deal. And I was shocked at the reaction when we would briefly show a little baby, a naked baby, you got . . . Now things have changed in the ten years that I've been here, you can get a flash of a rear-end, but it's remarkable the extent to which nudity is considered such a forbidden thing to show on network television.[12]

In Britain, adult nudity is screened only after 9.00 p.m. and must be justified by its context. Its purpose must not be exploitative. In 1995, the Independent Television Commission published the results of research into the use of nudity in television commercials. This followed the appearance in the previous year of the first British commercial to show a woman's nipple. In the Commission's view, the material was not inherently unsuitable for transmission after the Watershed, but it provoked the second highest number of complaints about a commercial to be received during the year. Unlike programmes, whose broad content can be learnt in advance, commercials are an unknown quantity, with a consequent increase in their ability to shock.

The research showed that a significant number of the public, amounting possibly to a majority, took a fairly open-minded view of nudity, although those who took a contrary view were substantial in number. One test of acceptability was the relevance of nudity to the product advertised. Another was the extent to which sex was implicit in the commercial since nudity and sex together were thought by some to be a dangerous combination. It followed that, for this group, single-sex nudity was less unacceptable than the showing of male and female nudity together. Stillness was generally more acceptable than movement. Where female nudity was used to promote a product used by women, it was considered less offensive than if its purpose were to advertise a product principally used by men. The quality of production was thought important, low production values giving an impression of tackiness.

Heterosexuality

If the couple are married to each other, then, for those members of the audience who maintain that only within marriage are sexual relations

[12] Personal interview, New York, 14 Jan. 1997.

permissible, the portrayal on the screen of their sexual activity becomes more tolerable. That view is held by significant numbers of people in both societies, particularly their older members, and remains the doctrine of the Christian Church. Christine Hikawa, of ABC, had told me that, in her view, American television portrayed the moral order as viewers would wish it to be. She said:

It used to be that television showed married couples sleeping in separate beds. It's probably a bit of a hold-over from that. We always think about people who are not married. Until recently, I will tell you, almost all commercials when they showed a loving couple in a bedroom scene, they were desperate to show that they were wearing wedding-rings.[13]

I said that the concern about wedding-rings recalled a controversial BBC series in 1970 on sex education for children. Protesters complained about the absence of references to love and marriage and the lack of a wedding-ring on a woman's finger. The BBC had replied:

The fact is that, in some areas, as many as ten percent of the children who might watch the programmes will be illegitimate, and we have no wish to cause distress to those children. Nevertheless, in creating the programmes, the BBC has been very careful to make them in a way that suggests warmth and family love, laying pictorial emphasis on the family group in which babies are conceived, born and nurtured.[14]

When, however, the actress Mrs Patrick Campbell spoke of exchanging the hurly-burly of the chaise-longue for the deep peace of the marriage-bed, she would have known that the marriage-bed with its deep peace is not usually of great interest to writers seeking drama and conflict. As always, there are exceptions to the rule, but the state of many television couples who reach the bedroom is to be unmarried. This would once have caused more anxiety than it appears to do now.

But Christine Hikawa pointed to a particular area for concern:

We think about it when we have unmarried people having sex . . . I think that many shows are much too quick to show young people jumping into bed. It's my personal view, but I think it's the view of many people over the age of 40 and it's something we think about. I'm not saying that we have an age-limit, but if someone is over the age of 25, we are much more lenient. The younger a person is, the tougher we are. We will not allow young people, be it 18 or 20, to . . . We think it's setting a bad example. We think it bothers people, we think it bothers the audience.[15]

[13] Personal interview, New York, 14 Jan. 1997.
[14] BBC archives, R78/2548.
[15] Personal interview, New York, 27 Jan. 1997.

The portrayal of casual sex, as distinct from the discussion of it, is less common than sex between committed partners. The behaviour patterns of characters in sitcoms or in dramas may include casual sex, but portraying their sexual encounters rarely serves the dramatic purpose of advancing the plot. To do so is, therefore, more likely to be gratuitous. Exceptions occur when the lack of commitment implicit in such behaviour, with its consequences, is the writer's theme. But in the majority of dramas which are about the development of relationships, there is little place for the one-night stand. At one US network, I was told that most of the values in sitcoms and dramas were extremely conservative and had their underpinnings in Judaeo-Christian values. The messages they conveyed were thought to be very positive, socially acceptable messages. While there might be joking about extra-marital sex, the notion that it was a bad thing and led to retribution was all around.

Incest

For many months in 1996 and the following year, *Brookside*, Channel 4's mid-evening soap, ran a storyline built around an incestuous couple. The conventional impression of an incestuous relationship is of a dominant parent or older relative exploiting a young child. In this case, the couple consisted of a sister and her younger brother, both in their early twenties, from a middle-class family. Their relationship was described as consensual so that there was no apparent element of exploitation. Physical contact between the pair was limited, but they were seen in bed together. In the sixteen years during which the serial has been playing, it has built up expectations among its audience that it will deal forthrightly with social issues, of which incest was the latest. Others have included lesbianism and domestic violence. The latter storyline, in particular, touched off a very positive response among people who had experienced domestic violence as victims, encouraging them to approach agencies specializing in the problem. Consensual incest, by definition, is not a problem for those involved in it until one or other partner wishes to break away from a relationship which is illegal and contrary to almost every prevailing moral injunction. The storyline did not, therefore, stimulate the same degree of interest as other controversial themes had done, but hostility to its inclusion in the serial was limited.

Pornography: Hard-Core and Soft

In 1994, Channel 4 ran a late-night season of programmes under the overall title of 'The Red Light Zone'. The degree of advance warning and the late-night placings given to the programmes diminished the number of complaints which the season provoked. The programmes, some of which had not been shown before, produced the comment among some critics that they were indistinguishable from pornography as they understood the word. I asked the Chairman of the BBC, Christopher Bland, whether the BBC would have broadcast material of the kind included in the season. He said:

> I think it couldn't, but I'm not sure that should be anywhere. That begs a different question. I think the public expects the highest standards from the BBC. The truth is that the public ought to get no lower standard from any other broadcasting arm in theory.
>
> Q. Really? You can walk into . . .
> A. I'm talking about taste and decency . . .
> Q. Well, I was about to give a taste and decency example. You can buy *Viz* or *Loaded* in the same bookshop as the *Field* or *Country Life*, so why shouldn't broadcasting have a Red Light Zone, using the term loosely?
> A. It does, it does. The question is only does that Red Light Zone conform with what the statutory standards are? Presumably it does, because otherwise it would have been stopped. Should the BBC do better than that? Yes, I think it should. It certainly does, it's a matter of observed behaviour. There are things which the BBC would not do which its competitors do.
> Q. Were you on the point of suggesting that 'The Red Light Zone' and the way Channel 4 did it should not have happened anywhere? Do you think it went beyond . . . treating broadcasting as a medium coming into the home?
> A. Yes, yes. But that's happily not my job. What I'm saying is let us assume, for it was shown, that it was within at least the outer limits of broadcasting. Does that mean that the BBC could and would do it? I think not.[16]

Paradoxically, in expressing the previously unmentionable, these programmes went further than the soft-porn channels licensed by the Independent Television Commission. These channels, more interested in portraying sexual activity than discussing it, are permitted to operate an encrypted service late in the evening or the early hours of the morning. Their audiences are so far too small to register on a scale of measurement which goes down to 0.1 per cent. They may show breasts, nipples, and female pubic hair, but, under the Obscene Publications Act, 1959, neither an erect penis nor any penetration. The standard of explicitness is, therefore, approximately the same as that of some premium cable channels in the United States.

Hard-core pornography is illegal in Britain. An attempt was made in 1992 to introduce a subscription service beamed into Britain by satellite from the Netherlands under the name of 'Red-Hot Dutch'. When evicted

---

[16] Personal interview, London, 6 May 1997.

from the Netherlands, it moved to Denmark and broadcast under the name of 'Red-Hot Danish', raising the prospect of a succession of flights and retitlings as government after government curtailed the broadcaster's activities. Its progress, however, ended in Denmark with its proscription by the British Government under the 1990 Broadcasting Act and, shortly afterwards, the company closed down. It remains possible, however, to receive similar services from other European countries, but interest among the audience has not been significant.

Homosexuality

When the couple are of the same sex the level of concern rises for those faced with editorial or regulatory decisions. The objections to the portrayal of homosexual relationships range from the belief that they have been proscribed in the Bible, through the view that they are unnatural, to the possible effects of the portrayal upon children, not least because of an assumption that homosexuals, the males at least, are always anxious to corrupt or proselytize. Although research in Britain has shown an audience anxious to demonstrate liberal attitudes towards the appearance of homosexuals of either sex on the screen, there is an undertow of reservation suggesting that homosexuals have some way to go before achieving complete acceptance. John Birt, the BBC's Director General, confirmed this view:

There is still a very substantial number of people in society which does not regard homosexual behaviour as being 'natural'. Clearly, there is a divide between those people and most of the people who work in the arts who are likely to feel not only that homosexuality is a perfectly natural state, but who would not be put off by the exploration of homosexual issues in drama or elsewhere on the screen. One of the most explicit things we have recently put on the BBC was the drama called *My Night with Reg*, which was about a group of homosexual friends. It contained a scene of reasonably explicit sex which, slightly to my surprise, elicited only two phone calls of complaint.[17]

The transmission of *My Night with Reg* had been on BBC2 and had been well and candidly signposted in advance. With that kind of preparation, Birt believed that it was possible for television to screen more explicit material.

Two different soap operas created controversies by showing kisses exchanged between characters of the same sex. *Eastenders*, the BBC's thrice-weekly serial, broadcast in the early evening on BBC1 and set in a

[17] Personal interview, 21 Apr. 1997.

working-class quarter of London, showed a brief kiss between a young man, whose homosexuality had been established earlier, and his partner. *Brookside*, whose treatment of incest was described above, had previously established the lesbian inclinations of a young woman, a member of one of the families around which the serial is built. She was shown kissing another young woman with whom she had not previously been in an acknowledged sexual relationship. Neither kiss was prolonged and each was discreetly shot. But each produced complaints from parents, among others. They did not expect to be confronted with a situation for which their children demanded explanations and for which they were themselves not prepared. John Birt observed with a certain wryness that the kiss in *Eastenders* was talked about as an 'absolute smackeroo', although it was not, but he acknowledged the difference between it and the play *My Night with Reg*:

Eastenders is a very different case to *My Night with Reg*, because the former will be watched by almost every different group in society, young and old. Broadcasters have to be very, very careful about this because we do not wish gratuitously to offend any group. Our responsibility is to ensure that there is a proper dialogue between groups, but not in any sense to act on behalf of any one of those groups to impose its views on other groups.[18]

He went on to say that homosexuals had emerged as one of those groups:

They have become a group of their own with pronounced views and I believe that it is absolutely necessary, in the interests of broadcasters helping society to communicate with itself, that this group is allowed to express its views. It is true to say, I think, that homosexual people today are acknowledged to be more present at every level throughout society. It was different when I was a child and would not have known what homosexuality was. And that's the context in which the *Eastenders* scene occurred.[19]

Gays and lesbians now have their own programmes on the two minority British networks, BBC2 and Channel 4.

In the United States, lesbianism has been denounced with the same vigour that is directed at male homosexuality. In the spring of 1997, the lesbian actress Ellen DeGeneres, after several weeks of extensive promotion, outed her screen persona, also called Ellen in the sitcom of the same name, to stand alongside her real-life persona. There had been other gay characters in sitcoms since the appearance of the first in *Soap*, but none in the leading role. The event undoubtedly had news value, greatly increased by the immoderation of some of the attacks on it from the

---

[18] Ibid.   [19] Ibid.

religious right. However, the running of the story as a news-item by *Ellen*'s producing company, ABC, stoked up the fires of publicity even more fiercely. The episode, when it eventually went out, was watched by more than forty million people, markedly better than the usual record of the programme, and gave an invaluable boost to ABC's performance in the May sweeps, that is, the sample week by which the broadcaster's performance in audience terms is judged by advertisers for future placings. The casting of Oprah Winfrey, the talk-show host, and Laura Dern, from *Jurassic Park*, provided valuable support for the principal performer as well as reassurance for any viewers who might feel disquieted. There was no physical expression of Ellen's lesbianism, simply further additions to the nightly toll on American television of talk about sex to which the Kaiser Family Foundation/Children Now report, noted in Chapter 4, had drawn attention.

Talking about Sex

The report commented on the degree to which sexual innuendo had become a significant element in American comedy programmes. When I discussed among the broadcasters whether the charge was a fair one, I sensed no strong denials, but the blame was laid on the writing rather than the subject-matter. For example, when the writing was good, it was possible, as it had been in one episode of *Seinfeld*, one of the most popular sitcoms in recent years, to treat a subject once wholly taboo. The episode had featured a masturbation competition between the programme's main characters. The kind of weary reliance on innuendo to sustain an indifferent script which characterizes much comedy writing was absent. It had produced very few complaints with the audience apparently enjoying the way in which the subject had been treated. In that case, it was both the quality of the writing, the playing, and the expectations of the audience which had influenced the response of the audience. At a much earlier stage in the programme's life, the response would have been considerably more antagonistic from an audience unaccustomed to the characters or to the comedic conventions which it had now established. On the other side of the Atlantic, the episode provoked few comments when it was shown in Britain. Earlier, it had been the audience's familiarity with the British series *Porridge*, the story of two convicts in a shared cell, which allowed an episode in one of its later runs to feature masturbation as a source of comedy.

Like the discussion of a number of other sexual practices, talk about fellatio in a serious discussion about sex is a question of finding the appropriate place in a schedule for such a conversation or piece of dialogue to take place. To simulate it, however, raises different considerations, including the justification for its appearance on the screen. As Alfred Schneider had said about bad language, 'Never say never.' At first sight, a justification for showing bestiality is difficult to imagine, but bestiality figures in the Italian film *Padre Pio*, in a way which robs it of the offence that, in a different form, it might have caused to many viewers.

Judging Sexual Issues

I was given a copy of a workbook issued by ABC in the early 1980s.[20] Written by Dr Melvin S. Heller, a long-serving psychiatric consultant to the company, it was intended as a guide for editors in the company's Standards and Practices Department. It contains a checklist of questions for editors to ask themselves before taking editorial decisions. In correspondence with Dr Heller as I was finishing this book, he told me that, in the circumstances of contemporary broadcasting, he would not adopt the same approach to the problems described in his book. Acknowledging changes in the sexual climate since that time, the workbook nevertheless provides interesting evidence of the considerations which were then thought proper to be borne in mind when sexual issues had to be weighed. In the search for answers to my overall question about the motives of regulators and editors, it offers some useful clues from an earlier time.

Many of those who work either as editors or regulators on both sides of the Atlantic do so against a background of codes and guidelines. That kind of document, as we saw in Chapter 3, is usually written in terms of principles to be observed, providing some ground-rules for the reader to interpret according to his or her experience. Even if it were desirable to provide closer-fitting models with which programmes had to comply, the growing diversity of programmes makes more detailed guidance impossible. Tony Hall, taking the most difficult range of editorial decisions in BBC News, set out for me some of the reference-points out of which individual judgements should be formed: custom and practice, the surrounding culture, the thoughts and actions of other broadcasters, the Press, political judgements, and viewer correspondence.[21] To which others may be added: research evidence and guidelines, for example. Making allowances for the special conditions of different genres of programmes, the kind of mulch of knowledge out of which Hall's judgements were formed is the resource on which most of the decisions must draw. As noted in Chapter 3, Christine

[20] M. S. Heller, *ABC Workbook*.
[21] Personal interview, London, 17 Apr. 1997.

Hikawa, from a later generation of ABC's Standards and Practices Department than Schneider, had told me that she had, over time, developed an instinct for knowing what should go through and what should not.

The significant point about the questionnaire in the *ABC Workbook* is the evidence it provides of a purpose rather different from the straightforward preservation of appropriate levels of taste or decency, guided by a sense of what is fitting in a particular situation. The great majority of editors or regulators would say that they had personal moral standpoints of which, in reaching their conclusions, they would not wish to lose sight. However, it does not follow that their individual moral standpoint should dictate those decisions. Making good appointments in this field is more difficult than in many others. Anyone particularly anxious to take up the work should be viewed with suspicion.

By contrast, the questionnaire appears to be pursuing a moral agenda. It is, for example, concerned with the need for consequences to be shown, including, in two instances, some kind of retribution: as part of a scenario denigrating family or moral values or depicting violent, sadistic sex. The glib portrayal of unspecified sexual deviations as alternative lifestyles or casual preferences is expected to give the editor pause for thought. The editor is urged to ask the question whether the portrayal of sex ignores 'the human values and potentials of sexual love'.

One question which is posed touches on a fundamental issue confronting regulators in dealing with the portrayal of sex on television: 'Would the sexual portrayal likely arouse many viewers? If so, what would fix it?' I acknowledge some unfairness in quoting a question which I would be surprised to find asked today, but it does reveal the risk of slipping off relatively solid ground into more treacherous territory in an area of judgement more than usually subjective. It is reasonable to ask, as the questionnaire does, whether a controversial subject is treated in a balanced way (the Fairness Doctrine still applied when Dr Heller gave his advice), whether factual information about sex is correct, whether risks are minimized, or minorities would be offended. But measuring a programme's potential for arousal and acting on the result is deeply problematical. It is as dogmatic in its vagueness as Justice Potter Stewart's definition of obscenity as 'I know it when I see it.'

The author presumably has titillation in mind and, if it is simply a gratuitous addition to the material, 'fixing it' can be achieved quite easily by editing it to an acceptable level or none. But the erotic has a legitimate role in drama which is not simply to titillate. In such circumstances, how many aroused viewers are too many? And what is so wrong about arousal that something has to be done to forestall it? And is being aroused by a poor programme morally worse or better than being aroused by a good programme? And is it appropriate, and therefore less troubling, if sexual partners are simultaneously aroused? These are not facetious questions, but necessary to ask for an understanding of an editor's perspective. In other words, in the name of what is he or she acting?

The author provides an answer to some at least of these questions, quoting Justice Potter Stewart in support. Some people, otherwise healthy, are not aroused, he writes. Other people are so readily aroused that the sight of a 'pretty girl sitting on a park bench' can provide satisfaction for the day. How, he asks himself, is an editor to establish a rule of thumb between attractive depictions of beautiful people on television and those which arouse or incite lustful thoughts? He is to trust to a visceral response. And if it occurs, then, whatever provoked it needs editing, unless the editor, presumably after checking with colleagues, alone experiences the feeling. But what if he should turn out to be one of those people never aroused? The cumulative difficulties of answering the question suggest that, here, a particular view of the nature of sex has been allowed to enter a set of considerations which are more general in their origins.

As a footnote to this section, it may be noted that the first, discreetly concealed, erection has now occurred in a British television commercial. It shows a nude male model posing before a mixed life-class, one of whose women-members arrives late. Her perfume provokes the young man's reaction, symbolized by a gently-rising feather and the movement of a clock's hands and evident in his expression of mingled embarrassment and pleasure. The ITC did not uphold forty complaints which were sent to it by viewers. Shown after the Watershed, its statement said, the innuendo in the commercial was not beyond the boundaries of good taste. It also rejected a smaller number of complaints which alleged that the commercial was sexist since it might encourage laughter at men having erections.

Rape

Rape is an abuse of power and, as such, is an issue of violence. Questions about its treatment in programmes do not belong in a chapter dealing with the portrayal of sex.

6

Language: And the Next Fellow Said . . .

> When I was at NBC, I didn't have to go to the President or the Chairman of the Board, I simply put out my own edict. 'No profanity allowed.' Period. You couldn't say 'Hell' or 'damn' in an NBC show. It wasn't because I didn't say 'damn' or 'Hell'. It was because I knew the next fellow was going to say 'son-of-a-bitch' or 'bastard'. And the next fellow was going to say something else.
>
> (Larry White, former Senior Vice-President, Network Programmes, NBC, 1996)

What is Bad Language?

When, in 1991, I was writing an introduction to a book on the limits of broadcast language, I began by considering the question of terminology. I face the same dilemmas in beginning this chapter. I thought it would be sensible, therefore, to borrow some of the words I used on that earlier occasion. Words, I argued, are neutral until they are put to use, given some additional meanings by their context, by the choice of surrounding words, or the tone of voice in which they are delivered. Much as Bernard Shaw said that, when the English talked of 'morality', they meant only sexual morality, so those who protest about 'bad language' often refer simply to 'language'. A lot of what was once considered bad language was so simply because the state decreed as much, for reasons which had more to do with power and politics than with morality. However, in the context of this chapter, none of the synonyms for bad language seems to me to replace it very well: neither strong language nor obscenities, swearwords, oaths, curses, terms of abuse, invective, nor profanity. Strong language may contain no words which are 'bad' at all. Swearwords, oaths, and curses cover the kind of expletives which cause offence or worse, but not discrimina-tory abuse. 'Terms of abuse', like 'invective', excludes too much, as does 'ob-scenities'. The 'No Profanity' warnings seen in public places in the United States are clearly meant to cover more than blasphemies, but 'profanity' is not in wide use in Britain. So, as bad language, if not just plain 'language', is the description used by many of those objecting to it on television or radio, bad language is what it will be called in the following pages.

I realized, even as I wrote that opening paragraph, that the neutrality which I was claiming for words is a falsity. What words mean is not simply what I, like Humpty Dumpty, intend them to mean, surrounded by other words and set in a particular context, but also what the listener under-stands from his or her own experience of them. They are a dangerous form of exchange, but the only practical one which we have, more precise than the images in which we trade a significant number of our ideas today. A young writer may say, quite truthfully, that 'God' and 'Christ' signify noth-ing to him or her and, accordingly, he or she is free to use them without further thought as expletives, but their casual, unregarding, use may be deeply offensive to some members of the audience. The latter may have no individual right of veto, although, in sufficient numbers, even the prospect of their disapproval may have a chilling effect.

The American television networks, in their supervision of schedules, demonstrate almost every night of the week the enduring importance of puritanism in the American tradition. Bad language, like sex, comes under more stringent control from the networks than either does in post-Watershed British television. On US cable services, it is less constrained. There is a greater element of choice in the viewer's decision to watch, actu-ally so in the case of premium channels, which are paid for individually, but more fancifully so in the basic range where, once the channels are in the house, they are as accessible as the free-to-air services. There is also, so far, a lesser pressure from advertisers, though they show their influence in the operators' selection of the channels to offer. As a surprising paradox in British eyes, puritanism seems to have less difficulty in coming to terms with violence as a major presence in the make-up of American schedules.

What Makes People Protest

More letters and telephone calls of complaint to British broadcasters and their regulators are prompted by bad language than by any other topic of this kind. The audience, research shows, is more anxious about violence, but complains formally about it much less. The practical explanation for this is that there is less violence to be seen than examples of offensive lan-guage to be heard. The greater anxiety felt by the public about violence is influenced by a broader anxiety about the way society is heading and the contribution which television may make to the changes which disquiet them.

The ITC's Programme Code requires broadcasters to take account of the rating given by the British Board of Film Classification (BBFC) to the video versions of the feature films they show: video standards being more restrictive than those for the cinema. Eighteen-rated feature films, which contain the most intense portrayals of violence, may not normally be scheduled on the three commercial networks or premium subscription channels before 10.00 p.m. The BBC, while not acknowledging the BBFC's classifications, makes much the same judgements about placings. The cable and satellite audiences, which are much smaller, complain less, possibly because of a more conscious process of decision-taking, possibly because of the different expectations which they have about such services in comparison with the mainstream broadcasters. If the product does not satisfy them, then they will simply not renew their subscriptions, ending a transaction they see in more frankly commercial terms than their payment of the licence fee.

If there is less correspondence with the American networks about bad language, it may reflect the tighter restrictions on its use in network programmes. Christine Hikawa, of ABC, described what had happened over the first series of *NYPD Blue*, the New York police series, transmitted by the company:

that show, you remember, was ground-breaking because it was going to have partial nudity and adult language. By adult language they don't mean 'fuck' and 'shit' because we could never ever say those words. They mean words like asshole and dickhead, sort of almost silly words that are sort of slang. And that show, for the first year, had very few advertisers. ABC lost about a million dollars a week just carrying it for the first year. And even now it's considered 'damaged goods'. And so no other show has ever attempted to do that. Commercially it made it non-viable. Now did it break down certain barriers a little bit? Yes, I think so. I hear partial language in more of the ten o'clock dramas and you occasionally see a flash of nudity in them.[1]

Being taken by surprise is a main cause of complaints. In the case of bad language, its unexpected appearance in programmes can breach the conventions of speech between the members of a watching family, creating anger as an expression of embarrassment. Although people themselves use bad language more freely than they did thirty-five years ago, they may still wish its use in the home to be governed by some rules. The rules are signs of parental authority which parents do not wish to see threatened by out-

---

[1] Personal interview, New York, 14 Jan. 1997.

siders of any kind. Bad language on television, particularly in favourite programmes or associated with well-liked personalities, might imply the endorsement of speech which parents are trying to resist elsewhere. As we noted in Chapter 4, bad language in children's programmes is, for parents and others, a matter of special anxiety. Both groups can be perfectly well aware that, in the playground at school, the children are likely, from an early age, to exchange the words between themselves. Parents are just as aware that their own parents, who may be watching television with them, are likely to be no less familiar with bad language. But the circumstances in which the words are acceptable vary from one family to the next and between generations within the family. The difficulties which families have determining their own limits are made greater by the tolerance given nowadays to words which, only a few years ago, would have been unacceptable except within clearly defined groups or situations.

British broadcasters try to reduce the occasions when unnecessary offence is caused. For example, once a series has become established, and has won the trust of the audience, it can introduce words and actions which would have been unacceptable in its early editions. As we noted in Chapter 3, an audience's expectations, in both the United States and Britain, are connected, among other things, with the timing of programmes. British audiences, for example, would not expect to hear any significant bad language in the early evening. As the evening progresses, so they would be prepared for some increase in the incidence of bad language. If, however, there were to be a significant rise in the intensity of bad language in a particular programme, for instance, a contemporary play or film, the audience would expect the programme to be preceded by a warning. That information may be delivered by one or all of several different means: verbally or by a caption on air, from information in programme guides, but always supplemented by what a majority of the audience may reasonably be expected to know already from its familiarity with similar programmes or the previous appearances of the same artists. That supplementary knowledge grows with the durability of particular performers or series.

With the passing of the 9.00 p.m. Watershed, the audience would be prepared for the use of those words which are capable of giving a higher degree of offence, with a specific warning given in cases of intensified use or the appearance of the words considered to give the most offence. The fact that the Watershed exists as a well-understood arrangement, observed by the broadcasters and aimed at reducing unnecessary offence, does not mean that it is constantly being evoked. Broadcasters are not expected to plead its existence as a shelter behind which, without any other justification, they may extend the conventional boundaries. Many of the programmes transmitted after the Watershed contain nothing which would meet any definition of bad language.

A note of despair sounds as a recurrent strain among the complaints: why should bad language be necessary at all? It was done without in both British and American broadcasting for a long time, making its appearance only recently. Fiction, in which the majority of bad language occurs in broadcasting, can achieve greatness without it. Great novels and plays, the argument continues, have been written for centuries without a single example of it. The play *Journey's End* and *All Quiet on the Western Front*, first a book and then a film, are two of the most profoundly anti-war works ever written. They succeed without any of the bad language which appears in *Platoon* or *Apocalypse Now*, though soldiers in the First World War in reality swore as monotonously as they did in Vietnam fifty years later. If the answer is said to be 'truthfulness', then is the altered perception of truth anything other than a matter of fashion?

It is tempting, but misleading, to regard the current omnipresence of bad language as a symptom of moral decline. Swearing has been a feature of earlier periods of history, its popular use waxing and waning from the restrictive era of the English Puritans in the seventeenth century to the bawdy freedoms exercised by their successors after the Restoration and back to the inhibitions of Victorian England. That bad language died out in the restrictive periods was untrue. The mixture of good and bad human needs which commonly prompts its use continued, but did so underground and unreported.

Bad language, as a matter of manners and fashion, is almost, but not entirely, a matter of taste. Will Wyatt, of the BBC, said:

broadly it all comes down in the end to some form of politeness. What you can say in public, what you can show in public, how you behave towards people in public. It's like language. I swear quite a lot, many people do, but you don't, on meeting someone for the first time, presume that you can use that language until certain signals have taken place and you know that it's all right or not. And on television or radio it's much the same and there's an area where you do or do not.[2]

Where it moves from politeness and taste to decency is the point at which the dignity of others is involved: in terms of racial or gender abuse, in abuse founded in disability, or where deeply held beliefs are insulted.

The Roots of Change

There are several changes to be noted. First, there is the decline in traditional centres of authority, starting with schools, churches, parliamentary

[2] Personal interview, London, 4 Apr. 1997.

institutions, the courts, and continuing with the family and reaching even the monarchy and the presidency. Deference, the unacceptable face of respect, has largely disappeared in Britain from the younger generation. Britons rarely use the word 'sir', thus losing the chance, which Americans have retained, to use it, as occasion demands, courteously or subversively. The abundant use of first names, except on the most formal occasions, is a reflection, sometimes a false one, of those changed relationships. Figures in authority have felt it important to present themselves as really not very different from those out of authority.

With authority weakening generally, the constraints on language which existed through the first half of the century and a little beyond slackened. The relaxation could be used to symbolize a wider liberation. Language of all kinds has traditionally been an instrument in the maintenance of authority, with strict conventions applied to what it is acceptable to say, where and when it is acceptable to say it, as well as to whom it might be said. Entire languages have been reserved for the use of the ruling classes, with penalties for outsiders who presumed to learn them. The use of inappropriate language posed a threat to an established order. That was why the defence in the trial of the Chicago Seven in 1968 adopted the tactic of using words intended to affront the court and demonstrate the defendants' contempt for the system of justice which was trying them. The words were to cause problems at the BBC when it later televised a dramatization of the trial. However, with the recognition that, if the words were cut, the programme would be fatally flawed, the production went ahead. It was screened, one Sunday night, in two parts, the first beginning at 8.00 p.m. and the second, following a break for the mid-evening news bulletin, ending after 11.00 p.m. Promoted with a series of warnings about the language, the transmission drew very few complaints.

A second change, which accompanied the first, was the emergence of a much greater consciousness of working-class life. Until the end of the nineteenth century, accounts of working-class life came mainly from outside observers. They were often confined to those areas of working-class life with which middle-class society overlapped, leaving other, much larger, areas with little documentation in fact or fiction. Wider educational opportunities and the increased interest of the middle-class public in the working class, partly from political motives, encouraged the production of first-hand accounts from within working-class society rather than the second-hand accounts available to earlier generations. As a result, society was now being reported and commented on from a fresh perspective. The working class moved nearer the centre of the stage, compelling attention, rather than occupying the anonymous walk-on roles which had been its lot in the past. It brought with it not only fresh insights, but also different styles and rhythms of speech, objects of comic wonder in *Pygmalion*, but becoming steadily more familiar as time passed. Descriptions became more realistic, as they also did generally, a process which extended to the language used in them. It was not that the working class necessarily used more bad language, as the stitching in sentences which might otherwise fall apart. The words it used were those over which the middle class observed a more powerful taboo, certainly in public. As the younger middle class sought to identify with the working class, it adopted new speech patterns which then spread until their novelty was forgotten and they became the standard for a large part of the population. A word like 'fuck' lost, for part of the population, the terrors with which it has for long been endowed. There was therefore a democratization of speech, inevitably striking some parts of the population as a levelling-down.

A third change came with the growth of equality between women and men. As roles changed, so the conventions governing the use of language changed. Those who went to work alongside men sometimes sought social equality in the workplace by adopting the speech of their male colleagues. As the authors of *Regulating for Changing Values* point out, one of the areas which saw the largest inflows of women was the non-technical communications industry.[3] It flourishes by, or at least on the shoulders of, creative processes which demand, whether justifiably or not in all cases, the fullest possible freedom of expression. The climate which is thus created is one which inevitably influences their work and the many people outside the industry whom their work touches. Writers and directors who want to explore boundaries and expand them have a special importance. John Birt, of the BBC, said:

Whether they be politicians, commentators, artists, comedians, or writers, the presumption one operates under is that they should be allowed freedom of expression. Talented people must be allowed to express themselves. Of course, those expressions must have worth and value. We would always want the maximum expression consistent with not causing unnecessary offence.

But the contribution which television and radio have made to a further change is not limited to the self-expression of writers and others. They have, in news and documentary programmes of many different kinds, brought together groups which had never previously met on terms of equality. Broadcasting therefore offers its own endorsement not only of

[3] M. Kieran, D. Morrison, and M. Svennevig, *Regulating for Changing Standards* (Broadcasting Standards Council, London, 1997).

[4] Personal interview, London, 21 Apr. 1997.

the attitudes it portrays, but of the manners which it observes, including those reflected in the use of bad language. Christine Hikawa, in talking of the first series of *NYPD Blue*, spoke of some barriers coming down as a result of its unprecedented freedom of language. Will Wyatt concedes that broadcasting has played its part in the process of change, but stresses that, rather than being its instigator, it has had many partners in the process.

People don't seem to mind and slowly the words lose some of their meaning. Are we contributing to that? I guess we are. On the other hand, it's also going on out there.[5]

One more change occurred with the recognition by the film industry in Hollywood that it could not compete with television on its existing terms, but would have to move into territory where television would find it difficult or impossible to follow. The industry needed to attract the younger audience which wanted to get away from home for its evening's entertainment. Epic productions, like epic emotions, were unsuitable for the television screen, so they provided the industry with one counterweight. Violence was another and bad language was a third. Greater sexual explicitness was a fourth, but its extent was limited by the national regard for more puritanical standards. Not only did these help to fill the gap left by television, but such shocks as they administered to a young audience were largely received as pleasurable, the satisfying shocks of witnessing the breaking of apparent taboos.

For all these reasons, bad language was within the consciousness of almost everyone by the 1990s in a way which it had not been forty or fifty years before. The Second World War had been reported in much the same terms as the First, although with the help of broadcasting technologies unavailable earlier in the century. There was a good deal less glorying in the struggle, a more practical expression of feeling for the suffering of casualties, but there were still few echoes of the language actually spoken by the armed forces of either country. The British had, indeed, been sufficiently sensitive to the feelings of American soldiers and airmen that officials of the BBC had expressed their anxiety about the possible effects on them of 'vulgarity' on the BBC.[6] Output departments received a plea from the BBC's own North American Service that the word 'damn' should not be included in broadcasts addressed to Americans still at home in the United States.[7] There, in 1942, CBS had banned the reporting of the word 'bastard' in a Congressman's speech referring to

---

[5] Personal interview, London, 4 Apr. 1997.
[6] BBC archives, R34/229/3, 'Vulgarity'.
[7] BBC archives, R34/291, 'Swearing'.

'bastard legislation'. A few years later, the BBC's Television Controller wrote: 'So far as comedy in general is concerned we should entirely avoid (as the films do) "damn, blast, hell, God, Christ, and—though improbable that it would appear—Jesus".'[8]

The immediate post-war period was not a time for radical change in the moral climate. It was a time for coming home, settling in, and taking stock. The British people voted in a Labour Government in token of a wish for change and, in turn, the new Government laid down the foundations of the Welfare State. But there was no immediate mood for change in broadcasting: that was not to come before the end of the next decade. In the meantime, secure in its monopoly, the BBC was able to rest upon the prestige it had gained during the war. And, in America, the networks went back to the business of making money within the old moral boundaries.

Words under Change

Changes in the attitudes of society towards bad language are paralleled by changes in the significance which is attached to individual words from time to time. Any mention of 'bastard', even if it is not being used as a term of abuse, is capable of upsetting an older generation to whom the stigma of illegitimacy remains real and abhorrent. But with the erosion of the stigma, the weight of the word in a context of abuse is clearly set to diminish, although abuse retains its capacity to sting even after the real meaning has largely drained away. When Mr Major, as the British Prime Minister, described some of his opponents in Cabinet as 'bastards', his use of the word conveyed a particular weight of fury to those, the great majority of the British population in fact, who were uncertain whether or not he habitually used the word in private. It is increasingly used in Britain, like 'bugger', linked to an admiring adjective, as in 'He's a clever old bastard.'

Both bugger and sod have lost most of their sexual connotations and it is doubtful how many younger people are conscious of the added condemnation its biblical origins once contributed to the latter. As a verb, however, 'bugger' remains forceful. To be accused of 'buggering up something' is to be reproached more seriously than for simply 'messing up something'. The imperative 'Bugger off' depends for its degree of offence on the strength with which it is spoken and, if someone has 'buggered off', there is an implication of a duty dodged, serious or otherwise, but almost certainly more irresponsible than merely 'sloping off'. 'Wanker' is another word which has acquired a new meaning and

---

[8] BBC archives, R34/274/4, 'Censorship'.

lost a good deal of its old as a masturbator. It is now more commonly used as a synonym for a wimp, which, with an implied lack of masculinity, is confined to men.

Among other nouns, 'Hell' has lost a lot of its force, as religion has declined in importance for many people, though I was told in the United States that the misuse of the word remains capable of giving great offence in some parts of the country. Despite the decline in religion, 'God', 'Christ', and 'Jesus Christ' keep their power to give deep offence, not only to many religious believers, but to a wider circle of people conscious of the offence which they can give to others or still tuned to the inhibitions laid upon their own use of the words when they were younger. The words are, however, extensively used, not least because they respond well to the heavy stress demanded in states of high emotion, and they are seldom used deliberately to affront or outrage believers, some of whom, nevertheless, consider any use of them to be blasphemous. The present age, however, with a greater proportion of unbelievers within once predominantly Christian societies, has found difficulty in accommodating the view that an offence can be committed by unbelievers against a deity whose existence they do not accept. That people have a right to hold the religious beliefs they choose is not in question, but that the beliefs themselves, rather than the right to pursue them without interference, should enjoy the protection of the law becomes harder to defend. However, it is argued in response that it is not the deity, of whatever religion, which needs protection, but the believers to whom religion is a central part of their lives. Although it may be suggested that the use of 'God' is less offensive, because its meaning is less specific, and the word therefore considered to be less sacred, than either 'Jesus' or 'Jesus Christ', my conversation with David McCormick, reported later in this chapter, confirms that this view is not universally held.

In recent years, more traditional words of abuse, often derived from sexual roots, have been joined by words implying discrimination based upon unalterable characteristics: race, colour, nationality, and disability. In the last case, words like 'schizo' or 'spastic' have been used to mock the behaviour of people not clinically defined as either, but have become much less common. The near-elimination of 'Mongol' in favour of 'Down's Syndrome' provides a remarkable example of how habits can be changed within a relatively short time. However, the hope that 'crazy' or 'blind' will be confined to those clinically identified as insane or sightless seems likely to take longer to fulfil. In such areas where political correctness is a constant presence, its zealots as daunting as its extreme opponents, the broadcaster is faced with the problem of balancing its reasonable demands with the need for effective communication with the audience. I discussed political correctness with David Glencross, former Chief Executive of the ITC:

Q. What about the coming of political correctness, sometimes daft, but sometimes making a stand on behalf of individual dignity? Some aspects of political correctness seem to me entirely good.

A. You mean in terms of racial abuse?

Q. Racial abuse, gender abuse . . .

A. I think that television has played an important part in that, both BBC and ITV. I suppose one should say particularly, Channel 4. As you say, it can sometimes fall over into a ridiculous posture. On the whole, I think that . . . and you know, it finds expression in soap operas too . . . that's a healthy development. People say that broadcasters set the agenda and I think in this case it's entirely justified and in the public interest.

Q. There is a point at which, presumably, you think you're moving into the business of social engineering. Which usually rises up and hits those who try.

A. Yes, I think that's what you call falling into a ridiculous posture. And I think the Americans have suffered from that. But in terms of, say, a television programme reflecting the fact that women have as much right to opinion as men and showing black people who are neither drug-takers nor super-athletes nor pop-stars, you're getting away from stereotypes which are not always harmful, but can be harmful. And I think that is all to the good. It's interesting, although it's not only to do with broadcasting, that the widespread anti-Semitic sentiments which were quite commonly expressed in the 1930s and 1940s are now unthinkable in broadcasting and, indeed, elsewhere. People don't talk about 'Jew-boys' any more, except . . . in a play set in the 1930s. But it was an expression, I can remember from the time, used quite openly by all kinds of people. It isn't now. I'm not saying it's only because of broadcasting, but I think broadcasting is right to see that certain terms cause offence and upset people and can do harm. I think the experiences of the Second World War did bring that home to people.[9]

Bad Language Now

As a result of these changes, we live in times when many people are more tolerant of bad language and prepared to use it in their own lives, particularly among younger generations who are frequently genuinely surprised at the degree of offence which their choice of words can give their elders. Some of them, of course, use it as a weapon, a symbol of the challenge which the new always presents to the old, serving to bind them more closely by its use and confronting taboos they believe to be outdated. Whatever the reason, this causes problems not only within the other sections of broadcasters' audiences, but among programme-makers within

[9] Personal interview, London, 5 May 1997.

individual companies. What may seem to a young producer a suitable choice of language may seem needlessly offensive to his older editor or manager. David McCormick, Executive Producer, Broadcast Standards, for NBC, said:

I have conversations with younger producers, I don't know if this will show my age, I'm not that old, but obviously they are a generation below. I still think that the basic principle we ought to operate on is that we are guests in people's homes and that any gratuitous use of language which is not acceptable household language ought to be considered strongly before it is used on the air. I think it is very difficult to say, 'You can't use this word, you can never use that word', because we don't know the context necessarily. But any words that any of us have questions about, we ask them to flag them. And somebody will say, 'Yes, but in the entertainment show at ten o'clock opposite us, they're using that language.' And my answer is, 'That's fine, that's an entertainment programme, we're a news programme. And maybe every-body likes that word over there.' But I want that discussion.[10]

Although there are plenty of examples where Britain and the United States share examples of bad language, there are differences. We shall come to 'fuck' shortly, but 'son-of-a-bitch', for example, has not secured a firm place on the British side of the Atlantic. Alfred Schneider, formerly of ABC, told me of the problems he had encountered when ABC proposed to show *Patton*, the film about the controversial American general in the Second World War:

It was the first time it was on the air and the question came up were we going to allow . . . 'son-of-a-bitch'. And the decision I made was that I would not edit that out. It would destroy what the character said and we ran it, with an advisory, at 9.00 p.m. We took some things out, but that went in. That was a first . . . So I guess you can never say 'Never'. What we're really talking about is 'Quality, time and content'. 'Time, manner, and place.' The Supreme Court talked about 'time, manner and place', reasonable standards for the things that needed those kinds of decisions.[11]

I asked Schneider, if he were still doing his old job in Standards and Practices, where he would run *Platoon*, in which there is abundant soldier-speak. Shaking his head, he replied, 'Never,' repeating the word when I told him the BBC had run it, uncut, with few complaints, at 10.00 p.m. on the mainstream BBC1. Later in the conversation, he said, 'But I did retire in 1991. I guess it might go at midnight. Now.'

I was surprised to find the amount of resistance in America, voiced by both David McCormick and Christine Hikawa as well as by others, to the use of 'shit', a word which still leaves many people uneasy in Britain. It is

[10] Personal interview, New York, 3 Feb. 1997.
[11] Personal interview, New York, 21 Jan. 1997.

still most commonly understood in its scatological sense, although American films have made it seem commonplace in a variety of meanings. It serves in the States as an expletive varying in strength according to the user's perception of it. It can also be a term of abuse directed at someone who has behaved badly or may be expected to. It is used for 'rubbish' or 'trash', but it can also be applied to possessions, even when the owner has no intention of disposing of them. 'I've got to move my shit,' said one of my students in Philadelphia, somewhat to my alarm, but meaning no more than that he was changing his lodgings. David McCormick told me:

That word I am very tough on. I think 'crap' has probably transcended the meaning that we first learnt in school. The other word I find unacceptable, again other than in some actuality situation which would be out of the ordinary. No, it's pretty tough in terms of those words.[12]

McCormick told me that, like 'shit', he would also debar 'Oh, Goddam'. He thought, however, that 'Jesus Christ' was slightly less offensive on the ear than either 'God' or 'Christ', although varying 'Jesus Christ' with an initial between the two parts or an accompanying adjective would not be acceptable.

I asked the Chairman of the BBC, Christopher Bland, whether those religious believers who experienced real distress at the casual use of the Christian names were expected to take it in their stride.

They certainly don't take it in their stride and the BBC pays attention to their complaints. But . . . and they are in a minority, but it is a very strongly held view and gives a very high degree of offence. If you say 'Jesus Christ' thirty-seven times in a programme during peaktime, you will cause great offence to a small number of people, a relatively small number of people, speaking of the total audience. I think the BBC, and the ITV companies, have to pay some attention to that. It is not simply statistical, it is also the degree of offence caused. It's not only Christians, but Jews and Muslims. I think that's part of your decency definition, really. It's a different kind of offence than is caused to those people by saying 'bugger'.[13]

The Particular Case of 'Fuck'

As Christine Hikawa had told me and others had confirmed on behalf of their own networks, 'fuck' would not be carried at any time. There are, however, rare exceptions. One occurred when NBC screened the network premiere of *Schindler's List* in the late winter of 1997. In deference to the subject-matter of the film, it was shown without commercials apart from two short breaks. These indicated with a caption that the Ford Motor Corporation had made the transmission possible. The nineteen obscenities,

---

[12] Personal interview, New York, 3 Feb. 1997.
[13] Personal interview, London, 6 May 1997.

eight profanities, and several vulgarities listed by the Christian Film and Television Commission on the film's release in 1994 were uncut despite the 7.30 p.m. transmission time. At least one Congressman declared that the broadcast had been an all-time low which would offend all decent-minded people, claiming that it challenged the sincerity of the networks' protestations about the restoration of decency to their programming. However, within twenty-four hours, he was saying that he was referring only to the time of the transmission. In the meantime, NBC took satisfaction from its own boldness. Its audience had shown, according to a company spokesman in a newspaper report, that broadcasters should not be pressured into providing bland, non-controversial programming to appease over-zealous watchdogs.[14]

'Fuck' in Britain has acquired a kind of iconic significance in the British vocabulary, contested between generations, but also between programme-makers, broadcasters, and their regulators. While some writers and directors have wanted to use the word in their programmes in order to make a statement about themselves, as an act of defiance towards an authority which they believe wants to control them, others have done so because the word comes naturally into the mouths of their characters or from the people with or about whom they are talking in documentary programmes. But despite its growing familiarity, the word has stubbornly retained its power to offend a section of the British audience.

The struggle has being going on since 1965 when the drama critic Ken Tynan used the word on air for the first time in a late-night discussion on BBC1. It caused a major outcry. The kind of hyperbole previously deployed during the campaign against commercial television was redeployed against both Tynan and the BBC. Tynan, aware of its effect, had quite deliberately chosen to use the word not as an expletive, but to illustrate a serious point. None the less, it was, for one journalist, the 'bloodiest outrage' he had ever known, a remarkable statement at any time, but particularly so hardly twenty years after the death of Hitler.[15] For a BBC already under attack from moralizers in and out of Parliament, the incident could only make matters worse, with calls for more effective means of bringing to an end the possibility of further outrages to taste and decency. However, they eventually came to nothing.

As the quotation from Larry White at the start of this chapter shows, the problem with efforts to control bad language, as with other aspects of taste and decency, lies in holding the line. Then, once a first breach has been justified, proposals for subsequent breaches become matters for negotiation.

[14] Report in *Los Angeles Times*, 26 Feb. 1997.
[15] A. Briggs, *History of Broadcasting in the United Kingdom*, vol. iii (Oxford University Press, London, 1970), 529–30.

Anecdotes about the process are plentiful, often growing more absurd in the retelling, with trade-offs allowing one word to remain at the expense of another. Absurd as they may be, they represent the only compromise between the demands of the two constituencies the broadcaster is serving, the outright ban sought by one or the complete freedom looked for by the other.

Tynan's use of 'fuck' on BBC television in 1965 was without any kind of official sanction and did not, in fact, produce a rush of imitators. However, as the word itself it became more of a commonplace in society at large, further incidents involving became inevitable. David Glencross, then a programme officer at the Independent Broadcasting Authority, described one situation to me:

it must have been the early 1970s, when . . . a documentary [was accepted for the network] about a Canadian psychiatric hospital which was developing new techniques, treatment, one of which was to encourage the patients to express themselves, not violently in a physical sense, but in terms of what they said. And frankly it would have been impossible, for there was a lot of 'fucking' in this piece of actuality . . . and there were long debates about whether this should be allowed to be transmitted and in the end it was agreed that it should be, I think at eleven o'clock at night, carefully hedged around with all the usual warnings. So that it would not set a precedent and so on, but it would have been unthinkable certainly right through the 1970s to have 'fuck' in a drama, in a scripted piece.[16]

For the BBC, the word continues to have a particular importance. All requests to use the word have to be approved at a very senior level. Phil Harding, Controller, Editorial Policy, at the BBC, believes that is the right policy. Although there may be less resistance to the use of the word than before, he argues, it retains a special power to offend which has to be recognized.[17] Will Wyatt, as Chief Executive, BBC Broadcast, told me:

Over the years, it's been clear that there are places where it doesn't cause any offence, well, not the level of offence that usually sets off all the triggers which we have had over the years: complaints to us, phone calls to the Broadcasting Standards Commission, anything else. . . . We never use it before 9.00 p.m. on either channel and it's pretty damned rare on BBC 1. And it's usually a mistake on BBC1.[18]

Harding provided an illustration of the volatility of responses to 'fuck'. The BBC produced two series which featured the Scottish actor and comedian Billy Connolly. Each was a mixture of travel-documentary, as Connolly visited parts of Scotland and Australia, and his stage-act. Each was transmitted in the later part of the evening on BBC1, despite Wyatt's forebodings about the fate of the word on that channel. Harding said:

[16] Personal interview, London, 5 May 1997.
[17] Personal interview, London, 17 Apr. 1997.
[18] Personal interview, London, 4 Apr. 1997.

With Connolly you know what you are going to get. In the first series, the tour round Scotland, the f-word appeared mainly in the stage-act. In the first series, he was playing in small Scottish theatres, much more intimate venues, and you got much more the sense that the audience was laughing with him. And because of that the use of the word was less offensive. . . . In the Australian series, he was playing very big venues, with very much a sense that he was on one side of the footlights and a distant audience on the other side of the footlights so you didn't get the sense of endorsement. And also, because he was playing such big venues he was shouting at the audience and strangely enough I thought that made it . . . I don't mean it was unacceptable, I think it was acceptable in the end, but I can see why some people thought it was less acceptable. The other interesting thing with Connolly was that, for the first series, we didn't put out a warning before the first programme. There-fore, although many viewers would have known what to expect, we clearly did take some viewers by surprise and they complained in quite large numbers. From the second programme in that series we did put out a warning beforehand and the number of complaints dropped just like that. And I think that's reasonable because we give people a chance to find out what they're viewing.[19]

David McCormick described it as a word which would not be accept-able on an NBC news programme:

A. That is a word which would not be acceptable on a news programme. Period.
Q. What about actuality?
A. I'm talking about news programmes now. If it were actuality, that is a word which would certainly never get on the air without some kind of man-agement approval. And I cannot tell you how many times I've struck it out of the news. One thing, I suppose if some extremely famous person utters this . . . as he or she is taking a bullet in the chest. that's one thing. It's another thing to hear it.[20]

The balance in the use of 'fuck', as often in issues of taste, can never be a rigid one. The right place for it, perhaps better described as the least-wrong place, can only be determined in relation to the programme's in-tentions, its execution, in short, upon its quality. And that, inevitably, is a subjective judgement.

It also depends on its placing. In Chapter 3, we noted judicial support for the FCC in the case of the 'Seven Dirty Words', uttered on radio at a time when children would be in the audience.[21] There is, of course, a more-than-reasonable risk that some children will be in the audience at any time of the day. There is an even greater risk that children may watch pro-grammes, by means of a video-recorder, at times different from those at which the programmes were originally scheduled. For neither of those

---

[19] Personal interview, London, 17 Apr. 1997.
[20] Personal interview, New York, 3 Feb. 1997.
[21] *FCC* v. *Pacifica Foundation*, 438 US 726 (1978).

possibilities is the broadcaster in any position to take responsibility, short of imposing an outright ban on all bad language which is as questionably practical as democratic.

'Fuck' is the word whose use is most debated because it stands at the boundaries of acceptability. The word 'cunt' is less widely debated, simply because, for the moment at least, it lies beyond the limits of acceptability, except in the very rarest circumstances in British television. The sexist message which it is seen to carry as a term of abuse has also contributed to its isolation. It is uncommon in America whether as a description of the genitals or as a term of abuse. British regulators face problems over one of its less offensive synonyms, 'twat'. The difficulty with twat lies with two other words, one of which is 'twit' and the other 'prat', neither considered more than mildly offensive. It is compounded by the two pronunciations of the word which are current, one with a long 'a', the other short. Twit, prat, and the two forms of 'twat' tend to be used interchangeably, especially by children, even though the genital meaning is, at least in some parts of Britain, as offensive as its synonym. Neither motherfucker nor cocksucker is commonly used in Britain and, indeed, the words themselves have appeared to be unknown to quite large numbers of people. Motherfucker is more commonplace in the States, particularly among blacks, but the acquaintance which most Britons have with it comes from its use in American movies or in the lyrics of rap music, frequently unintelligible to the uninstructed ear.

The arguments over the admissibility of bad language in programmes, as well as in many other aspects of life, will go on. There is a human need for it to express various degrees of shock or outrage, although the force which we attach to one or another word changes, just as the strength has departed from many of the expressions which had Christian roots or the power to offend has increased with abuse centred on disabilities. As for 'fuck', the arguments are also likely to be sustained for a long time. It is now much more than just a word. It is a cause of war. For some, the fuss seems disproportionate, akin to the plot of land for which Hamlet watched Fortinbras's troops set off to do battle, neither 'tomb enough nor continent to hide the slain'. For others, it serves as a symbol which, if overthrown, will carry down with it much which is of great value to them. In this particular struggle over bad language, as over the use of some holy names, we may be closer to perceptions of decency than to taste.

7

News and Reality Programmes

The Programmes

'Human kind', wrote T. S. Eliot, 'cannot bear very much reality.' Yet reality is brought to us in wagon-loads by television and radio every day. A mother carries her dead baby as she takes the handout from the famine-relief truck, the general shoots a suspect in a Saigon street, *Challenger* explodes on camera: these and innumerable others are the images which television has brought to almost every inhabitant of the planet in the past forty years. Less often now, but once as frequently and memorably, radio brings us the words with which to paint our own imaginative pictures: the destruction of the German airship *Hindenburg*, as it approached its mooring in New York before the Second World War; Ed Murrow reporting the blitz from the streets of a fire-lit London; Richard Dimbleby entering a Nazi concentration camp to make plain its horrors as the war ended. The sounds and images are unforgettable, haunting, in the strength with which they convey human despair, cruelty, selfishness, and greed. We have been witness to the murderous attack on the students in Tiananmen Square, to rescuers scrabbling to find survivors in the desolate aftermath of earthquakes, bombs, and volcanic eruptions, to the recovery of bodies from the wreckage of trains, cars, and aircraft. We live in the reflection of other people's tragedies.

We watch and listen to news programmes from a variety of motives: because, in our common humanity, we are curious; because there is an excitement to be had in following a story spiced with the special flavour of reality; because we want to discern signs of hope and possible relief; because, as the electorate in a democracy, we feel it our duty to be informed about the world, ours and other people's.

117

The BBC's Director General, John Birt, made clear the BBC's interpretation of its duty:

A fine balance must be struck between portraying dreadful events—massacres, for example—in ways which help our audiences understand the incident and its consequences, but without showing images which will cause people to turn away or, eventually, numbing viewers' reactions. And we must always remember the responsibility the broadcaster has to the humanity of people affected by such horrific circumstances.[1]

David McCormick, Executive Producer, Broadcast Standards, at NBC in New York described the broadcasters' duty as he saw it:

I think it is our responsibility to report the truth or what we know. We have a certain responsibility, obviously, to be the gatekeeper in our society and we're sitting on a lot of information. It's up to us, in a responsible manner, to stack it up, as you will, in an order of importance or relevance to the viewership or readership. I think the viewer looks to us as their eyes and ears and it's our responsibility to report back to them on what we think is important as well as important to their lives. On a daily basis.[2]

Coverage of the news, however, consists of more than the reports of it which appear in the heavyweight nightly bulletins. Television stations in the states may run local news programmes for up to two hours in the early evening, compared with thirty minutes in Britain, and a further thirty minutes in the late evening. They are popular and, for commercial services, highly profitable. News provides the raw material for current affairs programmes, whether they take a documentary form, supplying background information to contemporary events, or are studio discussions among experts. And it feeds the crop of news magazines, more potent and numerous so far in the United States, which derive style and values from the tabloid Press.

News programmes present reality in one way, marking the large or small changes which are considered by the journalists compiling them to be of interest to their audience. Talk-shows, which have increased in numbers in relatively recent years, stand on the border between the news and the large number of other programmes reflecting a different kind of reality. At their best, they can throw a different light on aspects of the news, underlining moral issues as they are seen at street level, whether they are discussing race relations, abortion, or capital punishment. At their worst, they are shamelessly exploitative, contemptuous of feelings in pursuit of confrontation, morally null. As Jerry Springer, the host of one of the most outrageous of

---

[1] Personal interview, London, 21 Apr. 1997.
[2] Personal interview, New York, 3 Feb. 1997.

American talk-shows said, 'We're a television show, people don't come on to get help.'[3] And then, under the broad heading of reality, there are programmes built around a number of public services: hospitals and ambulance crews, air-sea rescue teams, the fire service, and, most commonly of all, the police. The last enables programme-makers to exploit the fascination with crime and criminals which has been common in both the United States and Britain for centuries. The greater licence enjoyed by American programmes through the absence of the strict rules on contempt of court which operate in Britain was noted in an earlier chapter.

The News Revolution

Richard Wald, Vice-President, News, at ABC in New York, told me:

News is an artefact . . . there's a man, not famous in America, who was writing a book about journalism. It was called *Somewhere a Baby is Burning*. His theory was that the more big-time news there was, the further back the baby-burning came in the newspaper. The less big news there was, the baby-burning came closer and it got on the front-page when there was absolutely no news at all. And that's true. The *New York Times* fills up eight full columns on the front page no matter what the world is, and we do too. The question of what is more important and what is not is an interesting one because I think you can use the same analysis to say that there is almost no important news. News is whatever you think is news.[4]

Whatever their sources, the artefacts have to be shaped for the particular market, with its hierarchy of interests, which the journalists are serving. Principles which serious journalism regards as its stock-in-trade give way, as the market moves towards middle-brow outlets and the tabloids, to human interest and the greater personalization of stories. What starts as 'Shipping-line shares hit by liner disaster' emerges at the opposite end of the market as 'Cabin-boy saves dog as hundreds drown.' As readers influence the form of the news which they receive, so broadcasting channels tailor their news programmes, and the standards they observe, to the audiences which they wish to reach.

This practice, long common in print journalism, made a delayed appearance in broadcasting, thanks, in the United States, to the semi-monopoly enjoyed by the three networks. According to Don West, then Editor of *Broadcasting and Cable* magazine in Washington, they observed a kind of agreed-upon convention in the selection of news.[5] In Britain, the BBC had no competitors as a news service until the appearance of

---

[3] Jerry Springer on *Midweek*, BBC Radio 4, 4 Mar. 1998.
[4] Personal interview, New York, 19 Feb. 1997.
[5] Personal interview, Washington, 10 Feb. 1997.

Independent Television News in 1955 as part of the new commercial service. Even then, the years of the duopoly between the BBC and ITV, which lasted until the mid-1980s, saw few differences in the news agenda between the two services, although there were, to begin with, sharp differences in the style of presentation. In each country, because no real alternatives existed, the respective news services, in radio and then in television, established a particular kind of authority. In the United States, the level of authority also owed something to the importance attached by the networks to maintaining the prestige of their news operations, often at a cost which paid none of the regard now given to the bottom line. 'News was the place', wrote Peter J. Boyer in *Who Killed CBS?*, 'where people went in the morning and proceeded to spend the company's money.'[6] The close involvement in programming of the most senior men in the companies, a factor now almost wholly absent, meant that their individual standing with their peers was at stake. News programmes were an acknowledgement of the public's right to be informed, a prime demonstration of service of the public interest. News coverage of the kind considered responsible won valuable friends in Congress and elsewhere in Washington. More dubiously, other valuable friendships within business corporations were maintained by a certain reticence in dealing with corporate news. The faces and voices of the news teams became the individual hallmark of each network.

Richard Wald described how news had risen in public esteem and then, more recently, gone into a decline:

It was the common patriotic effort [in the war] in which most news outlets joined and were exemplars that made them respectable. That, and the advent [in the USA] of the Newspaper Guild which raised the prices for newspaper reporters, attracted a more educated middle-class kind of person, and created a system of people whose sense was that they were part of the middle class, they weren't outsiders, and whose work was appreciated by readers and listeners as being approvable because they brought you news of victory or defeat, with, after that, the great decisions of this country. And as that general national consensus decreased as the Cold War came to an end, the urgency of the news went down and I think that the result, all part of the same bundle, is that news has become less important and, as less important, less interesting. No, I don't think you can have in these years the kind of powerful news force which you had in the 1960s, but you could again if there were another crisis. It's crises that make these things important.[7]

Howard Stringer, who worked for CBS for thirty years, including two as President of CBS News, spoke to me about the decline in the authority once wielded by the networks:

[6] Peter J. Boyer, *Who Killed CBS?* (Random House, New York, 1988).
[7] Personal interview, New York, 19 Feb. 1997.

It's virtually impossible to have the great impact which you had . . . it's complicated by the fact that you have so many news-magazine shows, so many bits and pieces on the all-news channels that it somehow feels that every story has been covered in bits and pieces. And it's very hard to hold the audience's attention, very hard to hold the attention of Washington, very hard to capture imaginations . . . Nothing is a surprise to anyone any more, so I think the sheer flood of media has defanged the serious news organizations in a way that we probably wouldn't have imagined. It has to be so dramatic to cut through the clutter that it feels that news divisions are doing less of a job than they are. They're out there scurrying and scurrying and scurrying, but it's not the same, it's a different world.[8]

I asked Don West what he thought about the effect of all the new channels:

The time given to news is so much greater now and the length of time . . . The newscasts back then were only twenty-two minutes of which six or seven might have been about Vietnam and an item about . . . But now, CNN would be there all day. You would never have a movement which wasn't covered now unless people were bored with it and turned it off, but I don't think so. [People are] watching news in greater numbers than before. And in greater types . . . Now you've got *Hard Copy*, you've got all these other people on the edges, on the periphery, putting out news and people are watching it. There's a far greater dimension of news.[9]

Boundaries of Taste and Decency

To say that taste is a relatively minor matter in news and reality programmes is not to dismiss it as unimportant, but the fair treatment of individuals, which is so often at risk in these programmes, ensures that decency, rooted in a moral judgement, is often of more significance. In fiction, the reverse is usually true. The elements of fiction are present as the result of their creator's choices and are therefore more capable, when justified, of being presented and promoted in ways which reduce their capacity to offend gratuitously.

Issues of taste can, however, arise from the use of language or, from time to time, in the choice made of language recorded or relayed outside the studio. Crowd-sounds at sporting events sometimes contain swearwords differing in their intensity. People under stress use strong language and its retention in material actually transmitted has to be judged on the relevance it bears to the story being reported. Occasionally, it may be too difficult to excise it without significant loss of other material.

[8] Personal interview, New York, 7 Feb. 1997.

[9] Personal interview, Washington, 10 Feb. 1997. *Hard Copy* is a nightly news magazine.

The Treatment of Death

Sentimentality has been called emotion beyond the facts. It is a dangerous criterion to apply, however. The amount of emotion and its visible or audible expression which societies consider acceptable varies from one to another. What would be condemned as mawkishness in one would be regarded as no more than appropriate to the circumstances of another. Nowhere does this hold more true than in the treatment by television of death. It provides illustrations of the borderlines between decency and taste.

Where attention is concentrated upon a single, identifiable, individual, a soldier shot down by a sniper, for example, or the victim of a road accident, the televising of the actual moment of death clearly raises issues of decency. As a rule, it would seem that it should be treated as a profoundly private moment. Not only should there be a concern for any relatives who might be confronted with the image without warning, but such a moment, in the case of a private individual, is one at which strangers have no right to demand a presence.

For example, it does not appear easy to justify the live televising of a suicide on a Los Angeles freeway in the spring of 1998. A number of local stations broke into normal programming to show the incident, including programmes intended for children, even though the dead man and his motives were unknown.

Yet there are circumstances in which the rule may require to be broken. In contrast to the Los Angeles episode, a good case exists for reporting with pictures, at least after the event, the suicides by burning in the name of political protest which took place in Vietnam and in Czechoslovakia. In some circumstances, even a live transmission may be legitimized. Though doubts were to be expressed about the authenticity of the pictures, the execution of the Ceauşescus after the Romanian revolution which overthrew them in 1989 was shown on Romanian television as the proof demanded by the populace that the couple's tyranny was over. It was, therefore, the symbol of a profound change in the country's history, so essential that the abnormal circumstances, which included the risk of further killings if uncertainty about the Ceauşescus' deaths continued, may be thought to justify its transmission live. In countries where it was less directly significant, there was less justification for televising the pictures, certainly at a time when children could be expected to be watching in large numbers. The arguments are not straightforward. It could be argued that the images on the screen as the couple toppled over were not distinguishable from a score of other, but fictitious, killings which children would have witnessed. But to hold that this makes it possible to show the executions in the general run of programming might suggest that no real difference existed between the real-life event and a similar event created as part of a piece of fiction. In fiction, death is carefully choreographed, the moment calculated to achieve a certain effect on its audience. In reality, it is often sudden, arbitrary, brutally uncontrolled. Violent death forms so conspicuous a part of television's output that the distinction between fact and fantasy has to be preserved.

The live televising of judicial executions, or their recording for subsequent showing, might be defended on the grounds that, since the public, through the courts, has determined the sentence, the public has a right, or even a duty, to witness its ultimate consequences. Public executions, when they were a commonplace happening in both countries, were attended by large crowds. But public executions ended because of the growth of public feeling that such events were debased by their reduction to a public spectacle, not altogether lacking a touch of carnival. To reinstate public executions by presenting them on television to an audience even more promiscuously assembled raises profound issues of decency. The fact that it might deter some future crime could hardly be sufficient to outweigh the degradation of all those involved. The subsequent showing of the event beyond the boundaries of the country in which it took place, and therefore before an audience ignorant of almost all the circumstances which led to the conviction and sentence, lacks even the defence of the audience's ultimate responsibility for what was being shown.

Will Wyatt, Chief Executive, BBC Broadcast, described to me the BBC's approach to the killing of a public official, caught on film by a cameraman who had been present for a different purpose:

three or four years ago, a local planning inspector was shot dead in the northeast. Now that was all filmed, everything. We didn't show it [all], but you saw on television the indication beforehand, the man firing the gun, and then nothing after that was shown except people running away. But actually it was a continuous shot and I was shown it at a seminar we had, the whole bloody thing. Now that, by and large, that is the way we would continue to behave and I would hope so. Because I think there is a thing about people's death . . . the moment is a specially difficult one.[10]

There was no live coverage of President Kennedy's assassination, but the amateur film shown shortly afterwards signified its political and historical importance. A different kind of significance was attached to the murder on film of a Vietcong suspect in the streets of Saigon. There should be grave doubts about showing the death of an anonymous man or woman about whom nothing more is known. In this case, however, the manner of the

[10] Personal interview, London, 4 Apr. 1997.

shooting, arbitrary and brutal, was an illustration, beyond the power of most words, of the barbarity of the conflict into which American troops were being drawn.

Questions of decency do arise, however, over the subsequent repetition of these sequences, as they do over re-showings of the *Challenger* explosion. In Britain, the Saigon shooting was included in a television history of pop music, where its appearance was generally considered unjustifiable in the context of the programme. Because such images are so arresting, it matters greatly that they appear only in a context which does not debase or trivialize them, exploiting and ultimately diminishing their original significance.

Covering the deaths of children raises particular questions of taste and decency. Examples can be found on both sides of the Atlantic. In the first, the murder of JonBenet Ramsay in Boulder, Colorado, at the end of 1996, the child's body had been found in the cellar of her home. The mystery surrounding her death, for which nobody had been arrested by the spring of 1998, and the fact that she had taken part successfully as a junior beauty queen on the child pageant circuit produced great interest among the media. One television network interviewed the parents for forty minutes, another described the manner of the child's strangulation, two fought one another for photographs, while the police themselves were accused of leaking the photographs which a tabloid paper published. Pictures appeared widely of JonBenet and other participants in the parodic versions of grown-up dresses and make-up worn by children on the pageant circuit. Critics said that the coverage bordered on the paedophiliac, going beyond anything justifiable in the context of the child's death. While the social phenomenon of the pageant circuit and the doubtful values which, however lawful, it could be said to reflect were legitimate matters of interest, not least because their significance for the tragedy was at that stage unknown, the accompanying illustrations raised serious questions of taste. They implied connections between those matters and the murder which remain untested nine months later.

A different example of the same dilemma also occurred during the winter of 1996/7. Another young girl, older than JonBenet Ramsay, had been abducted and killed. At the trial of her murderer, he took advantage of an opportunity to speak in court after his conviction to make accusations of sexual interference against the girl's father. In its nightly news at 6.30 p.m. that evening, CBS broadcast the man's statement, saying that, before the transmission, it had carefully considered the propriety of doing so. The company then said that it did not accept the credibility of the accusations. It may be fair to ask what public interest was served by giving wide circulation to the convicted man's accusations which the broadcaster did not believe, so adding to the pain and distress of the family, particularly the father, at whom the accusation had been directed. The television audience, of course, heard the words and, to that extent, an end was put to possible rumours about what was said. Whether that was sufficient to warrant the broadcasting of such an obvious outrage against decency provides a very difficult question to answer.

There was controversy in Britain in 1995 about a documentary broadcast shortly after the conclusion of the trial of a nurse eventually convicted of murdering children in hospital under her care. The documentary included an opening sequence, backed by music, which showed the silhouette of a nurse-like figure advancing with a raised syringe. Criticisms centred on the appearance of conventions, used in feature films to increase tension, in the treatment of a factual story of that kind, one whose conclusion was by definition known.

The same kind of issue of decency arose in the days after the conclusion in Liverpool in 1996 of the trial of the two boys accused of murdering the 2-year-old Jamie Bulger. As noted in Chapter 3, the child's murder by other children, who were 10 at the time it took place, administered a shock felt throughout Britain and, indeed, more widely. The event assumed a symbolic value as the focal point of feelings about a general decline in the country's moral standards, although less attention was paid to all the circumstances of profound deprivation in which the two defendants had lived. Both BBC1 and ITV produced documentary treatments, making use of tapes released by the police and containing lengthy interviews conducted with the two boys before the trial began. Neither programme escaped criticism, but the ITV programme was criticized in particular for employing techniques more appropriate to fiction in an attempt to increase the drama.

Fact and Fiction

In the kinds of programme described above, questions of decency arise more often than in any other kind of programme. They frequently deal with people at their most vulnerable, in situations of suffering or at the extremes of emotion, when they are most open to exploitation, whether in pain or in elation. Those situations are rarely of the news journalists' own making. They may be created by natural disasters or through the actions of other people, most notably in wars and accidents.

By contrast, as we noted in considering the treatment of death, writers and directors, whether in drama or sitcoms, create their own situations. At least by implication, in doing so they set the boundaries of decency and taste which, in their view, are appropriate to the portrayal of those situations. The broadcaster who is buying their work knows the boundaries conventionally set, as described in Chapter 3, for the place in the schedule in which the material is to appear. The majority of writers and directors accept those boundaries, as they have to, with no significant disagreements. If they want to exceed them, then they must argue for the freedom to do so, as Barney Rosenzweig argued his case for the 'abortion-clinic' episode of *Cagney and Lacey*. With the advance of a successful career, however, the arguments usually diminish: the evidence of its popularity with the audience creates a demand among broadcasters for the work of a writer or a director. There is confidence that, in the right slot, its quality will outweigh any offence created within the audience or, in a commercial service, any hostility among advertisers. A Woody Allen can, therefore, insist on transmission of his films uncut on television. So can Steven Spielberg and a handful of others. In making original drama for television, Steve Bochco, with a long list of successes behind him, exercises a much greater right to freedom of expression than someone setting out to make a name. The playwright Dennis Potter earned the same right in Britain.

Even if the broadcaster's confidence is from time to time misplaced, the career of either a writer or a director will be proof against occasional failures, provided there continue to be enough successes to counterbalance them. Now and again, in pursuit perhaps of the 'larger agenda' mentioned in Chapter 3, a commercial broadcaster will be prepared to challenge the reactions of both audience and advertisers. The public broadcaster may understand that such challenges, by promoting the individual voice of a creative talent, constitute a proper interpretation of the public interest it exists to serve. In comparison with the making of news, the making of broadcast fiction is an orderly process. Time can be found, or made, for debate.

Whatever its sources, news-making is different. The sources of news, in comparison, as we have seen, are often unpredictable. The urgencies of deadlines compress the time available for considered judgements. The rawness of an event as the reporter sees it may not travel as he or she intends to a destination several thousand miles away. Once, when such news was carried on film and hours, or even days, could pass before it eventually reached the audience, there was time for editors in their newsrooms, facing no more than one or two deadlines in a day, to consider how the report should be presented. It could be given a context to make it, if possible, more comprehensible to the audience. Now deadlines are often non-stop on one outlet or another. The modern reporter may be feeding the same story to several different markets and, therefore, preparing different treatments for each. He or she may be feeding a story into a live programme, with no editor to intervene if the reporter's judgement on the spot, many miles away, seems faulty or inappropriate at the receiving end.

We can have our fill of disasters. Coming to terms with a natural disaster is often easier than with one whose origins are man-made. It rains, there is a flood, lives are in peril, lives are lost. But tribal hatreds, precipitating the flight of thousands from homes and safety into the blind uncertainties beyond a frontier, are less easy to understand for those who do not share them. The phenomenon of compassion-fatigue has already been identified, suggesting a limit to the number of disasters which audiences can digest within a given period of time. A Canadian scholar has referred to the way in which the treatment of disasters for news purposes has become, perhaps as a form of response, a matter of routine, calling it commodification. We can predict the stock items: the wide-eyed African child in a famine, the shoe abandoned in the grass after an air-crash, the helpless survivors picking purposeless ways through the havoc of an earthquake. We have seen it all before or something so like it that it becomes as indistinguishable as our responses themselves can become.

The threat to decency, to the preservation of the dignity of the people portrayed in the news, lies in the dehumanizing effect of the torrent of events into which the flow of news can develop. Meaninglessness is a constant danger. The reporter's purpose, at its best, is to inform the audience, often of things which, in scale, callousness, barbarity, or suffering, outrage decency. If the reporters are honest, therefore, they do not, in their reporting, conceal that sense of outrage, sanitizing the words they use or the images they show so that the audience will understand less than the truth. In doing that, however, they have also to avoid the dangers of desensitizing the viewer or provoking a visceral response with too much undigested detail, both of which stand in the way of communication. It is one thing to dwell on horror in the midst of it among people sharing the emotions of a common experience. It is another to pass on those emotions to an audience whose involvement is inevitably less and whose capacities for grief and anger are restricted. The price for miscalculating that balance is often paid by decency, in the loss of such dignity as remains to the victims at the centre of an atrocious act. Tony Hall, Chief Executive, BBC News, made the point in telling me the story of a correspondent reporting from the scene of an East African famine:

he went into a straw-hut where a woman was staying . . . where a child had died. Five or six years ago, he would simply have said, 'This woman lost her baby' [and the question was] do you dwell on the baby? He actually said, 'This woman invited me in because she wanted you to know what is happening and wants to know what is the world going to do?' As if he was saying that we are here by invitation, not because we simply poked our cameras, offered them dollars, and said, 'We want the pictures.'[11]

Hall's anecdote had arisen in the context of a conversation about the BBC's coverage of the shooting at the Dunblane Primary School in 1996. He had taken the decision not to cover the funerals of the sixteen murdered children and their teacher and had, as a result, been asked by an American network where the pictures they expected of grieving relatives were. It was a departure from precedents stretching back into the mid-1960s when, as described in Chapter 3, at another school, in South Wales, more than a hundred children and some of the school staff had been buried beneath a tide of slurry from a colliery tip behind the building. At Dunblane, the incident itself lasted only a few minutes, but in Wales there was live coverage of the attempts at rescue which went on for forty-eight hours. It made a running news story until the moment when all hope of finding survivors ended and a different, more private and personal, phase began. Yet the images, transmitted over two days, of the waiting villagers and rescue teams, in a place where the history of mining had taught bitter lessons in collective grief, the arc-lights and the ambulances, had drawn in the rest of Britain in a way quite different from the emotions provoked by the tragedy at Dunblane. To have stepped back, to use Hall's expression, from Aberfan and left the relatives and the rescuers to themselves would have been a different issue from deciding to step back from Dunblane. Hall believes that the BBC's conduct at Dunblane will create a precedent if a similar event occurs in the future.

As I noted in Chapter 3, such a decision would have been much more controversial in the United States than it turned out to be in Britain. The argument would be that, if an event was considered significant enough for coverage, then that coverage ought not to be compromised for any reason to do with the supposed sensitivities of the audience. Yet, every day, many stories end up on television's equivalent of the spike. Neither reticence nor explicitness, however, has a monopoly of virtue if the objective is to communicate the story truthfully. John Birt said:

British broadcasters are probably among the most restrained in the world in not exposing people gratuitously to the full horror of events . . . There are issues carefully to consider, including the dignity of the dead. And there's a very, very fine balance to be struck. We don't often show dead bodies on the BBC and when it happens, it is done with very great care. None the less, without confronting people with horror, they should be under no doubt that horror was committed.[12]

---

[11] Personal interview, London, 17 Apr. 1997.
[12] Personal interview, London, 21 Apr. 1997.

Birt had acknowledged earlier in my conversation that he regarded the communication of horror to the audience in the way he had just described to me as a legitimate expression of the public interest in broadcasting. Tony Hall had outlined for me the factors which he took into account in finding answers to particular questions about the extent of horror which it was permissible to screen: custom and practice, audience response, the practices of other broadcasters, political judgements, personal instincts. I asked whether he thought the public interest was represented by an amalgam of all these factors or whether it was a separate factor. He was in no doubt that it was quite separate:

No, there is something separate, which is the public interest. Because what the public interest might do . . . It's an open question because on the one hand you've got public pressure which is what you distil to be the public's view of what you do and that comes from a number of sources . . . It's like the [news] agenda. Who sets the agenda? It comes from ranging over a number of sources. And then [on the other hand] there's the public interest which might go directly against that public judgement, that public pressure. If we take the example of the George Alaghia piece [an account of a massacre], you could say that, because it offended many people, that in the sense of being decent to the people who we were portraying massacred, the piece should not run. The public interest defence of that is that there are moments when you must shock and you must say to people, 'We are going to describe the real horror of events which we would otherwise sanitize. Sanitize because we know you would find it offensive, sanitize because we know that it is not right for us to intrude into others' human dignity for our journalistic purposes.' It's in the public's interest that you should report to them fully the implications of a carbomb or of a massacre, whatever it happens to be . . . But you need to be sparing in your use of violent images in most occasions. Why? Because if you do it all the time, I actually do believe, and [at] seminars, that seems to be the consensus, though that doesn't necessarily mean it's right, that you will desensitize people to acts of violence.[13]

The Issue of Desensitization

Issues of taste and decency raised in news and reality programmes cannot be separated from the possibility of desensitization of which Hall spoke. The allegation is that both television fact and television fiction may eventually leave the sensibilities of the audience dulled, indifferent to the reality of pain and suffering and therefore, as the argument continues, readier to tolerate the sufferings of others in real life or even readier themselves to inflict pain. There is no conclusive evidence of this effect, only the belief, which Hall expressed, in talking about the news, that such consequences could follow.

[13] Personal interview, London, 17 Apr. 1997.

Over the five decades during which television has been watched in the majority of homes in both Britain and the United States, fictional and factual violence have moved closer together, with greater realism replacing in fictions the more stylized sorts of violence, often apparently bloodless, which characterized many earlier dramas and films. Technical developments have made possible the production of action movies which amount to a series of pyrotechnical displays punctuated by no more dialogue than is needed to give the displays an apparent motivation. The slaughter in them is frequently on a large scale, but the characterization goes no further than is necessary to ensnare the audience's emotions enough for them to enjoy the spectacular effects. The result in the case of many such films is to create a kind of gross cartoon. An audience of young people in California, watching *Schindler's List* in the cinema, was, however, reported to have laughed at the violence displayed in the film by the Nazis against the Jews. Unaware of the historical background and, therefore, of the context in which the violence actually occurred, they saw the film as simply another in which violence was displayed as a kind of sport. If there is a parallel danger in the anonymity of much real-life violence portrayed on the screen in reality programmes, then at least a partial response to it lies in greater contextualization of news stories where it is practical. The reporter's actions in speaking for the woman in the famine village, of which Hall had told me earlier, conferred on her, however scantily, an identity which rescued her from the silent and anonymous suffering with which most reports of that kind have made us familiar. It had the further advantage of demonstrating that the anonymous suffering was made up of many more individuals like her, countering the tendency of repeated scenes of the more familiar sort to create stereotypes of the Developing World.

I raised the issue of contextualization with David McCormick. I had spent several months in Philadelphia at the beginning of 1988 and been struck by the number of crime stories which were reported in the local news programmes. It had, however, seemed to me from other visits to the States that they provided the staple of such programmes far more widely than that.

Our local news does seem to be preoccupied with crime after crime after crime without stepping back a pace and really trying to figure out why we are doing those stories and is there any significance at all. Does the fact that there was one murder on a certain corner in a certain city have any impact on the larger audience to that television signal? That's a debate that continues. Off the top of my head, my personal hypothesis about why we do so much crime on a local basis is obviously somebody, I guess, has perceived that the viewer is interested in this kind of stuff. But I also think, on the other side of the coin, that one of the reasons we do it is, frankly, that we are not very smart in what we cover. Murders, fires, whatever, they're easy to discover, they are all on the police scanner, it requires no intelligence, no thought . . . And of course the figures are just the opposite, some of these major crimes are abating, particularly in New York City here . . . Part of the reality, and this is no excuse at all because there is no excuse, but just in terms of resources, particularly in local news organizations, if you have a one-hour or two-hour local news broadcast in the early evening, you have virtually an insatiable appetite for picture-stories and you know, as an assignment editor, that you can rack up a good count by covering a lot of spot-news and it doesn't require a lot of reporter-time. So that I think is also the driving force, certainly at the local level.[14]

Crime, however, makes its appearance in a wide range of reality programmes, not simply in news. The news magazines which, on the US networks, customarily follow the nightly news programmes, crowd many short items into their running times of twenty-two minutes. As many as a dozen items may go through in a commercial half-hour, several of them likely to be centred on violence of different kinds, intermingled with gossip about movie-stars. As in the case of newspapers, some victims of crime, children, nubile teenagers, and the elderly, lend themselves more readily to treatment in this context. There is, literally, no pause for thought.

As George Gerbner has pointed out on many occasions, the effect of constant emphasis on crime is to increase the sense of the pervasiveness of crime, especially among those who are heavy viewers or who, like members of some minorities, more readily identify themselves as potential victims. Fear of crime is a necessary part of human baggage. Like the fear of being burnt or the fear of falling, it alerts us to the dangers around us. But if it is developed too far, stimulated regularly by the casual reporting of violent incidents because violence compels attention and draws audiences, then its effects are socially destructive. They diminish the quality of people's lives, exaggerating the degree of danger to which they are exposed and robbing them of their right to what lawyers call 'quiet enjoyment'.

The justification for some programmes is the broadcasters' intention to give help to the police through the cooperation of the audience. The programmes may include reconstructions of the crimes for which suspects are being sought. One such programme is the series *Crimewatch*, which has now been running for many years in Britain. Will Wyatt described its origins:

I was instrumental in starting *Crimewatch* in this country . . . it was actually a German idea which we changed quite a lot because it showed things in a way I said we can't possibly . . . I remember seeing the tape, which [had been] brought to me [with the question] 'Do you think you can do anything like this? and one of the

---

[14] Personal interview, New York, 3 Feb. 1997.

re-enactions showed a rape from the rapist's point of view. And I said, 'In a pig's ear are we going to do that.' But the principle was a good one. Then when one has seen other versions of it, in the States and so on, they went far beyond the kind of thing we would do.[15]

In both the choice of crimes and the presentation of the reconstructions, certain kinds of crime may be over-emphasized, often those involving violence, and, as a result, exaggerate their place in crime statistics, increasing the fear of crime which is prevalent in both countries. Television, as we noted earlier, is more effective in conveying emotion than thought and it is emotion which tends to be evoked when the treatment of violence is perfunctory. I asked David McCormick what influenced the belief that the viewer had too short an attention-span to justify, for example, putting crime stories into a deeper perspective. Was it the view of advertisers? He suggested, as Don West had done, that there was now such a variety of news outlets that the viewers, if they looked for it, could find almost any treatment of the news they wanted.

somewhere if they crave it, they can get it. But it takes an active viewer, an active news-consumer to seek it out, whether you're looking at MSNBC doing five minutes on something or CNN doing five minutes on something or thirty seconds on the evening news. But in terms of just local news, a thirty-minute eleven o'clock news just for example . . . a thirty-minute news broadcast which probably runs twenty-two minutes, taking out the commercial breaks and all that, and must also include sports and weather, and just by its nature you are not going to get very much in-depth coverage. So that I am not sure whose responsibility it is to lead. So I guess you have fundamentally to go back to the original question, what do you believe to be your charter in life? And whose responsibility is it, knowing that you can be the most . . . you can put on what some people consider to be the most responsible . . . if nobody watches and nobody is buying advertising time, you're going to go out of business. So there is this balance between responsibility and survival.[16]

Talk-Shows

Talk-shows, which have increased in numbers in recent years, stand on the border between news programmes and the large number of other programmes which present different kinds of reality. Celebrity talk-shows, in which guests, usually from the entertainment business, trade judiciously chosen parts of their life-stories for publicity, are one thing, since both parties know the nature of the contract. Talk-shows involving ordinary people are another. The American versions are generally more unequivo-

[15] Personal interview, London, 4 Apr. 1997.
[16] Personal interview, New York, 3 Feb. 1997.

cally grounded in show business than the British, their presenters more obviously in that tradition, and the odds usually more heavily stacked against the participants. They may take some of their discussion topics from the news, but they rely heavily for others on freakish aspects of human behaviour. Their continued success depends largely on the personality of their presenters and the collusive exhibitionism of many of their participants. Paradoxically, although American news programmes were said to include a higher proportion of ordinary people than their counterparts in other countries, the role of the ordinary people is commonly reactive or intended to provide some human-interest material as light relief. Talk-shows share with many of the new breed of radio-presenters in the States in giving a platform to people who rarely speak, but may be spoken for, in other kinds of mainstream broadcasting. As Tracy Westen, President for the Center for Governmental Studies at the University of Southern California in Los Angeles, said:

That may be the only way in which they can be heard, but they are being heard on a very narrow slice of the issues that concern them. In other words, if you're in the lower middle class and you can get your concerns aired if they involve incest, but you can't if they involve education for your child. That's a mixed blessing and, in fact, it runs the risk that this segment of the population will become characterized by extreme issues when many of them are normal family people with normal family concerns. They are being offered access to the media only if their views are extreme.[17]

The participants pay a heavy price for their platform. Although experts may be on hand to add respectability by giving advice on handling the problems raised, they usually have little opportunity to offer more than perfunctory counselling before the host or hostess has swept past. The more ruthless presenters will turn the participants into spectacles for the audience's amusement and then, having drained them of whatever interest they hold, will move on, leaving them to pick up the pieces. Those are the worst of them. Others demonstrate more concern, showing greater respect for the individuality of participants.

But there are about some of the programmes elements of exploitation not unlike those that are characteristic of the more extreme forms of pornography. And there too it is said that nobody is under any compulsion to take part: there is no shortage of volunteers nor any shortage of sensational stories for them to deliver. The same question can be asked about both cases. Given that there is no compulsion, should society nevertheless find amusement in the humiliation of others? The answer in the case of hard-core pornography has been 'no'. But Stuart Fischoff, in an account of

---

[17] Personal interview, Los Angeles, 25 Feb. 1997.

his disenchantment with performing the role of psychologist-expert in a number of such programmes, wrote that people do not always have the sophistication to make the right choices or fully grasp the risks of parading their life-flaws for a few moments of cheap celebrity. Essentially, he wrote, it is the exploitation of the have-nots by the haves who encourage them to sell their misery to voyeuristic audiences as hookers sell their bodies. By contributing as an expert, he was giving legitimacy to a process which would not stop until shame and privacy had reasserted themselves among the nation's social values. The drawing of a line seemed to him a suitable subject for self-regulation among the broadcasters.[18]

Conclusion

The question raised by American newsmen about the absence of grieving relatives in the BBC's restricted coverage of the Dunblane shooting highlighted at least one aspect of the difference between the attitudes of the two societies towards coverage of the news. As I ended my conversation in New York with Richard Wald, he said:

One of the marks of journalism in this country is a certain lack of taste, rowdiness, and I like that. That is the way in which the culture works. But to be more refined and more decent and nice and kindly is an interesting and wonderful criterion of a kind that is not reflective of the country at large. In fact, the country offers a spectrum of attitudes, some quite highbrow and some very low, just the way the Press does. And I think that a Press has to be reflective of the country at large in order to talk to it.[19]

[18] Unpublished.
[19] Personal interview, New York, 19 Feb. 1997.

8

Privacy

The people of both the United States and Britain live in complex societies whose proper functioning demands the surrender of some of the individual's right to privacy: the right marmoreally defined in the last century by Samuel Warren and the future Justice Brandeis in the phrase, American to its bootstraps, to be 'let alone'. It is a right whose exercise has become more difficult since they published the words in the *Harvard Law Review* in 1890, not least in the past fifty years because of the actions of the broadcasting media. We all accept that some reduction of the right is inevitable, but we worry about the extent to which new demands are made, often, we believe, without either justification or consultation. At the heart of privacy lies the preservation of our dignity as individuals which, as I have argued in this book, is itself the core of decency. In this chapter, following our consideration of news and reality programmes, we shall look in more detail at the particular impact of news and news-making on privacy and then look at the way in which other kinds of programme also have consequences for privacy. First, however, we need to consider how attitudes towards privacy have been changing.

Changing Concepts of Privacy

It is one of the paradoxes of modern life that, as increased affluence and improved medical knowledge have enabled many of us to feel more secure, our privacy seems to have become more vulnerable. The threats created by technological advances are among the most disturbing for many people. The use of long-range cameras and microphones and the bugs placed in boardrooms, offices, and bedrooms are only the physical manifestations of the threats. We are also aware that mobile telephones are vulnerable to eavesdroppers. Many of us consider it unwise to assume that conversations on any kind of telephone will be shared only between the initiator of a call and its recipient. Faxes, by a single wrong digit, can end up in the wrong place, many times more dangerous than a bungled telephone call. Access to information about us and our habits seems, despite data protection legislation, to increase annually. Its electronic interchange across cities, countries, and continents is now a commonplace happening. Half a dozen printouts, carrying some information about us, may occur within minutes of one another in half a dozen places. We worry about the degree to which the computers on which the information is stored can be secured against determined or simply curious outsiders. Our shareholdings are checked, our grocery bills analysed, the closer to target our tastes. Curiosity about consumers for commercial purposes is resented by some people to the point of active protest, but, for others, it is little more than a nuisance and a cause of other people's wasted paper. We may even buy something as a result of a mail-shot. A New York man, to whom I had been grumbling about the volume of advertisers' mail reaching me in Britain, went into prompt rhapsodies about the suction-pump for an air-conditioning unit which, thanks to a mail-shot, had unexpectedly transformed his life. Our worries, however, grow more considerable over the confidentiality of our medical records and bank statements if these too appear accessible.

It is not only the abuse of otherwise-benign technology which creates anxieties about privacy. The pursuit of gossip, ranging from the urbane to the seamy and the prurient, has become a feature of almost every newspaper. It is conducted more aggressively as competition increases within the Press and between the Press and television which entered the field relatively late. The success of the Watergate investigators has spawned a host of imitators: 'gate' as a suffix has become shorthand for scandal. The growth in public scepticism about authority, however, means that resistance to some aspects of this intensified scrutiny, and to the practices which it employs, has become more equivocal. The same scepticism has its reflection in the plots of novels and films. They start with an assumption of the endemic corruption of those in power and develop in directions which, once dismissible as wildly improbable, have attained sufficient credibility to command large sales for their authors. Life, all too often, is setting precedents for fiction. In a culture of disparagement, almost anything becomes conceivable.

In the same period, in both the United States and Britain, as a sense of community has diminished, so individuals have become more protective of their own privacy and assertive of rights to be enjoyed without interference by others. The pressures of modern life make the need for somewhere in which to be oneself even greater, our time being burnt up in a bonfire of activities. Even children speak of a need for private space and greater affluence has made it possible for more of them to have it than before. If the public has a right to know, it has to be balanced against the right of individuals, as well as large and small groups, to be 'let alone'.

The great majority of people never figure in the public eye. When they do, it is often in the context of a calamity of some kind. It may be the violent death of a family member, an air-crash involving hundreds, or a natural disaster in which thousands are caught up and many do not survive. On occasions like these, the reaction of some of those involved will be to welcome the presence of reporters and camera crews as proof that they have not been overlooked. For them, relief comes from the sharing of grief and distress. The world is felt to care, or at least a part of it is. Being forgotten at that moment is not what they wish for. Others will resignedly accept the intrusion, distracted perhaps by all the other anxieties into which they have been so abruptly plunged. But a third group will be deeply resentful. The sudden death of a loved one will often be accompanied by sensations of guilt and people in the third group may be anxious only to get back to the seclusion and the imperfect security of their private existences. Only there, by themselves, can they come to terms with what has happened.

Privacy and the Law

We speak of a right to privacy, regarding privacy as an essential part of maintaining the quality of our lives. Without privacy, we lose control of those things about ourselves which we either do not wish to share at all or about which we want to make a free choice before we decide to make them known to anyone else. It shapes our perception of ourselves as independent beings in society. We agree to concede the right to others to intrude on our privacy with good cause, but we resist attempts to extend that right against our wishes. When we lose even a small part of our privacy without our consent, we feel diminished, resentful at the adjustments to our lives which have to be made as a result of its loss.

Because so many of the values cherished on both sides of the Atlantic are set out there, we might have expected something we regard with such importance to have figured explicitly in the American Constitution or in the Bill of Rights. It is there by implication in the Fourth Amendment which protects the right of the people to be secure in their 'persons, houses, papers, and effects' against unreasonable searches and seizures. It has also been implicit in decisions taken this century in the Supreme Court which were intended to protect individual self-expression: in particular the decisions on the right to abortion and the right to own obscene material for private use. The First Amendment, however, guaranteeing the free expression of opinion, has reduced the protection which an individual can claim against what may appear intrusions into their privacy by the Press and broadcasting. The right to be let alone is not unqualified. Attempts to assert it have to be taken by civil action and tell a story of mixed success.

The British have been agonizing for more than a decade about the issue of privacy and the need for legislation to protect it. It is now several years since a Cabinet Minister warned the Press that they were drinking in the last chance saloon. If they did not mend their ways, then the solution would be legislation to enforce compliance with principles of behaviour to be laid down in an Act of Parliament. It was not without a certain satisfaction that some of the papers reported the Minister's abrupt departure from office not long afterwards.

Each time that the Minister's threat of action to curb intrusive reporting seemed to be working and improvements in Press behaviour were said to have been noted, almost automatically, it seemed, one paper or another stepped out of line and stirred up the controversy again. Although broadcasters were not in the front line of criticism, there were occasions when, for example, aspects of news-gathering were criticized as unduly intrusive. With the death of Diana, Princess of Wales, in Paris at the end of August 1997, allegedly in flight from yet another group of pursuing photographers, the issue was given a fresh impetus, checked, however, by the manifest evidence that strict French privacy laws did not succeed in protecting the Princess. The Government has declared itself against legislation. The issue, however, will continue to be argued over. Any progress towards a decision is hampered by genuine concerns over the difficulty of drafting legislation which could not be used even further to fetter legitimate enquiries into matters of possible or real public interest. Substantial cover already exists for the wrongdoer in the English laws on contempt and defamation, as shown in my conversation with Harold Evans, reported in the opening chapter.

Towards the end of the Conservatives' term of office in 1997, the flurry of revelations about the sexual misconduct of Conservative Members of Parliament had the, no doubt intentional, effect of underlining how legislation on privacy, had it been in existence, might have frustrated the public interest in knowing what their representatives had been up to. Little consideration was given to the actual effect of their alleged misdeeds on their ability to do the work they had been elected to do. Impaled upon their party's much-trumpeted crusade for family values, the MPs had little alternative to suffering the assaults of reporters and photographers, apart from wondering why Opposition MPs, presumably no less fallible, were left largely unharassed.

Privacy and Regulation in Britain

The BBC and the Independent Television Commission, in their guidelines, provide clear advice on the boundaries of privacy and the circumstances in which it is permissible to breach them. They cover such matters as the undisclosed recording of telephone conversations and the use of hidden microphones and cameras, both of which require permission from a senior level within the broadcasting organization. The Independent Television Commission's Code examines the question of when it is permissible to put people on the screen without their permission if they have been filmed in institutions, factories, or shops. As figures in the background playing no particular part in the filming, no permission would be needed for showing them, unless the setting itself were thought sensitive: for example, if it were a psychiatric ward or an intensive care unit. When the people filmed are physically or mentally unable to give permission, then the ITC requires an approach to the next-of-kin. This may be difficult in practice in the case of elderly people or those with learning difficulties in long-stay accommodation. All their relatives may have died or moved away, severing any connections they may once have had.

The issue of privacy provided British broadcasting with one of the first examples of the independent scrutiny of the broadcasters' judgement. The BBC had had in existence since the autumn of 1971 a body, consisting of three independent people, to provide it with a second opinion on its response to complaints about unfairness in programmes. Although paid by the BBC, the first three members of the Programmes Complaints Commission could give assurances of their complete independence by pointing to their previous roles, as, respectively, the Lord Chief Justice of England, the Speaker of the House of Commons, and the Ombudsman (the official referee for complaints about government maladministration). About the same time, the Government had set up an official inquiry into the question of privacy and, when the Chairman of the BBC went to give evidence to the committee conducting the inquiry, he was invited to consider adding privacy to the remit of the Complaints Commission. The BBC subsequently agreed and the Commissioners could then deal with complaints about privacy on the same terms as they were dealing with complaints about unfairness. Complaints could be made only about programmes actually transmitted.

The Commission went some way to meeting the point made by the Labour leader Harold Wilson after a skirmish with the BBC in 1971, of 'public affront, private apology', with the BBC acting as judge and jury in its own cause. The BBC undertook to publish the adjudications of its new Commission in the *Listener*, one of its two weekly journals. If, in the opinion of the Commission, the BBC were found to be at fault, the fact would be widely publicized in the Press, eager to take the benefit of its rival's lapse.

The Commission served the BBC exclusively until 1980. The Independent Broadcasting Authority, with regulatory responsibilities for commercial broadcasting, declined an invitation to join in the work of the Commission. It argued that, even though it was at that time co-publisher of the commercial companies' broadcasts, it was better qualified than the BBC to act as an independent judge in cases affecting its franchisees. In 1980, the Government decided to institute its own statutory body, charged with handling complaints about unfairness and invasions of privacy whether they arose in the public or the private sector of the industry.

The Broadcasting Complaints Commission, the name given to the new body, had five Commissioners serving under a Chairman, all appointed by the Minister responsible for broadcasting. It lasted until the spring of 1997 when, as noted in Chapter 3, its work was merged in a new Broadcasting Standards Commission with that of the Broadcasting Standards Council. The latter was the creation of the Conservative Government in 1988 to conduct research into the portrayal in programmes of violence, sexual conduct, and matters of taste and decency and to deal with complaints from the audience. The members of the new Commission are also appointed by the responsible Minister.

The Commission deals with two distinct kinds of complaint. Complaints about violence and issues of taste and decency are rarely susceptible to precise and objective judgements. Some or all of the scheduling factors which were noted in Chapter 3 have a bearing on the formation of opinions about the appropriateness of the editorial judgements coming before the Commission for scrutiny. That is why the outcome of the members' discussions takes the name of a 'finding'.

Complaints of unfairness or of incursions into privacy, however, can be considered much more objectively on the basis of facts established by the Commission's inquiries. They are conducted on a quasi-judicial basis with their outcome published as an adjudication. Findings and adjudications may be ordered to be published at the broadcasters' expense either on air or in a newspaper chosen by the Commission. Neither adjudications nor findings are mandatory on the broadcasters.

The BBC, the Welsh Fourth Channel, and the regulators of the commercial companies operate their own machinery for dealing with complaints of the kinds considered by the Commission. That they have occasional differences of opinion with the Commission, or its predecessors, is not surprising, but uniformity of opinion on subjective issues would not, in any event, necessarily be a sign of health. The Commission, supported by its research programme, continues to provide a lay view of complaints independent of regulatory or publishing responsibilities for programmes. It exists, in a phrase applied by a former Chairman of the BBC to the role of himself and his fellow-Governors, to challenge the orthodoxy of the professionals.

Privacy in Disasters

The most terrible events may now be televised live. The *Challenger* explosion occurred during the routine coverage of a rocket-launch and the deaths of nearly a hundred football supporters at a ground in the north of England happened as the preliminaries to an important match were being televised. At a match in Belgium, a year or two before, when a wall collapsed after a riot started by British fans, some thirty Italian fans were crushed to death in front of cameras which were kept running. They were all, of course, public events, but they were also private events in the lives of the relatives and friends of those who died. People at home glimpsed their relations among those in the crowds at the matches, or believed they did: sons, daughters, husbands, or fathers. No previous generation has been faced with the same dilemma of whether to choose to go on watching. As for those without any particular connection with the episodes other than as spectators, they are watching in conditions quite unlike the conditions on the spot, their eyes and ears depending for their understanding on the programme-makers' selection of the sounds and shots available and the accompanying words of a commentator.

Whether, in such circumstances, the broadcaster's duty to the public interest, as opposed to any right he may have in the matter, is to carry on transmitting cannot be prescribed in advance. It is here that professional instinct comes into play, exercising whatever degree of restraint seems appropriate to the circumstances. On a strict interpretation, the only people who need to know immediately what is happening are those who are on the scene and in a position to help. The police, if they are having to direct the movements of large crowds, may find additional television pictures useful, but their value has nothing to do with providing the same pictures to an audience away from the scene. Even the ablest commentators, with the most skilled support, may be hard-pressed to make sense of the succession of events occurring before their eyes. However great their professionalism, they may be in something approaching a state of shock. There is a further factor to be taken into account. In 1985, following a fire in the grandstand at another football ground in the north of England, the transmission of scenes, including the sight of spectators with their clothes alight, took place in the afternoon when many children would have been watching television.

An analogy with the reporter or the cameraman on the battlefield only partly holds. He or she, and their audience, is prepared for the kind of incidents which may occur, including the sight of death, and such reports are, by their nature, very rarely transmitted live. Modern battles, in which set-pieces are a rarity, no more lend themselves to instantly coherent coverage than does the continuing turmoil of a major human disaster. As John Keegan, Defence Editor of the London *Daily Telegraph*, pointed out in an essay written in 1993:

The viewer cannot be shocked because the cameraman cannot capture, except by chance, the sort of image that has the power to shock. He must snatch what he can, often hoping that contingent factors—loss of focus, camera shake, bad sound—will, by indicating actuality, invest quite uninteresting film with authenticity and value.[1]

There will be times when the appropriate response for the broadcaster to make is to remain at the scene and to continue transmitting pictures, commentary, and sounds. There may be other times when it is right to concede the claims of privacy and allow the work of rescue to continue beyond the sight of anyone remote from the site of the disaster. The borderline between the display of compassion and lingering voyeuristically is often a narrow one.

The evidence in Britain suggests that younger people, as well as those involved in the rescue services, favour more explicit treatment of, for example, multiple car-crashes than do the rest of the audience. The young are simply that much more resilient, just as they appear more resilient towards the more extreme forms of fictional violence on the screen. People involved in the rescue services believe that the public will receive a stronger warning about the consequences of irresponsible driving if they can see its consequences at close quarters. This presents difficulties if the pictures are to be shown in news programmes shortly after an accident has occurred, at a time when relatives may not have been informed or have only just received news that the accident has taken place. Research in Britain has

---

[1] J. Keegan, 'Violence in Non-fictional Television', in Millwood Hargrave (ed.), *Violence in Factual Television* (Broadcasting Standards Council, London, 1993), 106–9.

shown that, after every accident, there are concerns among the television audience for the feelings of relatives and friends who may, with little or no warning, be confronted with dead or injured people whom they can identify.[2] There is the further danger of the desensitization which, as Tony Hall was noted in the previous chapter as saying, might follow repeated shots of carnage. Although there is evidence to suggest that public-service announcements warning against drink-driving are effective when they include realistic pictures of the results of accidents, the context in which the pictures are seen makes watching them an experience very different from that at the scene of an accident.

It has become a commonplace in cases of murder, especially when the victim is a child, for relations or friends to be interviewed, to make an appeal for witnesses or other kinds of information. This is often done at the request of the police, aware of the greater emotional impact which may be achieved by the visible stress of a parent or partner rather than by the appearance of a police officer using more official language. The cooperation offered by relatives on these occasions involves the surrender of their privacy which is usually made willingly. Inevitably, however, there will be, from time to time, cases where persuasion may overcome the better judgement of an individual or of a family. The normal circumstances of their lives have been destroyed and they are, as a result, vulnerable to even slight pressures from those who have come to help them. The programme-maker must be very certain of his own motives if he or she interferes in such circumstances and make sure that nothing is done for the purposes of a broadcast which might increase the existing level of distress.

Where the programme-maker is the initiator of such a broadcast, there is a case for saying that the same caution should be exercised, with a respect for the need not to aggravate any loss of dignity which the individual concerned has suffered or might later suffer. It has been argued that, in rare circumstances, the broadcaster may have to consider whether he or she has a duty to protect an individual or a family from themselves in the interests of the sensibilities of the watching audience.

This section has dealt so far with man-made disasters, but natural disasters, seeming to strip survivors of all their dignity just as they do the dignity of their victims, require the same consideration by the broadcasters. In treating natural disasters which occur in Britain and the United States, communication with the survivors and the rescue services is generally made easier by the use of a common language, although the existence of immigrant communities with a limited knowledge of English had added its own particular difficulties. Both language and a shared culture make it

---

[2] A. Shearer, *Survivors and the Media* (Broadcasting Standards Council, London, 1991).

easier for feelings to be understood, together with a sense that even the worst physical damage can, and eventually will, be made good by the country's own resources. There is less resignation and less cause for it. Natural disasters in developing countries, however, are more likely to be met with a fatalistic response and a knowledge that reconstruction, if it comes, is likely to be the result of individual or communal action rather than the fulfilment of some concerted, well-resourced, plan.

The coverage of disaster stories often concludes, for the time being at least, with funerals. The privacy of the bereaved is at its most vulnerable at such moments. The ending of one phase of their experience of loss and the beginning of the process of rehabilitation, however difficult it may for them to believe it, is marked by rituals in which strangers should become involved only with permission. Occasions of this kind are made no easier when they are taken over to advance a political purpose, sometimes contrary to the real wishes of the bereaved family.

Another Aspect

The increasing number of programmes which are built around what can loosely be called the emergency services raise privacy issues at the moments when they are likely to be at their most dramatic. The activities of the services frequently take them onto private property, not least when they are dealing with people who are not themselves the owners of the property. The police may pursue a burglar into a house, the fire service may be called to a factory. Or, as Ellen Alderman and Caroline Kennedy relate in their book *The Right to Privacy*,[3] a paramedical team may go into homes to treat the victim of a heart-attack. In the case they describe, which took place in Los Angeles, the team was accompanied by a camera crew collecting material for a future series. The victim died and, when the pictures of his final moments were shown, the family attempted to sue for breach of privacy. But the courts held that the privacy breached was that of the victim who, since he was dead, could not sue. The only ground on which an action could succeed would lie in trespass for the unsanctioned intrusion of the crew as they followed the paramedics into the victim's home. The television company went to appeal, arguing that the effect of the judgment would be to make impossible the fast response to news situations on which programmes depended and was contrary to the First Amendment. The issue was never carried to a conclusion, but ended in an undisclosed settlement.

[3] E. Alderman and C. Kennedy, *The Right to Privacy* (Vintage Books, New York, 1997), 176 ff.

Dramatizations

Courtrooms have always held a fascination for dramatists. The stylized playing-out within a confined arena of issues of right and wrong and, occasionally, of good and evil has furnished one popular plot after another, providing great actors and actresses with great performing opportunities. The plots have not always been fictitious and there have been many adaptations of famous trials for both the theatre and the cinema, as well as, more recently, for radio and television.

Murder is rarely a crime of old age. It usually occurs when the perpetrators are young or middle-aged. If their execution or a long spell in jail follows, they leave behind relatives with much of their lives left to complete. The relatives frequently choose to move away from the scene of the crime, hoping to create a new identity for themselves in a new setting. They change their name, as did Ethel LeNeve, mistress of Dr Crippen, one of those criminals whose story is most often retold, less for its mystery, of which the case held little, but for his capture, the result of an unprecedented radio signal sent to the ship on which Crippen and LeNeve, disguised as Crippen's nephew, were trying to escape from Britain. Where there is a mystery, then the prime suspect, untried or acquitted, may resume his life in the same locality. Flight would indicate guilt and offer, economically, no better prospects than those of remaining. Such people have a right to their privacy even if their stories retain, more than most murders do, a curiosity value greater than the fact of their occurrence. Unsolved crimes invite attempts at solutions, but the careless exposure of old identities or existing addresses constitutes a breach of privacy for which there can rarely be any justification.

Even where no such disclosure takes place, the individuals concerned, if they can be traced as a result of a programme, should have a right to be informed that a programme is about to be produced if it could draw them once again to public attention, despite the expectations and precautions of the programme-maker. In American law, they would be seen to be public figures and therefore have little chance of protection if they wished to object. Nor would their chances be much better in British law. Merely objecting would make them vulnerable since an unscrupulous programme-maker could make the fact of an objection known more widely.

Under the less burdensome American rules on contempt of court, it is possible to present a dramatization even before a trial has been held and a verdict reached. This was the case after two Texan military cadets had been accused of murder in 1995. The cadets, at separate military training schools, were engaged to be married when the male cadet had a brief affair with a young woman in his home town. His fiancée, from the same town, allegedly insisted, as the price of remaining engaged, that the young woman be killed. They were both charged with the subsequent murder. In February 1997, NBC broadcast a lengthy dramatization of these events called '*Love's Deadly Triangle*'. It included a sequence showing the murder being carried out by the pair at an isolated place on the edge of the town, followed by their appearance at the house of a friend where they asked for, and were given, a chance to clean up. At the end of the film, a caption stated that the accused couple were going to plead not guilty. They are going to be tried separately. The young woman, the first to be tried, was taken to court in February 1998. She denied her involvement in the murder which was, she said, carried out by her fiancé.

NBC replied to objectors by saying that the film was performing a valuable public service, alerting teenagers who watched it to the dangers of losing a sense of the value of human life under the pressures of teenage love. The *New York Times* quoted an NBC spokeswoman who said that it contained a lot of 'relateable things' that could have an impact on the teenage-audience.[4] Although the case had been closely followed in Texas, it had not been widely commented upon elsewhere in the States. Suggesting some confusion between the values of the courtroom and the values of the entertainment industry, the same report quoted the spokeswoman as saying that the case was unquestionably compelling and 'had not played out across the country'. The manager of the local NBC affiliate station, declining to carry the film despite the network's attempts to persuade him, said that local people would not see it as entertainment, even though the publicity differed very little from that given to the promotion of a fictional film, in its use, for example, of photographs of the leading players.

The murdered young woman's mother was another who did not see the film as entertainment. According to newspaper reports, she had not given permission for her daughter to be portrayed in the film, still less to be portrayed as promiscuous, which is how she believed the young woman would appear. She also objected to the portrayal of herself and the young woman's father in the film without their consent. However, the producer was reported to have argued in reply that she could not block her appearance because she had become a public figure. The threshold for identifying that status was, he said, increasingly low. If she had become, in law at least, a public figure, as indeed seems the case, it was quite involuntarily and, seemingly, contrary to her wishes.

---

[4] Article in *New York Times*, 3 Feb. 1997.

The case of *New York Times* v. *Sullivan* in 1964 established that the protection of the First Amendment would be given to attacks on public officials. It was held to be in the interests of free speech that citizens should be able to comment frankly on the conduct of public servants. Over the years, public officials have been joined as a class by public figures, a definition arrived at by a calculation of their relative newsworthiness.

It has, of course, always been true that a measure of privacy is inevitably lost when an event becomes the object of legitimate public interest, such as an accident or a crime creates. But that its loss should be aggravated or prolonged for the purposes of entertainment seems to be a fresh consideration. An American court has said that the boundary between information and entertainment is too elusive for the distinction to be made, but it seems to compound an individual's distress if third parties may stand to profit by the prolongation of exposure to the public gaze. Some crimes do catch the public imagination, because of the fame attached to one or other of the participants, as in the pre-war kidnapping of the Lindbergh baby, or some romantic element, like Crippen's flight with his mistress, or because of an enduring mystery where no criminal has been found. But it has usually taken time for such status to be reached and the re-creation of the crime to be warranted. Now it seems that, regardless of the fame, but mindful of the profit, instant re-creation has become acceptable, without thought for relatives and friends who may be trying to put their lives together again. Well-known crimes, such as that of the teenager Amy Fisher, who attempted to kill her older lover's wife, are more readily promoted on television than dramas featuring characters and plots never previously experienced.

The mother's were not the only objections to the transmission of the film. Lawyers acting for the male defendant objected to the inclusion in the film of a confession which, they claimed, had been obtained from him under a degree of duress which would make it inadmissible in a Texas court. They also objected to the interference with the judicial process which would follow if jurors who had seen the film had to be rejected. To which NBC's counsel responded by saying that jurors had proved themselves in the O. J. Simpson criminal trial to be capable of making up their own minds despite a wave of publicity surrounding that case which was even greater by the time the trial started than that surrounding the Texas case. He could see no difference between printing the information about the crime in a newspaper report and using it as the basis for a drama. Jurors were, in his view, perfectly capable of distinguishing between the two.

Some of the facts in the Texas case have their parallels with those surrounding the showing of *Beyond Reason*, a film transmitted on the ITV network in Britain in 1995. The film also told the story of a violent death under the influence of passion. This time it was the killing of a British army officer's wife in Northern Ireland, where her husband was stationed. Her killer was a young woman-soldier with whom her husband had been having an affair. She was subsequently convicted of the lesser offence of manslaughter rather than murder. The parents of the dead woman, like those of her husband, objected to the making of the film and it appears that the husband, although initially more inclined to cooperate with the production company, came to share that view at some stage in the production. Both families made strenuous efforts to dissuade the company responsible for its transmission from going ahead.

The legal issues in the Texas case have yet to be fully argued, but each case raises issues of privacy which may be looked at in principle. Both films thrust into the limelight three sets of parents whose lives had been brutally overturned. By the time the British film was shown, the British parents were some months past the particularly public experience of the trial and were, therefore, attempting, as far as possible, to rebuild their lives. The American parents had yet to reach that phase. The producing company in Britain claimed that not only was its story in the public domain, but it was in the public interest. It later withdrew this claim when the matter came before the Broadcasting Complaints Commission. In fact, neither story would appear to have any real pretension to serving the public interest, though there is a considerable degree of public curiosity about any kind of misconduct in the armed forces, not least when it involves officers or officers-in-the-making.

The suggestion was made that the British story showed up the vulnerability of subordinates in the army to exploitation, in this instance of a sexual kind, by their superiors, but it had never been raised as a matter of serious public concern at the time of the trial. The argument that the Texas case provided a powerful cautionary example to other teenagers is slender. Although some teenagers might be able to identify with the act of betrayal which prompted the crime, they would find it harder to sympathize with the couple themselves. It was not presented as a documentary since, in advance of the establishment of the facts at the trial, what was true and what was not true could not be stated with any degree of documentary certainty. Teenagers in America and elsewhere do not lack cautionary tales to warn them of the possible consequences of their behaviour, sexual or otherwise.

The Broadcasting Complaints Commission concluded that the broadcast of *Beyond Reason* was an unwarranted infringement of the privacy of the husband and his family, on whose behalf the complaint had been laid. It also agreed that his characterization in the film had been sufficiently distorted for the Commission to uphold his complaint of unfairness.[5]

There is no evidence that, in itself, such entertainment incites those who watch it to commit crimes on their own account. However, a distinction exists between the exploitation of trials long over and that of trials newly completed or still to be held. In the absence of a genuine public interest emerging from a recent trial or discernible in a trial yet to go court, the arguments for defying objections expressed by close relatives to the reconstruction of the crimes and their surrounding events seem weak, justified more by commercial advantage than by anything else. While the idea of compensating them financially for the intrusion into their private lives may be distasteful, so may be the thought of the commercial benefit being enjoyed by the producers of such material.

The evidence suggests that official curbs on outrageous assaults on privacy are impossible to maintain against the power of the market in satisfying the apparent wish of the public, even perhaps despite itself, to see the results of the violation of other people's privacy. Those who command the market are better placed to impose restraint in the name of decency. There is not, however, at present much evidence that they are very willing to do so.

[5] Adjudication by the Broadcasting Complaints Commission, London, 12 Oct. 1995.

9

In the Name of What?

In the opening chapters of this book, we looked, in turn, at the differences between the two societies and at the ways in which two differing regulatory structures have evolved. Then, in the third of them, we examined the different meanings of taste and decency before setting out the ways in which standards were established and applied. In the final chapter, we shall look at the motives for developing and maintaining the regulatory structures and consider what role they have to play in the very different future into which broadcasting is moving, no longer constrained by the shortage of frequencies marking its first eighty years.

As we noted in Chapter 2, the 1927 Radio Act, using a phrase to be repeated in its successor seven years later, stated that, in awarding licences, regard must be paid to 'the public interest, convenience and necessity'. Although the British planned no comparable distribution of frequencies, there was an expectation that the founding Governors of the BBC, who took up their work in the same year, would act as trustees of the national interest in broadcasting. The phrase had originally been used by the Crawford Committee in describing the role it was prescribing for the governing body of the new body it recommended should replace the original British Broadcasting Company. Its significance was real in a time when, less than a decade after the Armistice which ended the First World War, different attitudes prevailed towards the nation, still the possessor of a vast empire.

In neither country did its government define what was meant by the public interest on the one hand and, on the other, by the national interest. However, both rested on the idea that broadcasting was capable of carrying forward the ideal, then widely cherished, of a society embracing higher values, improved in that steady, but imperceptible, way described some years later by the BBC official quoted in Chapter 2. (Ironically, at the time he was writing that, other voices in the BBC were privately urging an end to the tradition of paternalism.)

By taking the commercial path in developing American broadcasting, however, the ideal was inevitably compromised by the needs of individual companies, even though it remains in the insistence that the FCC's licensees should have a limited number of public obligations imposed on them as a return for the benefits they derived from the use of a publicly owned asset. The best-known challenge to those obligations, which occurred in the *Red Lion* case, was rejected on the grounds that there were insufficient frequencies for all who wished to use them and that, as a consequence, the obligations, in that instance to provide a right of reply, were not unconstitutional.[1] Despite the abundance of new technologies and new forms of distribution, Congress and the American courts continue to acknowledge the distinctiveness of broadcasting stemming from the retention in public hands of the frequencies it depends upon. In the Telecommunications Act, 1996, Congress indicated that public interest requirements, yet to be precisely defined, must be met by broadcasters using the new channels. Whether enforcement of these requirements, whatever they turn out to be, will be more effective than enforcement in a previous age remains to be seen. As with the demands for public service programmes placed on the British terrestrial television licensees, much depends on the continuing financial buoyancy of the broadcasting sector and the willingness of commercial interests to accept the trade-off which such obligations represent. Neither cable and satellite services nor commercial radio stations are placed under similar obligations.

But regulation can exist for more reasons than alleviating the consequences of scarcity.

The Arguments for Regulation: Diversity and the Market

In broadcasting, regulation has been used to compensate for the deficiencies of the market, requiring the production of those programmes which commercially cannot pay their way, but whose presence is considered to be important to society. The needs of children provide an obvious example which is impervious to all but the most intemperate charges of elitism. Regulation can also be used to ensure that particular commercial interests do not dominate the market and influence the output of programmes to their own advantage. It is, after all, regulation in Britain which underpins

[1] *Red Lion Broadcasting Company* v. *FCC*, 395 US 367 (1969).

the innovative and experimental output of Channel 4. If the objectives of sustaining diversity by compulsion and controls on ownership seem removed from the issues of taste and decency with which we have been dealing, the impression is misleading. As those issues arise in programmes, the judgement applied to them by broadcasters or their regulators is in many instances, as we have noted earlier, a matter of context, of public expectations, and, inescapably, of quality. Quality is inseparable from intention. The blandness of much commercial broadcasting, justified by the broadcasters' obligations to advertisers and the sensitivities of the public, can be a curb on high-flying intentions with their risks of disaster. Such programmes, whose purpose is sometimes described as pushing out the envelope, require the existence of a sympathetic regime if they are to be attempted, let alone fulfilled. The substance of regulation, therefore, plays a crucial part in the evolution of a climate in which, as an essential ingredient in a responsible broadcasting service, conventional standards, whether of decency, taste, or other things, may be challenged as well as protected.

Although controls on the ownership of broadcasting stations have existed in the United States, they have not been directed, as a primary purpose, at ensuring a diverse range of output. The dangers foreseen in a concentration of ownership have been primarily political. The FCC has frequently been subjected to heavy criticism from the industry for any kind of involvement in the field of content. Two areas, in particular, which have appeared to be of particular concern to the Commission, children's programmes and coverage of public affairs, have not gained much ground under its tutelage. The greater pressure placed on companies from September 1997 to improve their output for children, as was suggested earlier, will not show positive results on any scale for some time to come.

The principal exception in the States to the deficiencies of the service provided for children has come from the publicly funded PBS. This has happened despite the severe constraints imposed on its finances over the years in an environment which strikes an outsider, and no doubt still more an insider, as habitually hostile. Among commercial broadcasters, in the States but also increasingly in Britain, much coverage of public affairs, reflecting changed emphases in the policies of a new breed of owners, has tended to become more closely identified with the idiom of entertainment which predominates on the networks. It is an idiom which demands, with only rare exceptions, simple stories quickly told. In this field, PBS has proved a consistent exception once again, but its increased dependence on commercial backing, as public financial support declined, puts it at risk from even the most high-minded of its supporters. In the autumn of 1997, there was, however, news of a proposal which, if congressional approval were secured, would enable PBS, modelling itself on the British Channel 4, to take a limited amount of advertising. This would be used to fund the making of a range of new American programming dissimilar to the normal run of advertising-supported material which provides only a limited range of subject-matter. The regular audience for PBS has traditionally tolerated boundaries to taste and decency wider than those prevailing on the networks, with a consequent widening of the range of its output.

The British have described as 'public service broadcasting' that balance of programming, brought about by regulation, which equitably, as opposed to equally, reflects majority and minority interests, in acknowledgement that very few people do not, at different times, move from one group to the other and back again. It is a phrase which fell out of fashion during the 1980s when it was falsely equated with a kind of elitism and accused of pre-empting for itself alone the concept of public service which others, including commercial interests, fulfilled no less. It also suffered during that decade, when an Orwellian simplicity of 'Private good, public bad' prevailed, in a general assault on the broad tradition of public service for its failure to lend itself readily to mathematical measurements of success.

That public service broadcasting responds to the needs of the audience rather than to their wants is true. Wants can be defined relatively easily by the size of respective audiences, running the risk that ever smaller lists of wants which satisfy the largest numbers of people will emerge as the process continues. Needs, however, are defined by more careful analyses. Their definition does not have to be elitist, the choice of those people whose goodwill a previous Director General of the BBC thought had to be justified.[2] It can be established by a combination of experiment and experience: the experiment of developing programmes in new subject-areas or with fresh talent and the experience gained by the response to their transmission. The positive injunction to innovate and experiment laid upon Channel 4 in legislation is a specific expression of an ideal of public service broadcasting. When John Birt, the BBC's current Director General, told me that he considered the BBC's legitimacy came as much from the audience as from the state, he was, in effect, saying that it was the satisfaction of the audience's needs which justified the BBC's claim for support from the state.[3] Selection there has to be in any system and the treatment of the market as the only expression of democratic choice reflects a narrow view of democracy. If everyone could trade in the market in equal terms,

[2] See pp. 22–3.   [3] Personal interview, London, 21 Apr. 1997.

153

then perhaps it would come closer to the ideals of equality which underlie democracy, but it cannot be forgotten that, in commercial broadcasting, the market is one for audiences, not for ideas.

The similarity between the apparent state of broadcasting and that of the Press has grown more striking with each new technological advance made in broadcasting. In both countries, competition between newspapers has led, in certain markets, to the emergence of a single, dominant, force through the elimination of its less economically successful rivals, reducing the variety of opinions available to the readerships in those markets. In the United States, the editorial freedoms of the Press and, to a lesser extent, broadcasting are protected from government interference by the First Amendment and, in the case of broadcasting, also by the Communications Act. In Britain, there is a tradition of independence which is embodied in the constitution of the major broadcasting institutions and exists in the Press, although qualified in the numerous ways described by Harold Evans in the opening chapter of this book. There are, however, no protections from the kind of interference which can arise from economic pressures, not simply with the expression of opinion, but, if only potentially, with the selection of news. Many modern proprietors of print media, as well as owners of broadcasting companies, are involved in a variety of activities. Their expansion is almost inevitable, big has to grow bigger in order to survive. Some of these additional interests are close to the media, but others are quite remote, although of legitimate interest in their own right to the public. The dangers of news management in the interests of the proprietors must, therefore, be added to the dangers of the circumscribing of opinions. The traditional role of the Press in keeping watch on politicians was a reaction to the power which politicians exercised. In modern society, industry and business are frequently at least as powerful. Theodore Roosevelt's claim that big business needed big government may be currently unfashionable, but the public has need of strong and independent media if industry and business are to be held accountable to a constituency larger than their own investors.

The Arguments for Regulation: Editorial Oversights

To the arguments for regulation in the interests of avoiding what the American navy called in 1910 'etheric bedlam' and of diversity of output, we must add a third which bears most directly on the concerns of this book, the oversight of editorial content. In comparison with newspapers, there has been much greater concern about the effects of television and radio on their audiences. In the particular fields of taste and of decency, with the exceptions of obscenity, indecent speech, and profanity, it is an area into which the role of the FCC extends only as far as is compatible with the First Amendment and the absence of censorship required by the Communications Act. The concern over taste and decency is not as exclusively about incitement to antisocial behaviour as it is over violence on the screen. It is also about the 'harm' and 'hurt' which might be caused by, for example, dismissive or degrading treatment of disabilities or forms of racial or religious abuse which diminish individual dignity. Regulation, therefore, in Britain, is expected to ensure that, as far as possible, the audience is made aware in advance of, and ultimately protected from, those things which might, in one way or another, be damaging to them, particularly to children. It is also intended to protect the audience from unnecessary affronts, whether as individuals or, more generally, as a group within society, such as the followers of a particular faith, or society itself.

There is a day-to-day responsibility on the part of the commercial broadcasters in Britain to comply with the regulators' requirements, part of the compliance procedures which in the past ten years have come to employ large numbers of staff in the commercial companies. The codes and guidance notes which lay down the rules to be followed, as a condition of their licences, are a form of advance regulation which, if not observed, may lead to intervention by the regulator after transmission. In the absence of close official regulation in the United States and of any collective code, the work is done, in the companies' own commercial interests, by the networks' Standards and Practices Departments, with responsibilities divided between news and entertainment. Advertisers, on whom the companies' fortunes depend, are reluctant, as history has shown more graphically in the United States than in Britain, to buy into an audience which is discomfited by any aspect of the programme it is watching.

The Arguments for Regulation: A Public Appetite

The belief that the British public wishes to be reassured about the quality of the programmes it is being offered and protected from, or least alerted to the possibility of, any 'harm' which the programme might cause ran as a persistent current throughout many of the conversations which I had with senior British broadcasters. Peter Rogers, Chief Executive of the ITC, cited the evidence for this belief in research conducted for the Commission in 1996.[4] It showed that, of the sample of 1,752 people

---

[4] MORI poll result, commissioned by the ITC, 1996.

questioned, 59 per cent believed that regulation was very important and a total of 7 per cent felt that it was either not very important or not important at all. A marginally smaller percentage of 57 per cent considered that the level of regulation of commercial television was currently about right. These figures have to be set against the percentages of 67 per cent and 61 per cent who wanted more regulation respectively of violence and swearing in daytime and the early evening. Forty-one per cent of the sample considered that more control over violence should be exercised in the late evening, that is, after 9.00 p.m., the Watershed hour described in Chapter 4.

Rogers's predecessor as Chief Executive, David Glencross, agreed, saying that there had always been support for regulation. The public wants to feel, he said, that there is somebody in charge of what is being broadcast.[5]

The same point was made rather differently by David Lloyd, a staff member at the Radio Authority, responsible for overseeing the commercial radio stations:

> I think that people are definitely reassured by the existence of some sort of regulation of this thing which is seen to be all powerful, called media. I think if you look at the number of letters which we receive, the way in which they are written, and the tone of the telephone callers to us, they really do want to talk to somebody about this and to get something done. They want to get it off their chests and they want to talk to someone who has some influence in it. And they want to talk to an independent body . . .
> Q. What is different about broadcasting?
> A. . . . There is a great tradition of broadcasting in this country being very carefully and heavily regulated. And people still look to that and expect those standards to be carried forward . . . and, of course, in radio . . . there's the way it's consumed.[6]

I put the same question to Michael Grade, then in his final days as the Chief Executive of Channel 4. He agreed that there was a public wish for regulation in the particular field of taste and decency.

Television is still a very big part of people's lives and, therefore, the regulatory paraphernalia which has grown up, imperfect as it is, has obviously given the public a degree of confidence in their broadcasting. It's hard to quantify, and hard to touch, but I think the level of patronage of television, reports of television, the relationship between the public and their television sets, is unlike any other country that I have been to. There is an intimacy, a loyalty and a feeling of belonging. Television is so important to people's lives in this country . . . the tradition in this country is one of trust and all the great institutions before broadcasting,

5 Personal interview, London, 5 May 1997.
6 Personal interview, London, 30 Apr. 1997.

they're all about people who are entrusted to look after things on behalf of the nation . . . In all the recent privatizations of the public utilities, you have a very complex regulatory framework that's been placed there to watch over the public interest.[7]

I was made aware of no similar feeling in the United States about the desirability of regulation directed at the protection of the audience. Children provided the only exception. A lawyer to whom I talked in Washington suggested that parents, increasingly aware of their powerlessness in impressing children's needs upon the broadcasters, were inclining towards regulation of sexually orientated speech or speech directed to children, as an alternative to the present situation. Newton Minow, with others, saw regulation as a means of providing better programmes for children in the States and reducing the output of programmes unsuitable for the child-audience, aims which he considered fell squarely within any definition of the public interest which the FCC was required to consider. It could no longer be done, he thought, through pressure on the schedules of the commercial companies in the United States.[8] There had been sufficient failures of that approach, as Henry Geller, with his long experience of the FCC, agreed, to make it vain to try it again. The solution of a separate channel for children's programmes, funded by a levy on broadcasters for their use of the spectrum, was a ghetto solution, but that had to be better than no solution and only a continuation of the present neglect of children's needs.[9]

Since both Rogers and Lloyd might be expected, as regulators, to say what they did about a wish for regulation among the public, it is useful to provide the different perspective put on their work by Andy Allan, Director of Programmes at Carlton Television in London:

I think that there is an assumption among some regulators that the public will be disturbed by something when, in fact, the public will not be in the least disturbed by it. The regulators desire to intervene where there has not been registered any public complaint. It seems to me that the regulators are sometimes making assumptions not based on knowledge, not based on science, but based probably on their own feelings and I think they have to be wary about that. Where there is no public outcry, this is dangerous territory to assume . . . If you can establish that similar things have caused harm, I don't think that you can just assume that with no factual basis whatsoever that [harm has occurred again] . . . I think there has to be some empirical evidence . . . You can define 'harm' in a very esoteric way. You can talk about the coarsening of society . . . I think that there is a political agenda which would cheerfully like the media blamed for all the evils of society because it's

[7] Personal interview, London, 30 Apr. 1997.
[8] Personal interview, Chicago, 11 Nov. 1996.
[9] Personal interview, Washington, 12 Feb. 1997.

easier to do that than deal with other things. It worries me when regulators start by seeking to please their political masters by taking that on board.[10]

Allan may be exaggerating the extent to which regulators, in their interventions with companies after the transmission of a programme, respond to the wishes of the Government or even of the Minister responsible for broadcasting. In my own experience, ministerial pressure was usually exerted over issues of taste and decency when there was public anxiety about an aspect of broadcasting, most commonly violence in television programmes. Ministers may wish to be seen to be taking action, even if only of a symbolic kind.

The expression of ministerial concerns over the portrayal of sex has become more rare in recent years. As I described in Chapter 2, ministerial pressure on the BBC in the 1960s to subscribe to the same conditions over taste and decency as the ITA came, in a very different climate over such matters, as a result of a build-up of feeling among a section of the public about declining moral standards, by which they meant primarily sexual conduct. The borders of public sensibilities shift backwards and forwards, in the way that Andy Allan described earlier in this chapter. The pendulum of opinion has swung in both directions, in particular over taste issues, many times in the past seventy-five years. In the case of decency, it is not unchanging, but swings more slowly. Being responsive, after careful scrutiny of the reasons, to such shifts is a proper part of a regulator's duty. I was told at the ITC that, nowadays, they would be unlikely to give their approval, retrospectively as the law now stands, to the showing before the Watershed of a love-scene in the film *Ryan's Daughter*, although, in the 1980s, it had gone out at 7.30 p.m. The 1980s, the Commission believed, was a more abrasive period than the 1990s.

Regulators, like broadcasters themselves, may take action in response to complaints. They may also be prompted by their own sense that a programme has gone further than is justified in comparison with a similar programme at a similar time, or, in the absence of any close comparison, by a feeling that the boundaries of acceptability have been breached, the 'know-it-when-I-see-it' feeling expressed about obscenity by Justice Potter Stewart, but also sensed about several other issues by experienced regulators.

Evidence of a breach may be offered in written or telephoned complaints. Such complaints always need to be treated with caution. Apart from their use by pressure groups, they are often too small in numbers to be regarded as a fair reflection of the feelings of an audience, often thousands or even millions of times larger. David Lloyd agreed that the Radio

[10] Personal interview, London, 12 May 1997.

Authority, with a large number of small stations within its jurisdiction, would regard five letters of complaint about a single topic as a signal of an unusual degree of concern among the audience. The ITC, whose television licensees typically serve much larger audiences, like the BBC, receives rather larger number of letters and telephone calls, occasionally running into hundreds, but rarely more. The sense of individual involvement with the BBC produced by the payment of the licence fee is clear in many of the letters addressed to the Corporation, especially from an older generation of correspondents.

I was told at one of the US networks that, in a single season, they might receive no more than 3,000 letters on all topics, confirming perhaps a different relationship with broadcasting in the States from that existing in Britain and described by Michael Grade earlier in this chapter. As for the involvement of Congressmen in individual complaints, this was much rarer than interventions by British MPs on behalf of their constituents. Some of the interventions are no more than those of a forwarding agent, but others involve much deeper engagement, sometimes with a political purpose, with the issues raised by a complainant. Two Members of Parliament were, for example, very active in pursuing the privacy issues of *Beyond Reason*, described in Chapter 8. Few complaints can simply be dismissed as so untypical that no notice should be taken of them.

Where a complaint about the standards of a broadcast is laid before the statutory Broadcasting Standards Commission, which is empowered to act in response to a single complaint, broadcasters will usually defend their judgements, but may concede the justice of the complaint, as they do in a significant minority of cases. If a single complaint seems an inadequate cue for starting what may be a process of investigation costly in time and money, the response has to be that a determined complainant could quickly rally sufficient support to reach a minimum total, but also, more importantly, that a viewer or a listener with a grievance is entitled to have it considered if it falls within the Commission's remit.

The increased attention which is paid to complainants in Britain is a development which has gained pace since the early 1970s, quickening again at the start of the 1990s. It is a form of increased accountability to the audience, its growth a response to the changing mood of British society more generally.

The uses of regulation which I have described in the last few pages take their authority from the duties laid on regulators to observe the public interest, or, in the case of the BBC, the national interest. I discussed the meaning of those phrases in both America and Britain, but asked first what were the moral responsibilities of governments towards broadcasting.

Moral Responsibilities

In creating a series of broadcasting institutions, the two governments were putting at arm's length the oversight of broadcasting, partly an administrative function, partly an exercise in moral judgements. I asked Don West, Editor of *Broadcast and Cable* magazine, what he thought were the moral responsibilities of the US Government towards broadcasting. West, a First Amendment absolutist as he had made clear in the conversation reported in Chapter 7, replied, 'None.' When I repeated the question as 'None at all?', he again said 'None,' but added, in a cautionary phrase he had used before in our conversation, that if you gave the Government an inch, it would take a mile.[11]

I put the same question to Keith Spicer, the former Chairman of the Canadian Radio/Television and Telecommunications Commission (CRTC). Canada has one of the most highly regulated communications systems anywhere in the West. The Commission has oversight not simply of technical issues in communications, but also of their social and cultural aspects. Central to its duties is the preservation of the Canadian national identity and its cultural sovereignty, the constant concern of a small country with a neighbour large and powerful, not least in the activities of its broadcasting media. Spicer, after stating the Government's obligation to ensure the fair distribution of frequencies and providing for fair competition, then listed the protection of vulnerable minorities, including children, laying particular stress on protection from violent material, and the preservation of the heritage.[12]

Christopher Bland, the Chairman of the BBC, to whom I also put the question, extended the Government's practical responsibilities to the active encouragement of the broadcasting industry to take a leading place in the global development of broadcast communications and added a responsibility for ensuring that the educational possibilities of broadcasting were properly exploited.[13]

Neither mentioned the assurance of the conditions for an accurate and impartial news service as an obligation on governments in democratic societies. Both Bland and Spicer, however, mingled issues which are more obviously of a moral kind with practical issues which are the administrative concern of governments, such as frequency-allocation and fair competition. But, in fact, a moral dimension is not entirely missing when frequency-allocation is a matter for judgement between rival bids. In

---

[11] Personal interview, Washington, 10 Feb. 1997.
[12] Personal interview, Paris, 29 Apr. 1997.
[13] Personal interview, London, 6 May 1997.

Britain, with the exception of the BBC and the Welsh Fourth Channel which are allotted their frequencies directly by Government, the choice of licensees to use the frequencies allocated for commercial broadcasting is the responsibility of the independent regulatory bodies. In the United States, the responsibility rests on the FCC. With its obligation to consult the public interest, the FCC must satisfy itself that its potential licensee will observe certain minimum standards in conducting its activities as a broadcaster. The same is true of the Radio Authority in Britain and the Independent Television Commission, although neither is specifically charged with observing either the national or public interest. However, as we noted, the ITC, in issuing licences for its terrestrial services, is required to take account of the quality of programming proposed by the licensee, which can raise moral concerns.

In considering, next, the history of the national interest in broadcasting, it is inevitable that attention in this section of the present chapter should be focused mainly on the BBC. It alone, in both countries, had the national interest invoked at its birth and, indeed, gave unchallenged expression to it for three decades. It remains, moreover, a publicly funded body, distinguished by the source of its income from the Welsh Fourth Channel in Britain and by the source of its income and its function as a broadcaster from the American Corporation for Public Broadcasting.

The National Interest in Broadcasting

The idea of a trust in broadcasting has stayed at the heart of thinking about broadcasting in Britain. It underlay the establishment of the BBC and, nearly thirty years later, of the ITA. The BBC in its trustee-role faced no serious challenges to its position during the first years of its existence. There was little active demand from the public for an alternative service, although the listeners who tuned in to English-language broadcasts from European stations were evidence of a restiveness at the absence of a real alternative to the BBC. The commercial interests which lobbied for opportunities to advertise on British radio made little headway. They had to be content with placing their commercials on those European channels to which fugitive listeners in British were turning.

With the outbreak of the Second World War in 1939, the BBC was provided with the opportunity to consolidate its position at the heart of the nation. There could be no simpler, more urgent, definition of the national interest than the winning of the war. Everything was subservient to that. The BBC succeeded in resisting the intention of the Government to suspend the Board of Governors, but, for a time, their numbers were reduced to two. The BBC's output was carefully monitored. Taste and decency were not overlooked in the stresses of the conflict. In addition to its security advisers, one member of the BBC's staff was known, at least unofficially, as the 'dirt' censor, 'vulgar' programmes being thought to have an adverse effect on the morale of the audience.[14] How strong the evidence was for this is not clear, but the BBC's preoccupation with 'vulgarity' had been of long standing.

Although the return of a large Labour majority in the general election in 1945 signalled a deep-rooted wish for change, it did not significantly alter the position of the BBC, greatly strengthened by the near-universal respect it had gained since 1939. The breaking of the television monopoly by the Television Act of 1955, described in more detail in Chapter 2, was a concession less to popular feeling than to the pressures on the old guard of the Conservative Government, headed by Churchill, from people outside Parliament and a minority of MPs. The BBC no longer exercised uniquely its trust of the national interest, whatever precisely that was. The two bodies might not agree on the interpretation they gave it. While no trustee-role had been conferred on the new Independent Television Authority, the two bodies were thought of in similar terms. In 1965, a newspaper, criticizing the conduct of the BBC's Governors, compared them unfavourably with the ITA as a trustee of the national interest.[15] The new Authority consisted of men and women drawn from the same sections of society as the Governors of the BBC. Later, a Chairman of the Authority was to be made Chairman of the BBC, a move described resentfully in the BBC as resembling the appointment of the German Field Marshal Rommel to take command of the British Eighth Army during the war. A few years afterwards, the then-Vice-Chairman of the BBC became Chairman of the Authority with no significant comment.

The Suez crisis in the autumn of 1956 genuinely divided the nation with a particular urgency dictated by the circumstances in which Britain and France, in order to help the new state of Israel, were contemplating an invasion of Egypt. The Labour Party, out of office since 1951, were opposed to the venture. After the Prime Minister, Anthony Eden, had broadcast on 3 November, arguing that the invasion was intended to separate the warring Israelis and Egyptians, the BBC, taking a different view of the national interest, accepted the demand of the Leader of the Opposition, Hugh Gaitskell, for a right of reply. The broadcast followed on the next evening. Gaitskell claimed that the real purpose of the invasion was the recovery of the Suez Canal Zone, recently returned to the Egyptians after many years of British occupation.

[14] BBC archives, RH34/275/1.
[15] A. Briggs, *Governing the BBC* (BBC, London, 1979), 18.

In the subsequent debate, when Britain and France, under heavy pressure from the United States, had pulled their forces out again, the BBC was harshly criticized by some Conservative MPs for its lack of patriotism and failure to support the national interest as the Government had interpreted it. If, since 1955, there had been two bodies interpreting the national interest in broadcasting, now it was clear that the BBC and the Government could read the national interest differently.

There were to be echoes of the same resentment twenty-five years later when criticisms were made of the BBC for its treatment of the dispute with Argentina over the Falkland Islands. Particular anger was expressed about what appeared to be a sympathetic reference by a BBC official to the 'widows of Buenos Aires', a contrast to the the the *Sun*'s triumphantly headlined 'Gotcha' when an Argentinian warship was sunk.

The national interest had come increasingly to be equated with the interests of the reigning political party. I asked the present Chairman of the BBC, Christopher Bland, how relevant he considered any talk of the national interest in broadcasting remained today:

It is not our job, the Government right or wrong. Even in moments like the Suez crisis and the Falklands crisis, the BBC has seen itself not as being responsible for protecting the national interest as defined by the Government of the day, but for protecting the public interest which is to be properly informed about both sides of the argument both domestic and international. I think that's probably what's happened to it.[16]

The gradual merging of national into public interest was also decribed by David Glencross, Chief Executive of the Independent Television Commission from 1991 to 1996:

I think it's easier to hijack the concept of the national interest, you know, by flag-waving than it is to hijack the public interest which really has the meaning of public benefit, devoid of any sense of any kind of political party affiliations. Politicians who talk of 'the public interest' rarely mean it in the interests of their own political party, even at the height of elections. I think that's the difference.[17]

Between Suez and the Falklands War, the inappropriateness of the 'national interest' as an expression of the BBC's responsibilities grew more marked. The first post-war generation, as it came to maturity, lacked the same feelings about nationality as their elders. They launched successive challenges to the way things were, abandoning old conventions for new. At one extreme, when people took to the streets in political protests, the Union Jack became material for knickers.

---

[16] Personal interview, London, 6 May 1997.
[17] Personal interview, London, 5 May 1997.

Under the influence of a reforming Director General, Hugh Greene, many of the changes were articulated in BBC programmes. Greene, taking office in 1959, had been charged with rebuilding the BBC's audiences, which had been greatly reduced during the first years of commercial competition. Greene succeeded not by competing, as the conventions of television competition had it, with like programme placed against like, but by stimulating a range of programmes which caught the mood of change running through the nation.

Inside the BBC, as Asa Briggs has described in his essay on governing the BBC, it was argued that this was not in the public interest, the first, unheralded, use of the phrase in the essay.[18] (Charles Curran, Greene's immediate successor, also moves without preliminaries from 'national interest' to 'public interest' in his book on the BBC.)[19] Greene's policies, it was also feared, by concentrating on a minority of radical, controversial, programmes could eclipse in the public mind the great majority of other programmes which continued to serve other needs and so undermine political support for the licence fee. Greene's task, however, in restoring the BBC's standing would have been much harder if he had not caught the mood of challenge in the country.

It was he who, frequently and significantly, used the metaphor of a mirror in the debate about values in broadcasting. In an earlier phase, the BBC had believed that, as an expression of the trustee-role, it had a moral purpose to pursue, a view which, as noted in Chapter 2, was most energetically advanced by its first Director General. It was a Christian purpose, but one which accorded at the time with the general disposition of society. A bridge between the Greene position and that of Reith was supplied by Sir William Haley, Director General from 1944 until 1952. He said that, while Christian values should predominate in the BBC's programmes, the Christian faith could not become the criterion of everything the BBC did. One of its most important duties, said Haley, was the promotion of tolerance.[20]

But if it becomes easier, and more natural, to talk of the BBC serving the public interest, as other broadcasters do, rather than an elusive national interest distinct from it, it is important to note that, although the public interest benefits indirectly from a better understanding abroad of British national policies, life, and attitudes, the external services of the BBC primarily serve the interest of Britain as a nation-state among other nation-states. They would, if some politicians had their way, serve it with a more discernibly propagandist edge. Currents of opinion within the country

---

[18] Briggs, *Governing the BBC*, 18.
[19] C. Curran, *A Seamless Robe* (Collins, London, 1979), ch. VI.
[20] Curran, op. cit., 94.

which ran counter to the official stance would be disregarded, despite the evidence that acknowledgement of their presence strengthens the trust placed on the services by foreign audiences: the very tolerance urged by Haley.

Christopher Bland pointed to the use of education as one of the moral responsibilities of broadcasting, identifying a national interest to be served by broadcasting. As long as the nation-state retains a high degree of sovereignty, there will be a national interest in maintaining a distinct identity culturally and socially.

For a long time after the war, the BBC tried to insist on its position as 'the national instrument of broadcasting', protesting to the Government when the words were omitted from its announcements on broadcasting. The concept, however, began to be seriously eroded after 1954. Then, for the first time, the Corporation faced a rival television service to be regulated by a mirror-image of itself: a group of men and women chosen from much the same sections of society as the BBC Governors had always been, the reservoir of 'the great and good', as it is generally called. Nevertheless, as we have noted, there was no reference to any form of trusteeship in the statute governing the new authority.

Everyone in the BBC whom I asked about its role as 'the national instrument in broadcasting' replied that the phrase was out of date. They preferred the BBC to be thought of as the national broadcaster, providers of the service to which the audience turned when it wished to be reminded of itself as a nation: in times of national emergency, for instance, or the celebration of some national success or at Christmas. Several of them, including the current Director General, John Birt, mentioned the public's attitude to programmes in 1995 to mark the fiftieth anniversary of VJ-Day. The programmes, recalling a war fought long ago in a distant place, had, despite that, brought a response from a far wider section of the population than simply the dwindling band of veterans and their families. Birt said:

We are very pleased and proud of those moments when we have a sense that the whole nation is drawn together by something we do, whether it's great comedy like *One Foot in the Grave*, or the Christmas *Only Fools and Horses*, or the marking of the anniversary of VJ-Day.[21]

There was a phrase about the BBC which was current for some years from the end of the 1950s. The phrase was 'the national cement' and it was applied to the BBC for the role it played increasingly, as the influence of the Church declined, as a unifying force. It was used by the then-

---

[21] Personal interview, London, 21 Apr. 1997.

Chairman of the BBC, Sir Michael Swann, in talking to the Annan Committee, the Government-appointed committee of inquiry into broadcasting, which sat between 1974 and 1977. Not only did the BBC, as it is still capable of doing, draw listeners and viewers together when they were conscious of themselves as part of a nation, occasions which might be as solemn as Armistice Day or sporting, like the Soccer Cup Final, but it covered, in the course of a year, a number of events which, with large audiences or small, amounted to an annual calendar reflecting a variety of the nation's activities.

I referred to the 'national cement' with a certain apprehension in the States, afraid that it smacked of a society very different in temper from the one which I was coming to understand existed in America. The national calendar which I believed the BBC had reflected in Britain contained a number of events which involved an established church and an unelected head of state, for neither of which did any parallel exist in the United States. Moreover, the Federal Government, it had been explained to me, exists to protect the freedoms of the people in the way that the people want them protected and as the people had defined them in the Constitution and the Bill of Rights. The sound of a national voice, a characteristic of most European broadcasting systems until recently, most conspicuously in Britain, may, therefore, be inappropriate in such a very different kind of society. I should not have been puzzled when, having asked two or three different people for a list of major national events in the States, most of the list was linked to sport or other forms of entertainment. As exceptions, there was the President's annual State of the Union speech and an Inaugural Speech every four years. Thanksgiving and Christmas are holidays and times for family reunions, but, like St Valentine's Day, which appeared on one list, seemed as much of a sales opportunity as a genuine day for general celebration.

More than one of the people to whom I talked believed that it is entertainment, with its ability to carry the sharing of experiences into every corner of life, which has a strong claim to provide the national cement in the United States. The fragmentation of the television audience as new channels appeared was regretted by more than one of the people to whom I talked because it further threatened a sense of unity. It was said that the Superbowl would soon become the only event to draw together the people of America in a common experience. But fragmented or not, entertainment remains a dominant influence. It digests events to regurgitate them in a palatable form, wiping out the no man's land between fact and fiction so that real-life lawyers, policemen, and criminals are perceived through the conventions of the imagination, encouraged to play out roles as stereotypes. Entertainment supplies a significant part of the vocabulary in which

the national dialogue in America, and increasingly in Britain, is conducted. We have long grown accustomed to the use of 'scenario' in talk of
an impending war, the fortunes of the stock market, or anywhere else
where a hypothesis is under test. In Chapter 8, we heard of a murder case
which had not 'played widely' in the States, as if its possibilities remained
ripe for exploitation, as, indeed, they did. We perceive life as a succession of
stories, slightly surprised when we cannot immediately watch the replay
to relive the experience and impatient when they cannot provide a quick
resolution.

The Public Interest in Broadcasting

Definitions of the public interest are numerous, but none wholly convincing. David Glencross's definition of it as 'public benefit' is open to the question of who is to determine the benefit, particularly the extent to which, in
broadcasting, it covers issues of content beyond a basic trio of 'information, education, and entertainment'. Lawrence Grossman, former President of PBS, expressed the difficulties the words had caused in the United
States:

This society has been driven by commercial, individual, enterprise as opposed to
any sense of public, or state, or civic enterprise. It's all volunteer, so that the way
broadcasting grew in this country is very characteristic, with a kind of independence. The effort to regulate it . . . was always quite an operation. Nobody ever
quite knew how to do it. Even the public interest, the standard of 'public interest,
convenience and necessity', was taken over from the Commerce Department who'd
applied it to Transportation. But nobody knew what standard to hold it against. So
it's always been a uphill battle to try to figure out what standard . . . Here, unlike
the veneration for elite values that there is in other societies, such as Great Britain,
so that you can have a standard which everyone would bow down to, there's not
only not a veneration for elite values, there's an absolute distrust. And yet at the
same time, in many ways, there's a much more rigid sense of puritanism which is
concerned about religious faith and an orthodoxy.[22]

The FCC, taking the public interest into account when granting licences, has looked to the licensees, in return for use of the spectrum, to
observe certain requirements: an awareness of local needs and interests,
dedication of time to informational programming, and to cater for children. In the Blue Book, it categorized a series of fourteen different kinds of
programme as representing the public interest. It has not, however, given
indications of how much time is to be given to programmes of these particular kinds. I suggested in Chapter 2 that quotas of specific programming

[22] Personal interview, New York, 30 Jan. 1997.

imposed on companies are of dubious advantage. They give no indication of quality, with the cheapjack scoring equally with the best. Indeed, that was made clear yet again in the attempt of the companies, following the requirement in the 1990 Children's Act for a quota of informational programming, to pass off as informational material which, on examination, had no informational value at all. On the other hand, an absence of guidance about the volume of output called for by the regulator is open encouragement to evasion by licensees disposed to produce a minimum of non-profitable material. If a disposition towards quality does not exist in the broadcaster, then it is wholly unlikely to be achieved by any form of coercion.

Tom Krattenmaker and Lucas A. Powe, in *Regulating Broadcast Programming*, are, however, scornful of 'the public interest', dismissing it as simply a device for protecting the interests of the elite.[23] They reflect the strong body of opinion in the United States that the only practical interpretation of the public interest is in the market-place. Many of them are persuaded that, in broadcasting, any alternative definition will run contrary to America's traditional values of free expression. They can point to the fact that, each day, the large commercial sector of American television, whatever methods are used for distributing its signals, gives much satisfaction to its audiences across the country, with far fewer of the gaps in the market-place than were obvious a few years ago. Taking the same line, Don West, Editor of *Broadcasting and Cable* magazine in Washington, in his own words a First Amendment absolutist, regards commercial broadcasting as the true public service because of its ability to respond to the audience. He believes that the deficiencies which might once have justified the organization of Public Broadcasting to remedy them have now disappeared. Cable, with its high penetration of the audience and its ability to cater for minorities, is making them good.[24]

By contrast, Henry Geller, with a long experience of watching 'the public interest' at work, believes that it has failed to achieve its intended purposes. He was one of three people who cited the coming of competition, with its impact on profitability, as a cause of failure. Geller said that much damage was done by the decision of the FCC in 1982 to end its anti-trafficking rules, under which the sale of stations had been prohibited for three years after they had changed hands. The argument was that, if a station was transferred to a 'higher valued use', that was automatically beneficial to the public interest. Stations, therefore, found ways to increase their

---

[23] T. Krattenmaker and L. A. Powe, *Regulating Broadcast Programming* (MIT Press, Cambridge, Mass., 1994).

[24] Personal interview, Washington, 10 Feb. 1997.

profits by lowering programme standards and, in effect, fattened themselves up for market.[25]

Geoffrey Cowan, Dean of the Annenberg School in Los Angeles, also believed that the cause of the public interest was seriously damaged when FCC regulations were changed to make it easier for owners to sell to the highest bidder. Buyers found the cost of paying off the purchase price absorbed the surplus profits with which to pay for service to the public interest. He cited the example of a radio station playing classical music, from which the owner was content with a modest profit. After the owner's death, the station's new owner cannot afford to operate on the previous, low, profit level and must turn to the more lucrative operation of a station providing pop music, of which there are already several in the locality, but from which higher profit levels can be achieved. Cowan's definition of the public interest extended more widely to cover news and education:

A. I think the public interest is basically the notion of serving what is in the broad interest of the public, in terms of its need to be informed about a broad range of issues rather than catering purely for the private interests of its owner to maximize profits.

Q. Does the public interest include upholding certain values, asserting the value of great works of art, great pieces of music?

A. . . . The public interest to my mind includes education in a very important way.[26]

Tracy Westen said that, once there was real competition in broadcasting with the coming of cable and the licensing of low-power television transmissions during the Carter presidency, the fate of the public interest was sealed. He believed that the concept of the public interest, never strong, as the failure of the Blue Book had demonstrated, had been subjected to increased financial pressures. The companies which had enjoyed a near-monopoly found it more difficult financially to give subsidies to unprofitable programmes. Nowadays, whatever sells in the market-place stands as the public interest, a variation on the theme that what interests the public constitutes the public interest.[27] The Chairman of the FCC, Mark Fowler, expressed the point unequivocally at the height of deregulation in 1982 when he said, 'The public's interest, then, defines the public interest.'[28]

---

[25] Henry Geller, *1995–2005: Regulatory Reform for Principal Electronic Media* (Annenberg Washington Program in Communications Policy Studies of North-western Univerity, Washington, 1994).

[26] Personal interview, Los Angeles, 26 Feb. 1997.

[27] Personal interview, Los Angeles, 25 Feb. 1997.

[28] Quoted in N. N. Minow and C. L. LaMay, *Abandoned in the Wasteland* (Hill & Wang, New York, 1994), 103, from M. Fowler and D. Brenner, 'A Marketplace Approach to Broadcast Regulation', *Texas Law Review*, 60 (1982), 209–10.

Without some mitigating element, however, that condemns broadcasting, with its potential for providing a much greater range of material, to the tyranny of popular choice.

Lawrence Grossman considered that, as the public interest had not been protected under the existing system, if the range of programming available was to include the unprofitable, it could only do so on the basis of a levy on the commercial broadcasters. The values represented by the unprofitable programmes would be characterized as elite, but they were the values by which judgements were passed by nations on one another. The money raised by the levy, as Newton Minow has suggested in the case of programmes for children, would then be administered by an independent authority. Tracy Westen, who supported the levy proposal, was uncertain whether such an authority would have access to mainstream channels or operate through a network of its own.

When I raised the issue of the 'public interest' in Britain, Peter Rogers, the Chief Executive of the ITC, had interpreted the public interest as the safeguarding of the audience: from harm or offence, but also from the consequences of anti-competitive moves by the Commission's licensees. For the view of a programme-maker, I talked to Andy Allan, Director of Programmes at Carlton Television. He said:

I don't think there is one overriding public interest in broadcasting. I think you have to consider the public interest case by case . . . What interests the public could well be public executions. I think we may have to make judgements as we try not to be too far in front of the public mood. It's realizing that if you push your viewers, your customers, too far down ways they don't want to go, you lose them, they'll reject you and you lose their trust. So I think the broadcasters still have to seek consent in order to reveal things that we believe the public should get to hear about, although that can sometimes mean uncomfortable relations with the executive, the judiciary, and even the regulators . . . it is in the public interest to have challenging themes addressed to them in fiction or even in entertainment . . . It doesn't remain the same from one year to the next. But it doesn't go in a straight line upwards in terms of liberality.[29]

Conclusion

I have not found a single, clear, answer to the question which I put at the start of this book and repeated at the head of this chapter: in the name of what was the regulation or self-scrutiny of taste and decency issues carried out in British and American network broadcasting? The process may reasonably be described as regulation in Britain where there are regulatory

[29] Personal interview, London, 12 May 1997.

authorities for both commercial television and commercial radio, as well as two self-regulating bodies, the BBC and the Welsh Fourth Channel. The latter are overseen by government-appointed boards expected to protect the public interest. In the United States, with prohibitions on government intervention in editorial content, the process is more accurately described as self-scrutiny.

The nearest I can come to a simple answer is the public interest. However, my opening comparison of attitudes in Britain and the United States towards free expression, the role of government, and the place of commerce emphasized the considerable differences between the two societies of which I had been warned. The natures of the two democracies, one more individualistic than the other, mirror their origins. Although each would claim with justification that it cherishes freedom, it is clear that the concept is rather differently interpreted on the two sides of the Atlantic. Earlier in the present chapter, a further range of differences emerged, again reflecting the individual and the collective, in the respective attitudes of the two societies towards the public interest in broadcasting.

The differences were expressed most succinctly in the declaration, noted earlier, that in America the public's interest is the public interest. Laurence Grossman testified to the long-standing unease which the words caused in the United States. Underlining that statement were the observations of Henry Geller and others that the recognition of a public interest in broadcasting had been largely extinguished by the rush to deregulation which had begun under the Carter administration and intensified during the Reagan years which followed. Nevertheless, despite this lapse, the public interest standard in broadcasting, in its limited field of operation, has not been formally abandoned.

In Britain, the notion of a public interest in broadcasting is less contentious. The link between broadcasting and public service has been a strong one, helped by the small size of the country and by the centralized nature of government. The foundation of the BBC as a public corporation born out of a private company, the existence of the licence fee, and the strong public control instituted over commercial television in order to maintain the tradition of a diverse output, all these have also contributed to the perception of British broadcasting as a comprehensive public service providing much more than entertainment. The idea of public intervention, therefore, to ensure the standards of the service does not provoke the kind of resistance which it would arouse if it were ever attempted in the United States.

In matters of taste and decency, as with other matters of content, British broadcasters and the regulators in the commercial sector operate within a broad agreement between themselves and the audience about what programme standards should be. The audience consistently displays its understanding of such matters as the scheduling of programmes and the characteristics of individual channels which allow broadcasters considerable latitude in their choice of subject-matter and its treatment. On the other side of the coin, regulators allow considerations of intention to weigh in their judgements of programmes. The evidence is that many of the public support the existence of regulation directed at maintaining standards.

The concern of the American television networks is to ensure the presence of audiences of the size and kind for which their advertisers are looking. This has meant that, in general, the choice of subject-matter and treatment has been more restricted than in Britain. Company anxieties about bad language and sexual explicitness were apparent in several of the conversations I had with network executives. Within that narrower spectrum, however, many of the programmes excel, as the presence of large audiences in the States and throughout the world testifies each night. Such television reflects the public's interest as the advertisers see it. Whether that is the true extent of the public interest depends on one's faith in the market to get things right.

I believe that broadcasting serves democracy best with a plurality of voices. That, however, means more than a large number of television and radio stations, although, within the limits of the revenue available to support them, that is highly desirable. It must also mean that the stations themselves are free to reflect different values whose expression will, from time to time, cause offence. The old joke about the countryman's advice to the lost traveller, 'If I were you, I wouldn't start from here,' contains a profound, if unrealizable, truth. A democratic society needs a lot of different starting places.

To depend exclusively on the market is, I believe, as mistaken as depending solely on public funding. The contribution which broadcasting can make to democracy cannot be complete within the confines of priorities set wholly by considerations of the market, but the recent weakening of the public sector, both psychologically and economically, and the parallel strengthening of the commercial sector make this a real possibility for the future. Moreover, the commercial sector is dominated by commercial companies whose numbers are regularly diminished by mergers and takeovers. Commercial dominance can only be checked with an expression of political will, reawakened to the sense, currently dimmed, of the value of broadcasting as more than an economic activity.

There are three directions in which the political will can be exercised. First, there is the question of ownership itself and the influence which the growing concentration of power in the media has on society and not least on politics. Corporate portfolios now extend far beyond the media field, but a world in which broadcast communications are dominated by a handful of powerful corporations is likely to be a world materially enriched, but socially and culturally deprived. The temptation for large corporations is to avoid real controversy, but that, whether in factual or fictional programmes, should be part of the agenda which broadcasting sets before the public. Richard Hoggart has described democracy as a thoughtful state which, if it ceases to be such a thing, becomes a populist state in which the leaders have to manufacture consent. As they grow bigger and bigger, it becomes the business of the corporations to manufacture more and more consent.[30] The emphasis placed in both Britain and America on consumer choice in the past twenty years, to which Oliver O'Donovan referred,[31] has been allowed to obscure the narrowing of the areas in the mass media for intellectual and philosophical debate in popular terms. Television's role as a genuine forum has inevitably suffered with the fragmentation of audiences, as Howard Stringer pointed out,[32] and, despite their wealth, large corporations seldom put to challenge the societies in which they operate. Broadcasting, however, is essential to maintain that thoughtfulness of democracy, the people's essential safeguard against the domination of government or commerce.

Seondly, there is the acknowledgement by politicians of the need to support forms of broadcasting which, although some may be uncommercial, have other benefits for society measured by other values. The support needed can take more than one form. The revenue from the licence fee which funds the BBC is one example. The public service obligations placed on the ITC's terrestrial licensees in return for their lucrative licences provide another. In the case of Channel 4 in Britain, its original launch in 1982 was funded by a so-called 'subscription' ordered by the regulator from the individual companies of Channel 3 in return for their right to sell Channel 4's advertising time and to supply some of its programmes. For a period after becoming profitable, Channel 4 was required to pay a share of its profits to its former 'subscribers', a commitment eventually ended in the mid-1990s. Subsidies can also be paid directly by the state as in the case of the Corporation for Public Broadcasting or the Welsh Fourth Channel.

Whether in Britain, where that part of the commercial sector now carrying public service obligations may eventually be incapable of sustaining them, or in the United States, subsidies, in whatever form they take, are a

---

[30] R. Hoggart, *The Way We Live Now* (Chatto & Windus, London, 1995), 6–18.

[31] Above, p. 2.

[32] Above, p. 120.

recognition of the values of the society to whose support they are directed. There is no reason why, in Britain at least, the possibility should not be considered of extending public service obligations to those new services which become highly profitable. Moreover, the state of election broadcasting in the United States, with the parties progressively more indebted to the broadcasters, should give politicians in both countries further arguments for maintaining a sector of broadcasting independent of commercial pressures.

Thirdly, there is the enfranchisement of the audience, which carries with it the necessity of improving media education so that the public's understanding of all forms of media is deepened. At present, the audience is able to express its views through the machinery of the market-place. Pressure groups may have their impact from time to time, but there is a need to find ways to institutionalize audience opinions as part of the debate about broadcasting and its wider role in society. Such an institution should be equipped to conduct research and originate enquiries into specific areas of broadcasting, not in a combative way, but in the interests of putting to use all the potential which now lies before us.

I referred in the first chapter of this book to the choice offered to society in Lord Moulton's third domain between the rigours of the law and the anarchy implicit if we refused to set boundaries to the expression of our freedom. The measures I have briefly outlined above are the safeguards which I believe are needed for the future maintenance of standards of all kinds in broadcasting—diversity of appeal, quality, range of opinion, decency and taste. With them, as channels proliferate, I believe that the future of the public interest in broadcasting must lie increasingly in the third domain.

Select Bibliography

United Kingdom

BONNER, P., with ASTON, L., *Independent Television in Britain*, vol. v (Macmillan, London, 1998).

BRIGGS, A., *The History of Broadcasting in the United Kingdom*, 5 vols. (Oxford University Press, London, 1961, 1965, 1970, 1975, and 1995).

—— *Governing the BBC* (BBC, London, 1979).

Cmnd. 1753, *Report of the Committee on Broadcasting, 1960* (HMSO, London, 1962).

Cmnd. 9824, *Report of the Committee on Financing the BBC* (HMSO, London, 1986).

HOGGART, R., *The Way we Live Now* (Chatto & Windus, London, 1995).

KIERAN, M., MORRISON, D., and SVENNEVIG, M., *Regulating for Changing Values* (Broadcasting Standards Council, London, 1997).

MCINTYRE, A., *The Expense of Glory* (Harper Collins, London, 1993).

POTTER, J., *Independent Television in Britain*, vols. iii and iv (Macmillan, London, 1989, 1990).

REITH, J., *Into the Wind* (Hodder & Stoughton, London, 1949).

SENDALL, B., *Independent Television in Britain*, vols. i and ii (Macmillan, London, 1982, 1983).

WHANNEL, P., and CARDIFF, D., *A Social History of British Broadcasting*, vol. i (Blackwells, Oxford, 1991).

United States

ALDERMAN, E., and KENNEDY, C., *The Right to Privacy* (Vintage Books, New York, 1997).

BARNOUW, E., *A History of Broadcasting in the United States*, 3 vols. (Oxford University Press, New York, 1966, 1968).

Bayles, M., *Ain't That a Shame? Censorship and the Culture of Transgression* (Institute of US Studies, University of London, 1996).

ENGELMAN, R., *Public Radio and Television in America* (Sage, Thousand Oaks, Calif., 1996).

GITLIN, T., *Inside Prime Time* (rev edn., Routledge, London, 1994).

Select Bibliography

HAMILTON, J., *Channeling Violence: The Economic Market for Violent Television Programming* (Princeton University Press, 1998).

KRATTENMAKER, T., and POWE, L. A., *Regulating Broadcast Programming* (MIT Press, Cambridge, Mass., 1994).

MCCHESNEY, R. W., *Telecommunications, Mass Media and Democracy: The Battle for Control of U.S. Broadcasting, 1928–1935* (Oxford University Press, London, 1993).

MONTGOMERY, K. C., *Target: Prime Time*, Communications and Society (Oxford University Press, New York, 1989).

PRICE, M. E., *Television, the Public Sphere, and National Identity* (Oxford University Press, Oxford, 1995).

SANDEL, M. J., *Democracy's Discontent* (Belknap Press of Harvard University Press, Cambridge, Mass., 1996).

Index